Endorsements

In *Miracle Workers, Reformers, and The New Mystics*, John boldly challenges this present generation through revelation about former and contemporary radical followers after God. This book provokes and fuels the Bride of Christ, who through intimacy, will rise up and unveil the Lord's all surpassing power to ignite revival in the earth. John Crowder's work should be a foundational prerequisite for all who desire to minister in the realms of the supernatural.

—Marc and Lydia Buchheit
Healing the Northwest Ministries
Northwest Healing Rooms Regional Directors

I highly recommend John Crowder's new book, *Miracle Workers, Reformers, and The New Mystics*. This book offers a rich biblical and historic perspective of the contribution of past Christian mystics and seer prophets in the Voice of Healing revival and throughout the centuries. These pages will give you prophetic insight as to how these believers laid a foundation which has lead to the birthing of the present day spiritual revolution and corresponding resurgence of the contemplative prayer and "soaking" movement.

As you read *Miracle Workers, Reformers, and The New Mystics*, you will be provoked to hunger after God and to believe Him to do even greater exploits through this generation! John's book paints a powerful and captivating picture of the church's prophetic destiny as the Holy Spirit births a generation of radical abandoned lovers of God in a time like none other in history.

—Todd Bentley
President, Fresh Fire Ministries

John Crowder's new book takes the hunger you have in your heart to see the miraculous and ignites it on fire. He stretches your vision to believe for mind blowing miracles, signs, and wonders to follow your life today. John paints a beautiful picture of how the mystics of old helped prepare the way for the new generation of miracle workers that the Lord is raising up in this hour. You will be challenged and inspired as you devour each page of this book. The planet is waiting for the miracle workers to come forth and display His glory everywhere.

—Jason Phillips
President
Revival Town Ministries

John Crowder is an up and coming prophet of a new generation of an Elijah company. I have been on team with John in prophetic conferences, and he has great accuracy and sensitivity to the Spirit of God. His writings will challenge and inspire you in moving out of the norm of Christianity into a life of walking in the Spirit.

—Dennis McNally
Life Links International
New Life Christian Church

I have spent many years studying the way the Lord worked through the previous generations. I was greatly blessed when I picked up this book and began to dive into it. It will stir the gift of faith in readers to believe for the impossible to be possible. But it will also bring understanding of the necessity of being a finisher with what has been given. Enjoy this book, I did!

—Keith Miller
Stand Firm World Ministries

John Crowder's book, *Miracle Workers, Reformers, and The New Mystics*, is both enlightening and inspiring as he chronicles the radical forerunners of history who have paved the way for the moving of the Spirit in each generation. God is indeed raising up a radical new breed of revivalists who will inspire, confront, reform and help usher in a new wave of God's glory and power into the earth. Your heart will be captured with a passion to pay whatever price necessary to be a carrier of His glory in these last days!

—Matt Sorger

Matt Sorger Ministries

MIRACLE WORKERS, REFORMERS, AND THE NEW MYSTICS

JOHN CROWDER

Destiny Image® Publishers, Inc.
P.O. Box 310
Shippensburg, PA 17257-0310

"Speaking to the Purposes of God for this Generation
and for the Generations to Come."

For Worldwide Distribution, Printed in the U.S.A.

ISBN 10: 0-7684-2350-3
ISBN 13: 978-0-7684-2350-1

This book and all other Destiny Image, Revival Press, MercyPlace, Fresh Bread, Destiny Image Fiction, and Treasure House books are available at Christian bookstores and distributors worldwide.

For a U.S. bookstore nearest you, call
1-800-722-6774.

For more information on foreign distributors, call
717-532-3040.

Or reach us on the Internet:
www.destinyimage.com

2 3 4 5 6 7 8 9 10 11 / 09 08 07 06

Dedication

This book is dedicated to my wonderful wife, Lily, and our three oldest children, Maile, Jonas, and Nova, who endured many long months in a small Alaska shack as dad hovered endlessly over the computer, compiling the following chapters. It was your sacrifice that really made this book possible. Your personal support and willingness to chase hard after God, even in your youth, has been a great inspiration. Your lives are full of divine intimacy and power. There are few things more pleasurable to a father than seeing his children's hands placed on the sick, then watching them recover.

I would also like to dedicate this work to our youngest child, Ezekiel Sozo. It is no coincidence that his birth comes precisely as the first edition of this book is completed. You are Jacob's generation.

Acknowledgments

To our church family in Alaska, thank you for your many prayers and words of encouragement. Your intercession has been the fuel behind this project. Thank you for your understanding as the Lord has pulled us aside to focus on His call.

I would like to thank David and Darcia Bentley for your assistance in coordinating so many behind-the-scenes aspects of this book. We have enjoyed your company, and may the Lord reward you richly for your service.

I wish to acknowledge the work of Professor David Harrell and Don Stewart for both a journalistic and insider's perspective of the healing revival. Between the two, one gathers a comprehensive view of the majesty of God and the humanity of His ministers in a day of great power. I drew heavily from both.

I would also highlight the work of David Bercot, Fr. John Laux, Roberts Liardon, Lester Sumrall, the many rich resources offered by Christian Classics Ethereal Library and the many other historians and sources cited throughout this book. While I have substantive reportorial experience, I am no historian. Therefore, it is a blessing to be able to confidently build on research gathered by men of great caliber.

Special recognition is due to Rick Joyner, whose thoughts one may find echoed in many respects throughout these pages; it comes from long years of saturating in his insightful writings.

And to our parents, we appreciate your constant support and your confidence in all that we do. Thank you for your love and care.

Foreword

I want to highly recommend John Crowder to you. There are a lot of people we know who profess to be Christians but then you occasionally meet someone who really knows the Lord and has spent time with the living Jesus. John is a man who has real intimacy with the Lord, and for that reason I want to highly recommend his new book, *Miracle Workers, Reformers, and The New Mystics*. Allow this book to take you on a journey with those who have truly tasted of the Lord and brought something back to affect a whole generation. I believe this book will spark a fresh hunger in your heart to seek first the Kingdom of God and pursue the Lord with everything within you.

—Ryan Wyatt
Abiding Glory Ministries

Contents

"For the Kingdom of God is not a matter of talk, but of power" (1 Corinthians 4:20).

CHAPTER 1

Postmodern Prophets

TO fully understand the scope of power that is coming to the church in our day, it is important to consider the times in which we live. Society itself is on the verge of sweeping transformation, as we move into the postmodern era. The church is on the brink of spiritual renaissance and revolutionary structural change, to be set as a gem in the midst of a fallen world. Amid darkness and defeat at the end of the age, the church will shine like a beacon, displaying the power and glory of God's Kingdom as she arises as the spotless Bride. The Lord's intent is to bring the "restoration of all things" (Acts 3:21) first through His people. No matter what state the church appears to be in today, no matter the depth of apathy or traditionalism, we cannot give up on her. A cornerstone of the Kingdom is God's heart for redemption and restoration.

We read in the prophet Haggai that the glory of the latter house will be greater than the glory of the former house. We are living in exciting times—days that the fathers of our faith longed to see, as the latter rains of God's presence are poured out on His people. Life is being restored. The church is again waking up and moving in power. In this hour, God is again raising up dread champions, who are rebuilding ancient paths long forgotten. We are living in a generation of pioneers. A time of signs, wonders, and miracles for the last-day harvest. What will be the exploits of this emerging church?

The Lord has given us clues and keys all along the way, through His prophets, seers, and holy men—many of whose stories fell into obscurity over time. Their lives stand as signposts for what is yet to come in the corporate Body of Christ. In the following chapters, we will see parallels between early forerunners and the unprecedented move of God that is on the horizon. We are about to witness an entire generation of people walking in power that will surpass even the first century apostles. The work which they began in glory, we will finish in greater glory. The power, beauty, and authority of the Lord will be manifest in His Church like the world has never seen.

To see the extensive restoration the Lord is bringing to His Church at this time, we must look at the historical map He has already given us. In order to look forward, it is necessary that we first look backward. History repeats itself, and this message of understanding the past will continue to be a rallying cry coming from many major prophetic voices in the world at this hour. Throughout Scripture, God continually called His people to *remembrance* of His former deeds, even as He also says, "See, I am doing a new thing! Now it springs up; do you not perceive it?" (Isa. 43:19). After all, this is why we study Scripture. And this is why the early apostles exhorted the church to learn from the Old Testament fathers of the faith, despite the fact that God was already doing a new thing in their midst.

We still look to those biblical examples of old. We should also look at *church history*, because the Lord did not stop working when the canon of Scripture was sealed. Revivals, awakenings, and renewals have brought extraordinary acts of God since the first century. Church history, from the first century to the present, is full of mighty generals of the faith, into whose mantles of spiritual authority we have been invited to walk.

By digging into the past, we will find numerous keys to unlocking mysteries. After all, "it is the glory of God to conceal a matter, but the glory of kings is to search out a matter" (Prov. 25:2). I believe that the Lord often separates the mature believer from the immature by purposely concealing knowledge. He does not throw His pearls to the swine, and He does not give the children's bread to dogs. Likewise, there are many hidden truths and spiritual weapons that have lain dormant for ages, just waiting to be recovered. The extent of our prophetic perspective often hinges on our understanding of how the Lord has previously worked. But we are not simply studying to learn facts—the Christian looks at history interactively, because he is not bound by the element of time. The believer also realizes that, through the blood of Christ, he has access to the same spiritual feats and destiny as any great figure in history.

To take hold of all the Lord has for us today, requires that we move away from a strict scholarly approach to history, to a hands-on, experiential retrieval of ancient pathways. We must also look at ancient gates that have been opened and closed, for good and for bad, and it is important to have a basic understanding of how both generational curses and blessings have been passed down. The deeds of the greatest saints have sometimes opened huge doors of blessing, and on the other hand, those same saints have opened vast doors of error. It is important to understand that we have authority to open and close such gates (see Matt. 16:19), even if they have been forgotten for thousands of years.

There is now a call from the Lord for us to position ourselves for what is coming. Let us be prepared.

NEO-PILGRIMS

The emerging church is rising up from the confines of dead religion to take hold of new ground, *terra nova*, in the spirit. Every advancement in bringing the Kingdom of God to earth was paved on the backs of visionaries, martyrs and those who broke the mold in their respective eras. It is often said that Israel honored her prophets, but not until she had killed them first. Even today, those who are on the forefront of groundbreaking ministry are still catching the most bullets. But once their trails are blazed, multitudes follow behind them. We will be surprised at how commonplace ministries of radical signs and wonders will be 20 years from now, as the way is continually paved by scouts and seers.

Are miracles the only sign of groundbreaking ministry? No. However, "the Kingdom of God is not a matter of talk, but of power" (1 Cor. 4:20). We've had 2,000 years of talk, but only a few pockets of power here and there to back it up. That's about to change drastically.

"What now seems strange, risky and new will eventually be familiar, safe ground, because forerunner pilgrims will have tracked out safe paths to walk in," writes John Sandford in *Prophets, Healers and the Emerging Church.*[1] There are spiritual landscapes still to be discovered. The Lord is looking for those bold enough to forge new paths into the hinterlands where numerous pioneering Christian mystics, prophets, and miracle workers left off.

We will not be focusing heavily on reformers or great theologians—not even on the Christian *mystics* in the strictest sense of the word. This is a book about miracle mantles available to the average believer today. It is about spiritual wells of old that are being recovered in our time. Isaac redug the wells left behind by his father Abraham, and he was the child of inheritance. Blessings and mantles are released from one generation to the next. Isaac and Jacob released blessings to their children when they died. Elijah passed his mantle to Elisha when he died, and Jesus passed the very ministry of God to all believers through His death and resurrection.

As we read the lives of those who have walked in miraculous spiritual authority, their deaths and departure only open a door for us. Their testimonies can literally transfer power and become part of our own experience, until we have the faith to live life as they did. As you read their stories, you may want to pause at each one to pray, and ask the Lord for their mantles to come upon your own life. Each carries a unique flavor of the same God. The power of testimony is to strengthen our faith and enable us to both repeat and excel beyond what we have heard. In this era, we still overcome by the blood of the Lamb and by the word of our testimony (Rev. 12:11).

There is an upcoming generation which will carry these mantles of old, as well as new ones. They will walk in the spirit of Elijah, preparing the way for the return of the Lord (see Mal. 4:5; Matt. 17:11). Even as John the Baptist came in the spirit of Elijah before Jesus' first coming, so will that same spirit rest on an entire church before His second coming. Even the least of us will be greater than John. This will be an entire age of forerunners, heralding not just a new ministry or a new movement, but the Lord Himself. John and Elijah were not "Sunday school" Christians. They would not have been considered safe or conservative in our day. They were completely insane by modern standards. Many attend church today, strictly because Christianity is viewed as a status quo, mainstream religion. But the new mystics will not be looking for religious acceptance, nor will they fear the opinions of any man. Neither will they just eat what they are fed. They will hunt for themselves. They will not rest until they have personally heard from Heaven.

The history of the church is full of such radicals, men and women of no reputation who impacted their respective day by dwelling in the transcendent realm of Heaven. For the most part, these men were all ahead of the curve—shadows of what is available to each and every believer. They were fingers pointing not only to Christ Himself, but also to an entire host of men that will one day manifest the glory of God on a corporate level before He returns. Daniel prophesied of this coming generation of champions who would do great exploits. His words and revelation were sealed from that day until now, but the book is being opened.

The mystics, ascetics, and miracle workers of the past had lives that brimmed over with spiritual experiences, divine visitations, and supernatural encounters. In times of spiritual dryness, we have looked back on their stories as a thing of mythology or zealous embellishment. We have allowed our own *lack* of experience to dictate our beliefs about such men. No doubt, historical accounts are sometimes sketchy, and at other times, stretched. But many of their lives, especially those in the past two centuries, were documented in great detail with little room for historical error. For this reason, we will look extensively at the healing evangelists and miracle workers of the 20th century. And even today, the dead are being raised, the blind are gaining sight and deaf ears are opening around the world as the gospel is being preached.

Scripture itself is full of these men, who spoke with angels, split bodies of water with a word and made the sun stand still. Yes, men and women of this caliber still walk the earth today. But Jesus pointed out that we barely believe the accounts of Scripture.

> *[Jesus] said to him, "If they do not listen to Moses and the Prophets, they will not be convinced even if someone rises from the dead"* (Luke 16:31).

Our skepticism of the Bible itself runs deeper than we know. If Christians cannot believe the miracles recorded in Scripture, how will we ever believe for God to work similarly through us today? God made the world in seven days. He flooded the earth, and Noah's family escaped destruction with a boatload of animals that took more than 100 years to build. In the early days, men lived hundreds of years, and there were giants in the land. Moses turned water to blood, and when he spoke, phenomenal plagues overcame the Egyptians. Years later, when Elijah prayed, fire fell from Heaven to consume a sacrifice drenched in water. Even the water was burned. Some time later, the prophet Jonah was swallowed by a whale, where he stayed for three days until he was spit up on dry ground. These are big, dramatic, sensational things. Is this all allegory? All poetry? In our age of unbelief, many claim adherence to the Christian faith, or uphold the Bible as an inspired work, but they do not really believe such tales. How about the very resurrection of Christ? Charles Spurgeon went so far as to say, "There are very few Christians who believe the resurrection of the dead."[2] Is that possible? Many give the Scriptures lip service, but very few believe it in their heart. Even fewer believe it enough that they expect to imitate the miraculous on the same scale in their own lives. When we hear of people curing every manner of sickness and disease, multiplying food or walking on water *in our day*, we likewise disbelieve them.

But history—and the present day—is full of such radicals. More legitimate, documented miracles and supernatural healings have taken place over the past 50 years than are listed in the entire Bible, cover to cover.

As C.S. Lewis aptly put it, our faith is either the undeniable truth or it is the greatest cosmic scam job ever invented by man—but there can be no middle ground. "Christianity, if false, is of no importance, and if true, of infinite importance. The only thing it cannot be is moderately important," he said.[3]

Many want nothing to do with such a bizarre faith that is beyond their scope of understanding. To top it off, many forerunners of the faith were not only marked by signs and wonders, but by strange and uncanny lifestyles. Isaiah, who authored one of the largest books of the Bible and most clearly prophesied the coming of Jesus, walked naked for three years. Ezekiel ate dung cakes. John lived in the desert and ate grasshoppers. When one moves outside the established circles and into the company of fanatics—for that is what they really are—he will consistently encounter ideas long abandoned by the mainstream. Radical ideas. Ideas which were too unsavory to stomach, too inconvenient, or too discomforting to be discussed. Forbidden ideas. Yet these hidden regiments of fanatics—those who stow away in caves and hide from television cameras—they thrive amid such extremities. They are the final preservative that remains for unfashionable truths, before the collective memory of society discards them—loses them to the sands of time.

"One of the first signs of a (great saint) may well be the fact that other people do not know what to make of him. In fact they are not sure whether he is crazy or only proud: but it must at least be pride to be haunted by some individual ideal which nobody but God really comprehends. …He cannot seem to make his life fit in with the books," writes modern contemplative Thomas Merton.[4]

These are not balanced men. But they are soldiers, and many a regal principle of humanity and spirituality has been sealed in the annals of history by the blood of such men—when historians would otherwise have forgotten them. Such men are acquainted with suffering. With social distaste. With persecution and the theft of human dignity.

Of such a breed of men, we read in Hebrews 11:35-40:

> *Women received back their dead, raised to life again. Others were tortured and refused to be released, so that they might gain a better resurrection. Some faced jeers and flogging, while still others were chained and put in prison. They were stoned; they were sawed in two; they were put to death by the sword. They went about in sheep-skins and goatskins, destitute, persecuted and mistreated— the world was not worthy of them. They wandered in deserts and mountains, and in caves and holes in the ground.*
>
> *These were all commended for their faith, yet none of them received what had been promised. God had planned something better for us so that only together with us would they be made perfect.*

These are the men who forged paths, of whom the world was not worthy. But they were not untouchables. We are counted in their ranks, and God planned something better for us. Even now, the Lord is looking for a band of deliverers, through which He can fulfill the promises He made to these spiritual forefathers. They looked forward and saw into our day, longing to be a part of it. This is the last day people of promise. "Such is the generation of those who seek Him, who seek Your face, O God of Jacob" (Ps. 24:6). Jacob's generation is one that esteems its birthright. Their inheritance is the Kingdom of Heaven, demonstrated on earth in all its glory. Of the remnant people, the Lord spoke through Jeremiah the prophet saying, "I will give them a heart to know Me, that I am the Lord. They will be My people, and I will be their God, for they will return to Me with all their heart" (Jer. 24:7).

Those men of old died, not yet receiving the promise. And the things of Heaven that were owed to these forefathers will be released to us. We are their children, and the Lord has stored up an inheritance for us *through* them. We will not only pick up where they left off and finish what they started—we will also reap what they have sown. It is our time to walk in their mantles—that is, their place of spiritual authority. For too long, we have idolized the saints, as if their work was of some special dispensation to which we could not attain. But it is time we begin to look at the great miraculous works of the saints merely as blueprints for what is available to every believer. Blueprints for the latter house of God's glory, which will shine with unprecedented brilliance. As in Zechariah 4, the Lord's hand has laid the foundation of that house, "His hands will also complete it."

Will we be counted among this company of men who walk in a reckless abandonment for the things of Heaven? I have seen that, in men's lives, nothing is more radically transforming than the power and loving presence of God. Many times, have I seen a man violently redirect his entire life's goals because of one single *encounter* with the living God. Not just at the life-altering moment of conversion, for that is common. The same is true when a man is touched by God in a way that spins him headlong into a chase after the Lord's presence. I have seen many sell all that they own, in order to purchase the pearl of great price.

Many men have lived their entire lives, conscious only of the natural realm around them—realized only through their education or experience as perceived through the five senses. Their faith being nothing more than a dim, esoteric concept. Yet in one instance of tasting the glory realm of Heaven, their entire lives are thrown into upheaval. The awareness of a very real and viable spiritual reality, to which we have been blinded for years, always brings a sudden, irrevocable change that is, on one hand, utterly senseless—and on the other, completely sensible.

RESTORATION

To fully embrace the spiritual awakening that has already begun in our day, it is critical that we understand God's ultimate purpose for mankind, which is restoration. For 6,000 years, God's purpose has been to restore man into right relationship with Him. God always completes that which He begins, and He will not cease until mankind is again walking with Him like Adam did in the garden. From day one, since the fall, God has sought to restore mankind back to his original state of perfection. This was the very purpose of the atonement. So will this element of restoration be a central theme to retaking ground in the lives of believers in these last days.

We are about to see an entire host of garden-dwellers, who live transparent lives before God without the fig leaves. We may have an idea of what is coming and what that will look like, but it's better than we have imagined. The Lord told prophetic teacher Bobby Conner that he had personal permission to try and exaggerate what the Lord is about to do. The Lord will top it. Let us not forget that He is God. The wildest imaginings of Hollywood cannot comprehend it. The world has never seen that which is on the horizon.

It will not be so critical for us to have perfect eschatology—an exact understanding of the end times—prior to the Lord's return. However, even as the Book of Revelation promises blessings to those who read, hear, and take the book to heart, so there will be blessings to those who apply themselves to prophetically understanding the Lord's end-time purposes. But more important than knowing the dates, times, and details of the apocalypse, is knowing the Lord's heart. We can quickly become deluded trying to understand shadowy biblical prophecies without close communion and inspiration from the Holy Spirit. Intimacy is both the key to revelation and its goal. If we understand the heart of God, and His nature, we will better understand the details of His unfolding plan for the last days. The love of God is our guiding compass. We will return to this compass repeatedly in the following chapters.

> *For I am confident of this very thing, that He who began a good work in you will perfect it until the day of Christ Jesus* (Philippians 1:6).

This one verse speaks volumes about the intentions of the Lord, who always finishes what He begins. Even now, He is working to bring His labor to completion. Not only does the Lord finish His work, but He always saves His best wine for last. Whatever He started in former generations, He will finish with greater glory.

"Everything, which had a true Christian foundation, is going to be restored to the Lord. This includes every university, every city— even every nation. As we move closer to the 'period of the restoration of all things' which Peter talked about, we are going to see many such things that had a Christian foundation, but seem to have been lost to the spirit of the world, recovered for the purposes of Christ," writes prophetic teacher Rick Joyner.[5]

This is an amazing concept, one which seems too good to be true, until we consider the magnificence, capability, and sovereignty of the God which we serve. The same God, who created the earth in perfection, will ultimately restore it, supernaturally. Imagine everything completely restored to its original state, its original condition! We are reaching the fullness of time, when such things are starting to take place.

How extensive will this restoration be? Just think, we only use 10 percent of our brains according to scientists. Was that the case prior to Adam's fall? Did sin put a limitation on the very function and capabilities of our human bodies and souls? Of course it did. I would not doubt if Adam could even fly like an eagle or run and not grow weary (scriptural promises for us). Even Elijah was able to supernaturally outrun a chariot and a team of horses. Sampson had supernatural strength. Through Adam's sin came sickness, disease, hunger, poverty, corruption, environmental disaster, war, plague, abuse, and every evil thing. How much more will the entire earth be renewed through the second Adam, Jesus? If God had not allowed our capabilities to be limited after the fall, we would have destroyed ourselves long ago. But now, through the potential of a renewed mind, body, and spirit in Christ, incredible things are coming.

"No eye has seen, no ear has heard, no mind has conceived what God has prepared for those that love Him" (1 Cor. 2:9; Isa.

64:4). While we've used this verse to describe Heaven, we rarely put this in the perspective of a Kingdom that is just at hand. That which God has ultimately prepared for us is far more utopian than the Garden of Eden. And to the extent that we embrace the cross, we can access that realm of resurrection life *today*. The only question is, how much of it will we see on this side of eternity? How much do you want?

God wants us to ultimately thrive at a level of supernatural activity that looks inconceivable to us today. Remember, "Elijah was a man, just like us" (James 5:17). He had the same human limitations and struggles as we do, but he went on to perform some of the greatest miracles ever recorded. If our greatest imaginings are too small to comprehend what the Lord of Glory has in store for us, we may as well lift our vision higher, and expect more from Him with our lives.

In fact, we are not just being restored to the level of Adam; we are being restored to the image of God's Son. Did you realize that many of the men who walked closest to God in such a way were sucked right off the face of the planet? Let me whet your appetite with a few examples:

Enoch, the grandfather of Noah, we read in Scripture, "walked with God; then he *was no more*, because God took him away" (Gen. 5:24). Enoch was only seven generations from Adam—possibly speaking of the seventh symbolic day in history when the church would be carried away to be with the Lord. His life also speaks of a deep spiritual intimacy that is available to us all, as well as a last days "friendship with God" anointing that will be upon many. Like Elijah and others, Enoch was simply translated away to be with God. Imagine the revelation

Enoch

and insight Enoch must have received! The Book of Enoch, though not part of the biblical canon, provides an incredible glimpse into the fall of angels, telling how they slept with women to conceive giants and taught mankind all manner of sorcery and evil crafts, prior to the flood. It is interesting reading for any who have wondered about the Nephilim of Genesis 6 or the pre-flood era. Those days were not dissimilar to these in which we now live.

The Book of Enoch was written well before the birth of Christ, and was even considered Scripture by many early church fathers. Many of their writings made reference to it. Jude actually quotes from the book of Enoch in the New Testament (see Jude 14-15). While we do not consider the Book of Enoch to be Scripture today, there is solid basis to believe it carries some degree of inspiration, though our copies of the text are only in fragments. Justin Martyr, Irenaeus, Origin and Clement of Alexandria all used the Book of Enoch in the second and third century, and Tertullian (a.d. 160-230) called it "Holy Scripture." The Ethiopic Church put the Book of Enoch in its official canon. It was banned after the Council of Laodicea, and eventually went out of circulation. However, we must remember that many other things were banned at that council without merit, such as new songs and hymns (that would include just about everything we sing in church today). The council also ruled that no one could sing in church except for appointed singers— women could not even sing in public worship. In other words, the book may not be infallible, but it can certainly be profitable. The council that banned it obviously wasn't perfect.

After that council, the Book of Enoch was lost for centuries, until the explorer James Bruce found three Ethiopic copies of it in 1773. Since that time, other copies have been found as well. Enoch makes reference to a figure he calls "the chosen one," "the son of man" or "the messiah." Of further interest, the book's writer—quite possibly it really was Enoch—states that its revelations were not meant for Enoch's generation, but for a remote generation in the future. His writings also speak of a great judgment to come. Was this book meant for our day?

I believe Enoch was first of all speaking of the judgment in Noah's day. Enoch's son, Methuselah, lived 969 years—right up until the days of Noah. Methuselah's name means "when he is dead it is going to come," speaking of that judgment. But it is a warning to us as well. The apostle Paul essentially tells us that Noah had an open Heaven encounter, seeing into our day "from a distance" (Heb. 11:13).

Jesus said that "just as it was in the days of Noah, so also will it be in the days of the Son of Man" (Luke 17:26). There is actually a time period set aside, known as the "days of the Son of Man," and that is the period we have entered today.

Of further interest, the Epistle of Barnabas makes use of the Book of Enoch. Many of the aforementioned church fathers also used the Epistle of Barnabas in their early canons, though we do not include it in our Bible today. We must be careful as we read a number of these extra-biblical books, as many were phonies circulated by gnostics and other heretical sects (such as the supposed Gospel of Thomas, recently popularized by Dan Brown's book, DaVinci Code). Nevertheless, there is quite solid evidence that this epistle was the true writing of Barnabas who traveled with Paul the apostle. Barnabas also writes that the seven-day creation of the earth prophetically speaks of the age of the earth in thousand-year days.

> *The meaning of it is this; that in six thousand years the Lord God will bring all things to an end. ...Therefore, children, in six days, that is, in six thousand years, shall all things be accomplished* (Epistle of Barnabas Chapter 13).

If this writing is correct, and the earth is only 6,000 years old, such writings only confirm that we could very well be on the verge of seeing the last of the last days. For some, these days are the brink of disaster. For others, these are days of walking with God like Enoch.

There is another great mystic closer to our time, Sundar Singh, who surely walked with God this way. In a supernatural visitation with a saint, Sundar once asked, "Are there any other saints who were translated?" And he was told, "Yes there are many." Enoch and Elijah were not the only ones who entered Heaven early and bypassed death. In fact, God sometimes has need of such men in the Heavenly realms. We are still active after leaving the earth, as we see in the lives of Moses and Elijah, who both came back to earth and attended to Jesus many centuries after they had gone to Heaven. We should not seek, reverence, or pray to departed saints, but it is biblical to experience assistance or have visitations from believers who have gone to be with the Lord. They are all part of the great cloud of witnesses who are observing our lives and cheering us onward in Christ.

Sundar wrote that, "Our relatives and dear ones and at times the saints as well often come from the unseen world to help and protect us but the angels always do."[6]

Sadhu Sundar Singh

Sadhu Sundar Singh (1889-?) ranks as one of my utmost favorite mystics, as he so aptly exemplified a lifestyle of intimacy and revelation, as well as a demonstration of God's power within the most extreme context of his own culture—a culture that is still today far removed from the Western evangelized world.

Sundar was born in India to an upper class Sikh family, and from the age of 5, his mother taught him to pray for hours a day. He prayed so often that his father worried something was wrong with him. As a child, he was so zealous for his faith that he had burned a Bible and would chuck rocks at Christian missionary kids. His life's goal was to become a sadhu—an Indian holy man who lives a life of poverty and prayer. Sundar believed in a type of monotheism, that there is one God, but he was so frustrated at age 14 that God had not revealed Himself, that Sundar vowed to throw himself on the train tracks and die on a certain morning if God did not show up. When that day

approached, he began with his regular routine of prayer, hours before the
dawn. Suddenly, a bright light
appeared outside in the darkness. It
was Jesus Himself, in an open visitation, speaking to Sundar in
Hindustani, and saying, "I am Jesus,
whom you have persecuted."

Sundar was instantly converted.
He cut his hair—it is a Sikh custom to
grow it long from birth. In doing so, he
was immediately shunned by his family, and they even poisoned his last
meal, trying to kill him before kicking
him out of the house. His was a very
great sacrifice, considering he was

Sadhu Sundar Singh

being thrown from the top of the caste system to the very bottom.
It was shortly after this, that Sundar began to live out his life's dream
of being a sadhu. But, of course, he was a Christian one. Sadhus keep
no possessions, but are fed and taken in by families who want a
blessing on their household and want to hear their teachings.
Sundar adopted the customs of the holy men, to spread the gospel.
Sundar's only possession was his turban, which doubled for a blan-
ket, as well as his pocket New Testament. As he was taken into someone's household in the regular Sadhu custom, he would begin to
teach them about Jesus, seeing tremendous success in winning
souls.

Sundar lived much like Francis of Assisi, keeping nothing for
himself, yet trusting God for everything. He gave away any money
that he received, living literally one day at a time.

Sundar's life was marked by extraordinary levels of faith and
revelatory experience, as he continued in his discipline of spending hours a day in prayer. He was frequently caught up into
ecstasies and trances, and regularly met with the Lord Himself in
open visitations, where he asked questions and received answers.

Besides meditating on the Scriptures for hours, and sometimes all day and night, Sundar would spend much time in silent prayer and prayers of recollection. He also entered deep contemplation and fasted regularly.

Sundar was regularly persecuted for his faith. In one village where he preached, he was dropped into a well that was full of human bones, and he was left for dead. An unknown figure freed him from the pit late at night, and the next day he was seen preaching again on the streets. The village leaders, terrified at his miraculous escape from the locked well (the village leader still had the key to the lock in his robe), expelled Sundar from town.

Sundar was also beaten, tied to trees to be eaten by wild animals and was even tied up in a wet yak skin to be crushed to death as it dried up in the sun's heat. Often, he was rescued by a mysterious, hidden regiment of Indian Christians. Sundar's fame quickly spread to Christian missionaries, and as he became well known, he eventually traveled the international speaking circuit. He came to America where he spoke to overflow crowds and received wide press coverage. He was known coast to coast in America, but secular historians leave us little to no information about him today. The streets of major cities were literally packed with people trying to catch a glimpse of him. Sundar remarked on Western Christianity's shallow spirituality and the rampant materialism at that time. Throughout his life, Sundar wrote a number of books, including detailed documentations of Heavenly visitations.

Once Sundar visibly encountered satan, who offered him millions of followers if Sundar would only bow down and worship him. When Sundar realized what was happening, he rebuked the devil. Just as soon as he did this, he turned his head to see Jesus on his other side, face to face. The Lord told Sundar that he was well pleasing in His sight, and to ask what he wanted and he would receive it. From then on, Sundar was able to ask the Lord questions face to face and he went on to extensively document these detailed visions and encounters.

Another of his more profound encounters occurred in the Himalayan mountains through which he walked long distances on a regular basis. On one excursion to Tibet in 1912, Sundar was walking through the mountains when he fell into a hole. Surprisingly, there sat a hairy old man surrounded by numerous leather manuscripts. The man who lived in this cave claimed to be nearly 400 years old, and said he was baptized by Francis Xavier, the famous Indian missionary, in the 1500s.

"I pray for Tibet night and day," said the old intercessor, who Sundar called the Maharishi of Kailas. Sundar was persecuted severely by skeptical Christians for telling this story, and they often prodded him about the encounter with the old hermit. Nevertheless, Sundar returned to visit the Maharishi subsequent times, and the man gave Sundar specific words of knowledge for some of his acquaintances, whom the Maharishi had never met— detailed messages that might involve their names, issues of specific direction or even hidden sins that needed to be dealt with. Although Sundar offered to lead a group into the Himalayas to verify the Maharishi's existence, few could keep up with Sundar's pace in the rugged mountains—Sundar was used to walking many miles a day in the steep mountains—and eventually each one in the group gave up trying to follow him.

Equally mysterious was Sundar's departure from the world. Toward his latter years, Sundar had given up his world travel, in order to devote more time in prayer before the Lord. His intense revelatory experiences became more and more frequent. Setting out on a path he regularly took to Tibet, Sundar disappeared in 1929. His body was never found, and no one knew the details of his whereabouts. Many speculated that he went to live with the Maharishi, or that he took the hermit's place. Others feel that Sundar was simply taken into Heaven like Elijah and Enoch.[7]

Sundar and Enoch are models of what is coming. Translations from one place to another will become far more commonplace with the new mystics. When our only standard is the presence of God, the *favor* of God rests upon us, and all things become possible.

The enemy shivers at the thought of what access we have to God's power. He will do anything to keep us from picking it up. But as the church begins to step into the power we have as Christians, we will never again be on the defense against the enemy. We will always be plundering hell, whose gates will not prevail against us. As we press into divine encounters and begin to perform miracles, the work of the Kingdom will accelerate by leaps and bounds.

As Christians, we understand that our glorified bodies will be perfect in Heaven, that we will be renewed there and that the Lord will even create a new earth. But we must also remember that the Kingdom of Heaven is in our midst, and that the Lord wants to restore the church prior to her entrance into glory. Before the Lord returns, He will have a Church functioning in her prime. A pure and spotless Bride without blemish.

We usually do not think of a powerful, mysterious church when we consider the last days. Just how much of our end times theology is centered on chaos and devastation? We tend to think of the judgment of God when we consider the last days, and surely judgment will come. But the last days are when the church will shine her brightest. God has always brought His people *through* their trials and tribulations, and He always does so triumphantly. God brought the children of Israel through the Red Sea, through the desert, through the Jordan River, through the land of giants, and through years of captivity. The people of God do not bow out or get whisked away in times of trial, rather God carries them right through to the other side as they lean into Him. This is why, like Jesus, we can sleep through any storm.

Yes, the judgments of the Lord will be severe, and He will strip away all that is not of Him. Anything with a faulty foundation will not stand—all that can be shaken will be shaken. But the last days will not be a time of doom and darkness for Christians. It will be our greatest hour. As we focus on God's glory and dwell in His presence, He will be a refuge to us through it all. There will be suffering and even more martyrdom. But God is far more concerned with restoring than destroying. And while it seems that all hell is breaking loose around us, God's hand will be upon the Church, showing Himself strong through her.

In these last days, the Church will walk in the anointing of the sons of golden oil foreshadowed in Zechariah 4 and Revelation 11. Like olive branches, we will be *producers* of the anointing of God. We will walk in the power of Moses and Elijah, speaking as often as we desire to release signs in the Heavens and the earth. The distinction between light and darkness, sheep and goat, wheat and tare will continually become clearer as we enter these times. The final harvest will be a reaping of everything that has been sown into man, both good and evil. Good and evil are both coming into full maturity in the earth. Cults, pop religions, and outright satan worship will abound. Mockers and satanists will enter churches and openly confront leaders, making sport of services. But as our focus remains on the Lord Himself, in the intimacy of His secret place, we will see only light. We need only look to His face in worship to gain victory. And as Jesus is lifted up, He will draw all men to Himself. Those with vision will embrace such open encounters with the demonic, because Christians who walk in power will be on the offense, not the defense. Every power confrontation will be an opportunity for victory and saved souls.

The primary reason we must understand the principle of restoration in the last days, is to grasp the coming tidal wave of supernatural power about to be released on the church. The time could not be riper to bring all the jars into the house, because the oil is already beginning to flow. We must prepare for what the Lord is doing. The church may not look like a force to be reckoned with today, but this is largely because we do not understand the power and authority that is owed to us—that is legally waiting to be restored. The entire world is about to take notice of His Church again.

> *But this is a people robbed and plundered; all of them are snared in holes, and they are hidden in prison houses; they are for prey, and no one delivers; for plunder, and no one says, "Restore!"* (Isaiah 42:22)

It is time we demand restoration and take hold of that which is owed to us as the Church. It is sometimes as simple as calling for it. Our inheritance and right as believers is to walk in the power and intimacy with the Father that Jesus did. We must cry out for the lost mantles of former champions. And with the 20/20 hindsight of historical perspective, we will be able to see where they ended, where they succeeded, where they failed—then retake that ground and go further. There are many prototypes throughout history whose lives foreshadowed this coming generation. Of course, we will no longer be a church that lives in the past, but we will recover what those forerunners lost.

A NEW BREED OF SEERS

One of the most impacting moves of God we will see today is the merger of the postmodern and prophetic movements within the Church. As with two streams that flow together into one, there will be eddies and turbulence. Some charismatic circles will have difficulty embracing postmoderns, viewing their ideas and approaches as an erosion of fundamentals. And postmoderns will have difficulty embracing the spiritual heritage and giftings of their charismatic fathers. But the two will become one. They will not be able to stand alone.

Before we begin to explore some of the spiritual dynamics at hand, we must first consider the divine order of the ages to see where we sit on the brink of history. The church is right now transitioning out of modernism. "Postmodernism" is a trendy word thrown about in many crowds today, and while its actual meaning may seem elusive, we must recognize it as the cultural and societal backdrop of the next mighty move of God's Spirit. To some, a postmodern church is simply a culturally *relevant* church. To others, it means a *relativistic* church—one that waters down sound doctrine. Any emergent 20-something reading this chapter is probably sick of hearing the p-word, and anyone with a legalistic bone in his body has a "seeker-sensitive" red light flashing in his head right now, warning him to proceed with caution. We obviously need a brief history lesson.

In the strictest definition of the word, postmodernism is a trend in popular art, literature and culture, considered by many to be "extremely modern," or perhaps suggestive of the MTV generation. It is not a church trend, but a *societal* trend. While there are reams of philosophical books aiming to define the postmodern movement, the simplest way to describe it is life *after the modern era*. It would help us, therefore, if we first understand a bit more about modernism, to see where postmodernism takes off. This is because the church tends to approach God and Scripture from a *modern* mind-set. This is not bad, only incomplete.

I will oversimplify things by splitting church history into three big chunks. I hope to show a few general trends, to illustrate our present place in history more objectively. Here is my butchered synopsis of Church History 101:

Early Church - This period stretched from the first-century apostles through the fall of the Roman Empire around a.d. 500. This includes the Desert Fathers and the Patristic period, in which basic doctrinal issues and the creeds of the church were established. The early fathers battled heresies and Christological errors. The Emperor Constantine jumped on board with Christianity around a.d. 300, bought up the clergy, and made a big church/state hybrid. He ended Christian persecution but basically sold the church out to a political spirit that still remains today.

Middle Ages - This era stretches from the fall of the Roman Empire to about 1500 b.c. It ends with the Renaissance and the Protestant Reformation. This was a time of feudalism, kings and peasants, lots of monks. Black plague, knights, the whole works. Mysticism flourished in this time, as did ignorance, bad doctrine, and oppression.

Modern Era - This is the era of Protestantism, from 1500 to the present. It is marked by the Age of Reason, science and analysis. It is the age of conquer, colonialism, and the Industrial Era.

Modern does not just mean "new-fangled." Modernism is actually an era of history, beginning where medieval feudalism left off. The Protestant Reformation was sweeping Europe at the time, and the conquistadors were sailing the earth, taking native lands and people by force, and *imposing* Western European culture, religion, and philosophy.

The Age of Reason, or the Enlightenment, seems to be the defining crown jewel of this era. It brought a heavy emphasis on analytical thinking. The mind and rationalism reigned supreme, and this seeped heavily into the church. Never before had the intellect played such a prominent role in matters of faith. Author Brian McLaren describes this move toward analysis by saying, "If the universe is an intelligible machine—and science is the master screwdriver to take it apart—then analysis is the ultimate form of thought, the universal screwdriver. ...The fact that to us *thinking* and *analyzing* seem to be synonymous suggests how successful modernity has been at marginalizing all other forms of thought—imagination, intuition, pattern recognition, systems thinking, and so on."[8]

In modernism, everything was broken down into logical, understandable parts. Modern man has been consumed with science, practicality, and criticism. The mysticism of the Middle Ages became a filthy scourge to be washed away by modern scientific thinking. The supernatural was suddenly just *superstition*. Religion was thoroughly institutionalized, and spiritual *experience* was exchanged for the dissecting scalpel of systematic theology. God was quickly boxed up.

"Also assumed was the highest faith in human reason to replace all mysteries with comprehension, superstition with fact, ignorance with information, and subjective religious faith with objective truth," adds McLaren. "As a result, in modern times, narrative, poetry, and the arts in general (which yield softer, more impressionistic returns than science, math, or engineering) took a back seat...."[9]

Basically, modernism has been an age of *control*. Native peoples were conquered; nature itself was conquered. Production. Practicality. Consumerism. It was also the era of machines—highlighted by the Industrial Age—which obviously resulted from mechanistic, utilitarian thought. The analytical mind of the rationalist, or the scientist, sought to control the entire universe within the confines of the human brain. Reams of books, facts, figures, theory, and data from the collective mind of man sought to become the substitute for a simplistic faith in God.

And where was God during these past 500 centuries? For the most of society, and a large part of the church, He was relegated to the far blue yonder. The deistic overseer who sat detached and afar, having constructed His mechanical universe to run on legal, scientific principles. The world operated largely on its own without much of His direct interaction. This *deism* even flourished in early America, with many of our first leaders being direct products of the Age of Reason. Many thought God established physical and spiritual laws, then proceeded to kick back in the Lazy Boy, letting the world run on its own. Any immediate claims of divine inspiration were soon held in disdain and discredited as lunacy. Illogical. To this day, you can be thrown in the nut house for saying you personally hear from God. It's happened to me. But the medieval mind had no problem with something like that.

Some of the greatest mystics came out of the modern era, but many were reamed by the church. Eventually, the modern rationalist dismissed God altogether, and scientific atheism was born. All this time, modernism was infiltrating the church. *Individualism* and rugged independence—hallmarks of the modern age—were promoting the concept of having "your own personal Jesus." Remember, modernism was a time of control—control the environment, control native populations and, inevitably, control God. It was also during this time that a number of broad Kingdom principles were suddenly truncated down to a four-step gospel of *salvation only*, focused largely on a one-time legal transaction for the individual believer. This "legal" emphasis of the gospel largely overshadowed any romantic or passionate motivations for the atonement. Let's look briefly at where this started.

St. Anselm of Canterbury

St. Anselm of Canterbury (1033-1109) was a medieval philosopher and theologian, whose theories held over into the modern era, becoming a plumb line for modern, institutional religion. In fact, it was Anselm who first argued the idea of substitutionary atonement in his work, *Cur Deus Homo? - "Why the God-Man?"*

Anselm articulated that man's sin is an offense to God's righteousness, and that God cannot save man as long as the debt to this righteousness is unsatisfied. With all men being sinful, no one can satisfy God's demands. Therefore, God sent Jesus Christ, who died and was resurrected to satisfy God's righteousness and allow man to be saved.

Bravo Anselm. St. Paul said the same thing a thousand years before. It is clear that a legal transaction took place on Calvary, and we need to understand this. However, thanks largely to Anselm's influence, the *main focus* of the gospel shifted significantly away from an *act of love* to an *act of law*. The Bride of Christ suddenly seemed more interested in expounding on her marriage certificate than enjoying the Bridegroom Himself. Emotion was largely extracted from this objective, rational approach to the gospel.

We must realize that this was a very extreme departure from the medieval mystics, whose poetic discourses leaned heavily on erotic language and immediate, intimate encounters with the divine. Faith simply became a formal, legal interaction with God, where man's sin was exchanged for a ticket to Heaven, and modernity kept things on an analytical level.

Now of course, modernism also brought a lot of great advancements. None of us wants to be a feudal plebe dying of dysentery. Science is a gift from God and true science was never an enemy of the faith. Modernism also brought us greatly needed theological understanding and the resurgence of many powerful truths. The Protestant Reformation reintroduced an intellectual understanding of grace for crying out loud! And the modern era is chock full of revival and mighty moves of God. But culturally speaking, the church is still hindered by the analytical thinking, science, rationalism, conquer and control mentality of modernism gone overboard.

How then do we define postmodernism? Postmodernism is simply post-analytical, post-scientific, post-conquer, and post-control. It is also post-Protestant. We must remember that postmodernism is not *anti-modern*, it is simply *beyond* modernity. We don't reject modern thought, but we must transcend it. And what lies beyond the modern age? That is a question many are asking today. See, this whole postmodern deal really seems to be about a search for answers, or perhaps a search for better questions. People are *seeking* again—getting hungry for *spiritual* reality and discontent with analytical religion and scientific guesswork.

I would not say society is advancing, but society is changing. For the most part, society will likely not be throwing out rationalism, analytical thought, and the positive advances of the modern era; we will just go beyond those things. Eat the meat and spit out the bones. We will always glean from modernism, but we are moving forward into a new era. Likewise, we will see resurgence in many *premodern* ideas that previously went out of fashion. Ancient concepts will be revived, both in the church and in the world. For instance, the church will move in supernatural power as it did long ago, even as the world moves into more blatant pagan idol worship. Non-institutional, premodern ways of approaching God are being revived: Contemplative prayer is becoming fashionable again. People are regularly interacting with angels again. Strict denominationalism and religious programs are losing popularity. Miracles are back in style. People are seeing visions again—and visions usually begin in the realm of the purified *imagination*, before they extend to the open eyes.

In the church, I believe there will be a virtual renaissance, blending the old and the new. We will be able to get back to our roots, while becoming something entirely unique. Not only will miraculous power return corporately, but the arts, music, and even undiscovered forms of worship will abound. The church will become a cultural leader because of the creative anointing it possesses. No longer will we try to become culturally relevant. Not just copycatting the latest music style on our worship albums, etc. People will want to join the church because we've got the best gig in town. Spiritual creativity will ignite innovation. We will spearhead cultural advancement, as did the ancient Celtic church. Not only will we reach new realms of divine authority and experience, but we will also reopen deep wells of blessing that were abandoned prior to the modern age. We will get past the mind—past controlling, domineering Christianity—and demonstrate a spiritual life that attracts the world.

With any era, there are pitfalls to the "spirit of the age." Postmodernism is riddled with them, and many still have yet to surface. The ignorance of the Dark Ages led to war, pestilence, and short life spans. Modernism, as we have just discussed, was full of its own flaws and limitations. But on the whole, one cannot say that any *age itself* is good or evil. An age just is. Each one is marked with strong and weak points. When we discuss an entire era, we are not just talking about the *spirit of the world* in the biblical sense of worldly evil. We are discussing the traits common to a particular time period. We must remember that postmodernism is largely an amoral cultural platform—a backdrop—upon which either good or evil can be painted. Right now, both good and evil are coming into the church through the postmodern world. Of course, the trendy *postmodern movement* in the church is something different. It is probably just another fad, yet it is waking us up to the church's lack of relevance to the dying world. To say we must rid the church of postmodernism is about like saying we should rid it of Americanism—it's not quite that simple. Postmodernism is a cultural trend. One of its signature marks is that it embraces unknowns.

"The famously 'X' generation is really just the first of the screenagers to come of age and express...their acceptance of discontinuity and turbulence," says secular pop culture author Douglas Rushkoff, in describing the present postmodern generation.

Postmodernity does offer a healthy contentment with paradox that, on one hand can lead to confusion, and on the other hand, is needed to sustain a deep spiritual life. While some will abandon concrete, absolute truth in this age of fluidity, others will simply see that our guiding truths are *living* absolutes. There's a big difference. Christ is ultimately the *Truth*, and He is on one hand unbendable, and on the other, a living, flexible person. Postmoderns can handle this kind of paradox without pulling their hair out. There is a beauty to such mystery.

I am not supporting or renouncing postmodernism any more than I would support or renounce the Patristic period. Every era has its bright and dark spots. But the church must come to grips with the times in which it lives. Obviously, the initial flaw of postmodernism is its openness to moral and theological relativism. As the controls and restraints from institutionalized religion are lifted, many will flounder into syncretism. Many will compromise basic biblical doctrines. But on the other hand, society will also become an open window through which the Spirit of God can work mighty deeds in His Church, unhampered by dead religious structure and pat answers. It is truly a two-sided coin. There cannot be freedom to grow unless there is freedom to fail. Why else did God leave the tree of knowledge in the garden?

Christians have become so comfortable with their control spirit in the church that they panic when it leaves. We have become so rigid in our fundamentalism that God is trying to shake some life and movement back into our fundamentals. I find it ironically God-like that some of the greatest renewal is about to come out of the most theologically liberal seminaries in the country. You may not think it possible. But those places which most true Christians have learned to despise will suddenly produce spiritual champions to our utter amazement. We've become comfortable with God making leaders out of drunks and former drug addicts. But we don't believe He can actually transform a theological liberal. Lookout, the wind is about to blow.

The church is going to be putting aside petty theological differences anyway, and getting back to God. Overall, what's on the horizon will be a much more *spiritual* age, with the heavy chains of rationalism lifted. Society itself will more readily acknowledge and interact with the spiritual realm more than it has for centuries, for better or worse. Postmodernity is the cultural vehicle through which the spirit of prophecy will move in these latter days. Like the medieval period, this age will be much more conducive to Christian mysticism. However, thanks to the advances of rational thought, these post-mystics will possess a clearer intellect and safer theological understanding through which to experience the divine than ever before. The spirit and the mind of redeemed mankind will function at levels of cohesion never before realized. Mysteries will unfold like gangbusters.

The transition from the old school requires much more than a new program, a new style, or a hipper polish on the outside of the evangelical cup. It requires a complete death and overhaul of ministry as we once knew it. The move from program-based models to relationship-based models will be a big part of that. Anything less is a vain attempt to stuff ministry into old boxes. The concept of grabbing at the latest method to build our own kingdoms or improve the old system is still an old wineskin.

"Progress should mean that we are always changing the world to fit the vision, instead we are always changing the vision," said G.K. Chesterton.[10]

Yes, we need to become culturally relevant. But cultural relevance is not our goal. Our primary objective is to get closer to the Lord. When you get closer to the Lord, you naturally want to become more accessible to the people around you. In the church, postmodernism is not just a *movement* toward seeker sensitivity. It is an entire shift in the mindset of mankind that enables us to embrace paradox, mystery, and discontinuity. The postmodern mind can balance a lot of seemingly contradictory perspectives. In this sense, the postmodern can draw from multiple streams of the church of the ages, and find that single strand of divine DNA—the very essence of God—that holds it all together.

Let us begin looking at some of these streams this generation will reclaim.

ENDNOTES

1. John and Paula Sandford, Prophets, Healers and the Emerging Church (Shippensburg: Destiny Image Publishers, 2003), 184.

2. Charles Spurgeon, "The Resurrection of the Dead," sermon delivered 17 Feb. 1856 at New Park Street Chapel, Southwark.

3. C.S. Lewis, God in the Dock: Essays on Theology and Ethics, ed. Walter Hooper (Grand Rapids: William B. Eerdmans Publishing, 1994 ed.), 101.

4. Thomas Merton, Seeds of Contemplation (New York: New Directions Publishing, 1986 ed.), 69.

5. Rick Joyner, "Understanding." www.eaglestar.org, Word of the Week. 3 Sept. 2003.

6. Sundar Singh, Visions of Sadhu Sundar Singh of India (Armidale, Australia: Noah's Ark, 1996 ed.).

7. Janet Lynn Watson, The Saffron Robe, is a valuable source on the life of Sundar Singh, (London: Hodder and Stoughton, 1975).

8. Brian McLaren, A New Kind of Christian (San Francisco: Jossey-Bass, 2001), 16-17.

9. Ibid., 17.

10. G.K. Chesterton, Orthodoxy (New York: Dodd, Mead and Co., 1908).

CHAPTER 2

The Forerunners

W E are all aware of the great supernatural exploits and miraculous lifestyles of the first century church. The same apostles who had walked with Jesus traveled throughout the ancient
world, spreading the gospel and planting churches until all but one
reportedly died martyrs' deaths. Philip was scourged, thrown in
prison, and crucified in Phrygia in a.d. 54. Andrew, Jude,
Bartholomew, Simon, and Peter were crucified as well. Peter historically asked to be crucified upside down, as he felt unworthy to die
in the same manner as the Lord. Peter was warned ahead of time
that his persecutors were after him. But as he was leaving the city
gate of Rome, he saw the Lord in a vision. Peter asked, "Lord, where
do You go?" To which the Lord replied, "I have come again to be crucified." Peter understood by this that it was his own appointed time,
and he went willingly back into the city.

Matthew is believed to have traveled to Parthia, Persia, Media,
Syria, then Ethiopia, where he was speared with a halberd in a.d. 60.
James the brother of Jesus was supposedly thrown from a battle-
ment on the temple, stoned by the Jews, and his brains dashed out.
Like Bartholomew, Thomas took the gospel all the way to India,
where he was speared. Several were beheaded, including Paul, who
was put to death *more than once*; James the brother of John; and
Matthias, who replaced Judas, was stoned and beheaded in
Jerusalem. Mark went to Libya and Egypt among his travels. In

Alexandria he was dragged through the streets and his body burned. Luke was hanged on an olive tree by Greek priests.

John was boiled in oil in a botched execution, but did not die, leaving some to wonder if he is still alive today, following Jesus' mysterious exhortation to Peter, "If I want him to remain alive until I return, what is that to you?" (John 21:22). Christianity continued to grow and spread throughout Europe, Africa, and even the distant parts of Asia during the first two centuries, facing intense persecution from a number of Roman emperors. This era of persecution is when we read of believers being burned at the stake as living torches in the Emperor Nero's garden, being thrown to wild animals in the coliseums and often being labeled as "enemies of the human race."

BLOOD SEED

The first centuries of Christianity were marked by widespread persecution and martyrdom that has still not been avenged by the Lord. There is an over-arching spiritual dynamic to the principle of sowing and reaping that will fuel the end-time harvest in our day that legally releases Kingdom restoration. God is going to use all the prayers from all the saints and all the sacrificial blood of the martyrs together as seed, which has been sown throughout the ages. This will be mixed together with Jesus' own prayer and blood, then mingled in a censer with incense and a fiery coal from the altar. In these last days, He will hurl it all back to the earth to blow open the heavens and release all the power and glory of the ages on one generation (see Rev. 6 and 8). All the buildup of spiritual seed—the sacrifice, prayers and service of the saints—from the ages is coming down in one fell swoop. All the injustice satan has waged against the saints will be evened out by the just hand of God, and this will pave the way for the last day revival.

As we read in Hebrews 11, there were powerful forerunners who had tremendous testimony and favor, but still they did not receive from the Lord what was promised. This is because God had something planned for a future date. They were the sowers. And without us, those generations of saints would not be complete. While we respect the groundbreakers of the past, the baton has now been passed to us, and we are called not only to imitate their faith, but to take it to the next level. We will ride the wave they created.

When a prayer is lifted, or a martyr's blood is spilled, sometimes we see an immediate effect. But the greatest power of prayer and sacrifice has yet to be realized. Did you know that we have not yet seen the complete answer to any prayer? Nor have we seen the full reward of any sacrifice. The blood of the martyrs still cries out against the enemy, saying:

> *They called out in a loud voice, "How long, Sovereign Lord, holy and true, until You judge the inhabitants of the earth and avenge our blood?" Then each of them was given a white robe, and they were told to wait a little longer, until the number of their fellow servants and brothers who were to be killed as they had been was completed* (Revelation 6:10-11).

Martyrs' blood is a powerful seed. Their blood has a *voice*, and the Lord will not allow a single drop of it to pass away. While we may have seen a few salvations here and there as a result of their deaths, we have yet to see the full impact of the death of the martyrs in the earth. The saints of old are all crying out for the full release of God's just power. They saw glimpses of it in their day, but God has held in reserve the answer to their prayers for a later time. The very justice of God requires that the enemy cannot steal, without making restitution. All that has been stolen in the earth will be repaid at once in one massive decree of God's justice.

There are still martyrs to be added to the ranks of Revelation 6. Many are being killed for the faith around the world today, but there are still more to come from the West.

I was shown shortly after the terrorist attack of Sept. 11, 2001, that the Lord is going to be releasing His "suicide preachers" into the Islamic world. Even as terrorist suicide bombers give their lives, just to impact a street corner, a tour bus, or a restaurant with a few explosives on their bodies—so will the Lord begin to send His own missionaries into the Muslim world. Not with bombs, but with the word of God. These will usually be young, single radical men with nothing to lose in this world, who will freely volunteer their lives. They will go into the street corners and market places of Islamic cities, stand up, and begin to preach the gospel in the open air. Their words may reach only the immediate listeners around them, and a few people close by will be saved. But the natural effect may look just the opposite of an Islamic bomber. Instead of exploding out-ward and inflicting damage to the surrounding crowd, the crowds will sometimes implode on the preacher, immediately swarming him—beating and stoning him to death in an instant. This will have a heavy impact for the Kingdom. It will blow every church growth strategy out of the water. This is going to be a *movement* in the church.

Breaking open new realms always takes sacrifice.

There really will not be as many killed by this type of activity as one would imagine. More often than not, the crowds will actually stop and listen to these preachers, because people are hungry for truth—especially when they are walking in signs and wonders. Muslim people take miracles very seriously. Nevertheless, these preachers will always be prepared to lay their lives down for the gospel. The response will be better than many would expect, and many traditional missionaries will grow in boldness due to their work. They will realize how paranoid we have been not to just share the gospel plainly. Much of this fear may come from a subtle racism against Arab people.

Presently, most Islamic mission work is very slow and tedious, depending on one-on-one relationship evangelism. This will change. What are now the most unpopular places for evangelism will quick-ly become the *most* popular mission fields, because of this radical, thrill-seeking army that is on the rise. They do not want to build on other people's foundations. They want to pioneer in new areas. This extreme, death-risking preaching will actually become popular sport among young believers. They will go out in waves, until eventually it becomes so commonplace that Islamic governments seriously crack down on persecutors.

The forces of satan are very fearful of the new martyrs that are coming. Scripture says that the rulers of this age would not have crucified the Lord of Glory if they had known the consequences of their actions. In the same way, the enemy has learned how foolish it is to kill martyrs. Whenever he kills them, they multiply. The retribution that follows is far greater than if he left them alone. The only reason he takes them out is to stave off his appointed time of judgment. The enemy is frantically fighting back the waves, but he is also storing up a bigger payback.

I was once taken into a vision where I was standing on an aircraft carrier in the Pacific during World War II, when suddenly a Japanese kamikaze plane came hurtling down right toward me. Someone on the ship must have shot it on the approach, because it suddenly burst into a huge ball of flame. But shooting the plane did not stop it. This massive ball of flame and metal was coming right at us as clear as day, speeding down to only a few dozen yards away, and I knew it would take out the whole ship. The vision ended, and instantly, the Lord spoke to me about the new martyrs that are coming on the scene and how the enemy feels about them.

This is what I heard: *They will freak you out, dude.*

I knew that the Lord was releasing His radical kamikazes. They will be a holy terror. They will be hurtling down on the enemy, and he will have no way of escape—pinned in a corner. There is nothing he can do but sit there and lose when a man is so abandoned that we will give his very life for the gospel. Nothing is more precious to the Lord than the blood of His saints. We cannot expect the Muslim world to be won without the shedding of martyrs' blood. No major new ground has ever been taken in the world without it. Tertullian said, "Afflict us, torment us, crucify us—in proportion as we are mowed down, we increase; the blood of Christians is the seed (of the church)."[1]

There is a young company on the rise that is so desperate for something of substance, that they will pay that price. It is no surprise that many in the present generation now struggle with issues of suicide. Theirs is a generation built and called for such purpose and destiny, that they are geared to sacrifice it all for something of purpose. Without this higher purpose, that inner drive pushes them to self-destruction. They will be willing to make this type of commitment. This is a generation that can turn either toward extreme depression and self hate, or extreme reckless love of God to the point of joyful sacrifice. We are entering an age of extremes. "Greater love has no one than this, that he lay down his life for his friends" (John 15:13). Because these will be extreme lovers of God, they will also be extreme lovers of their fellow man. They will not count their temporal lives a loss, if it means reaching their fellow man with news of eternal salvation.

We often hear stories of martyrs, and *Foxe's Book of Martyrs* is a good source to learn about those who died for the faith. But we rarely hear of those accounts that were accompanied by bizarre miracles. Let us look at one of the largest mass martyrdoms ever; it occurred in Switzerland and birthed the longest-running, continuous worship service in the West. St. Maurice abbey has held a nonstop, 24-hour prayer service every day for the past 1,500 years, beginning in the sixth century. And it was built at the site of one of the most phenomenal martyrdoms ever recorded.

St. Maurice and the Theban Legion (c. a.d. 286) were 6,600 Roman soldiers under Maximian Caesar, sent to put down a rebellion among the Gauls, north of the Alps near the city of Thebes. The emperor had sent many troops to put down this rebellion, but they kept deserting him. In order to prevent this from happening again, the emperor sent

"Theban Legion" by El Greco (c 1580-1582).

this particular 6,600-man legion all the way from upper Egypt, since they had no regional ties in the upper Alps. That was a tremendous distance to send such a huge army in those days! As it turns out, this entire group of Egyptian soldiers were Coptic Christians.

This legion soon discovered that the rebels were also Christians. The reason they had been dispatched to kill them, was because the rebels were refusing to worship the emperor as a god. The Egyptian commander, Maurice, along with all 6,600 of his men, utterly refused to attack their fellow brothers, the Christian Gauls. But they were not trying to be disloyal to the emperor. Maximian repeatedly commanded the legion to obey his orders, but when they kept refusing, he had them decimated—that is, every tenth man was put to death. The Christian legion did not even fight against their emperor. They willingly submitted to martyrdom. After that, a second decimation was ordered, unless the remainder of the men obeyed the emperor. Instead, they gave a great shout throughout their camp, saying they would never carry out such an unholy order.

"Emperor, we are your soldiers but also the soldiers of the true God. We owe you military service and obedience, but we cannot renounce Him who is our Creator and Master, and also yours even though you reject Him," they wrote Maximian, both in loyalty and courage. "In all things which are not against His law, we most willingly obey you, as we have done hitherto. We readily oppose your enemies whoever they are, but we cannot stain our hands with the blood of innocent people....Christians we declare ourselves to be; we cannot persecute other Christians."

The second decimation was carried out, then finally every last one of them was slaughtered, without ever resisting in any way— 6,600 in all. During this ordeal, Maurice constantly encouraged his soldiers to worship only God and reminded them of their commitment to Christ. The soldiers simply lay down their weapons and even offered their necks to the executioners, despite their own obvious force as an army. This alone was a tremendous witness, but there were also phenomenal miracles during their martyrdom.

Shackles were miraculously broken off of some. In other cases, fires were extinguished so they could not be burned. After some were beheaded, their bodies began to glow like light bulbs with the glory of God. In Zurich, three who were beheaded—Felix, Regula and Exuperantius—miraculously stood to their feet, picked up their own heads, walked away, and prayed before laying down in death. These three saints still appear on the coat of arms and seal of Zurich today. Others were beheaded and thrown into a river. Then they walked up out of the water with their heads in their hands in a similar fashion.

In honor of this mass martyrdom, in a.d. 515, a regional king of the area instructed monks to begin the continual praise and worship cycle at a nearby church, where it has continued day and night ever since.[2]

If glowing corpses and talking heads stretches your faith factor, you will surely not want to miss the following:

St. Denis (c. a.d. 250) preached in Paris when it was only a small city, founding a church where Notre Dame now sits, and where formerly there was a pagan temple to Jupiter. Denis was a very successful missionary during the second persecution, and many people were converted under his ministry. But they were finally all persecuted. Three hundred believers were tortured and beheaded at a place

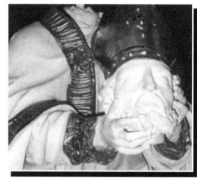

A statue of St Denis holding his own head after he was mertyred.

called Martyr's Hill, or *Montmartre*. As the story goes, after Denis' own head was chopped off, he picked it up and carried it up hill for two miles. Denis is the patron saint of France and is depicted in sculptures and paintings with his head in his own hands.

There are no written eyewitness accounts of Denis still in existence, but the story is passed down to us from St. Gregory of Tours in the sixth century. Some of the following accounts are equally sketchy, but this bizarre miracle of walking and even talking without a head during martyrdom seems to be common.

Saints Fulcian and Victorice (c. a.d. 287) were missionaries to the Morini people, and were taken in by the innkeeper St. Gentian, when persecutors came to martyr them. Their executioners put rods of iron through their ears and nostrils before taking off their heads. Then they arose by the power of the Holy Spirit, and carried their heads away from the place they were beheaded.

St. Nectan (sixth century) was a Welsh hermit who subsisted on wild berries before a local farmer pitied him and gave him a cow. One day, two thieves came to steal the cow and beheaded Nectan. To their surprise, he picked up his head and carried it back to his hut.

St. Nicasius (c. a.d. 451) was the bishop of Reims, France, and was martyred with his sister Eutropia and a group of believers. The Vandals were coming to kill this group of Christians, and Nicasius offered up his own life to them. While he was praying, they sliced off his head. After his head rolled off, he finished his prayer before he died. The wilder accounts of this ordeal tell that the Vandals saw a large Heavenly army appear after the slayings and they dropped their weapons and fled. Then the slain bodies of the martyrs began to glow with a luminosity that could be seen in the night.

We should realize that many miraculous happenings will mark this final wave of martyrs. At the same time, there will be a certain number in the Lord's last day army who carry a type of anointing that makes them physically invincible to those who try to harm them, as foretold by Joel. This may sound too "superhero" to be true, but we must remember the biblical precedent of Samson and David's mighty men. Some of them killed thousands of soldiers in a single battle with crude instruments, like the jawbone of a donkey. They were absolutely vicious. This anointing will not be given for carnal warfare, but the point is, we should not at all be fearful of our spiritual adversary, the devil. Even if we are killed for our faith, it will only ensure us front row seats when we get to Heaven. The spirit of martyrdom is not one of fear and worry, but of joy and exuberance. I do not want to belabor the headless martyrs—but the form in which they die is quite prophetic. I believe we will see another wave of Christians being literally beheaded before the second coming of Christ, which will speak of a greater spiritual reality. As peculiar as it may seem, there is a special authority given to headless martyrs:

> *And I saw the souls of those who had been beheaded because of their testimony for Jesus and because of the word of God. They had not worshiped the beast or his image and had not received his mark on their foreheads or their hands. They came to life and reigned with Christ a thousand years* (Revelation 20:4).

This passage speaks not only literally, but also symbolically of those who are detached from human wisdom and the wisdom of the age, and are submitted to the true Head, which is Christ. We will be a people who walk in revelation and possess the very mind of Christ. The enemy always goes after the head, because he knows God appointed mankind to crush his own head in the garden. It is no coincidence that the *mind* of Christians is a constant target of attack. We are stereotyped as nonintellectual, brainless fools for having faith. Our belief systems are constantly criticized, though we are categorized as being *biased* for critiquing ungodly belief systems. It is interesting that John the Baptist, the forerunner of Jesus, was beheaded. So will we live as a people separated from a worldly mind-set, trusting fully in the Lord even to our own hurt. I also do not believe it is coincidence that a common means of execution in the Muslim world is by beheading. There will be a new wave of last-day pioneers who will break open the Muslim world with the gospel at the price of their own lives. But it will take more than sheer commitment. It will take a love for the Islamic people, and it will take consecrated, holy vessels, who have thrown off the shackles of racism and a religious spirit regarding them. It is time we learn to live a delicate paradox of passionately hating the demonic belief systems of false religions, while unconditionally loving and embracing our fellow man who is trapped by them. Martyrdom is an act of love.

There are many brave and heroic tales of martyrs too numerous to mention here. But God's people "will volunteer freely in the day of [His] power" (Ps. 110:3). There is a level of anointing that releases such inebriated abandonment, that a man can literally count his life as nothing compared to the surpassing glory of Christ. When Stephen was martyred in Acts 7 he seemed stoned in more ways than one. He was in complete ecstasy, in the grace of God, as his persecutors threw rocks at him. I don't think he even felt a thing—he was feeling something much better. Stephen was so aware of the presence of God in the room—so enrapt with a greater spiritual reality—that he lost consciousness of the murderers around him. If a handful of men could attain this same awareness of the presence and nearness of God in day-to-day life, they could turn the world upside down with unprecedented boldness.

Eusebius writes of such fiery boldness in the early church:

"There were occasions when on a single day a hundred men as well as women and little children were killed, condemned to a succession of ever-changing punishments. No sooner had the first batch been sentenced, than others from every side would jump on to the platform in front of the judge and proclaim themselves Christians. They paid no heed to torture in all its terrifying forms, but undaunted spoke boldly of their devotion to the God of the universe and with joy, laughter and gaiety received the final sentence of death: they sang and sent up hymns of thanksgiving to the God of the universe till their very last breath."[3]

The enemy's advances against the church are very limited, and there is a turn of the tide coming quickly, as the enemy's time draws to an end. Daniel 7:21-22 says:

> *As I watched, this horn (the enemy) was waging war against the saints and defeating them, until the Ancient of Days came and pronounced judgment in favor of the*

saints of the Most High, and the time came when they pos-
sessed the Kingdom.

Even now, the church is beginning to possess the Kingdom of
Heaven here on earth. The decree of judgment is going out, and we
will walk in the victory owed and paid for by the blood of saints and
martyrs from the dawn of time. Abel's blood still cries out. When
satan saw that Abel's sacrifice was accepted by God, he knew Abel's
lineage would be the one to crush his head—and so he roused Cain
to kill him. But then Seth was born. Seth's name means "substitute,"
and out of his line would come Jesus, the Liberator. At the cross,
satan's defeat was ultimately sealed.

THE FEARSOME ONES

Forerunners have long planted the seed of God's Kingdom with
their lives. The forerunner spirit is primarily one of self-decreasing,
so that the Lord's presence increases and He is drawn into the present-day life of the believer here on earth. As Heaven impacts earth
in such a manner, a violent, caustic reaction takes place. The Lord is
unleashing a company of men who are completely sold out to Him
in this way. He is amassing a fearsome brood of champions who are
"powerful without number" (Joel 1:6), who will exhibit ferocious
zeal before His return.

> *Like dawn spreading across the mountains a large*
> *and mighty army comes, such as never was of old nor*
> *ever will be in ages to come. Before them a fire devours,*
> *behind them a flame blazes* (Joel 2:2-3).

The Lord is gathering a great army. We will look further at Joel's
Army in Chapter 10. However, I will note here that this will be a
people that strike dread into the heart of the enemy. Why? Because
they are possessed by a spirit of burning, a passion for purity. Their
lives will be utterly transparent before the Lord, and every impurity

will be purged from their midst by the white hot flame of the Lord. They will truly be spotless.

> *But who can endure the day of His coming? Who can stand when He appears? For He will be like a refiner's fire or a launderer's soap. He will sit as a refiner and purifier of silver; He will purify the Levites and refine them like gold and silver...* (Malachi 3:2-3).

God is making for Himself worshipers in this hour whose lives are enflamed with holiness, who are unattached to the things of the world. They desire only their Lover. We must move beyond acceptance of this cleansing fire. Let us even move beyond submission to the fire. Let us become the fire. Hebrews 1:7 says the Lord makes "His servants a flame of fire." This fire is synonymous with purging, and it is also synonymous with passion. It is burning desire. The great revivalist John Wesley said "I set myself on fire and people came to watch me burn." In fact, our God Himself is a "consuming fire," and to become one with Him is to take on His fiery nature.

God will have for Himself a people who drip the fear of the Lord from their pores, and it will rattle the enemy's camp like nothing before seen. With the fear of man absent from their midst, they will be consumed with holy fear. Like the great forerunner John the Baptist, these will not be soft-bellied people. John got in the face of King Herod and called him on the carpet for his adultery. There was no man-pleasing spirit in John.

> *From the days of John the Baptist until now, the Kingdom of Heaven has been forcefully [violently] advancing, and forceful [violent] men lay hold of it* (Matthew 11:12).

The fear of the Lord is a transferable anointing. Later, we will look at men who walked heavily in it. People are going to begin shaking again at the name of the Lord. Obviously, the Lord wants us to approach Him boldly, and with love. But we never abandon our fear of Him. It should only increase, though not in a slavish way.

When a slave learns to love his master, he is no longer a slave, but something else. He has progressed perhaps to a bondservant (a willing slave—a "love slave"), or even a friend. In fact, our goal is to move beyond slavery into an understanding of our sonship in the Lord. Romans 8:14-16 says:

> ...those who are led by the Spirit of God are sons of God. For you did not receive a spirit that makes you a slave again to fear, but you received the Spirit of sonship. And by Him we cry, 'Abba, Father.' The Spirit Himself testifies with our spirit that we are God's children.

There is a high calling in Christ to move beyond fear-based service, to which the law itself is limited to effect. Of course, there is a very valid type of ministry that aims to produce the fear of God in men. That is usually found in the office of the evangelist. The fear of God is truly the beginning of wisdom (Ps. 111:10), and without the conviction of sin, there can be no repentance. We never abandon the fear of the Lord, but we must grow into a maturity that produces the love of God. Fear of punishment will produce an immediate response, but only the love of God will produce a sustained relationship. The love of God is not divorced from purity. And righteous living cannot take hold in the depths of our heart without us being enraptured by the goodness and beauty of the Lord. When we taste His beauty, our hearts become undone, and we cannot help but to serve Him in righteousness. Only the inspiration of His unconditional love for us will draw us beyond fear and into bridal love.

> There is no fear in love. But perfect love drives out fear, because fear has to do with punishment. The one who fears is not made perfect in love (1 John 4:18).

Many people cannot seem to embrace the paradox of the fear of the Lord and the love of the Lord. This is why many seek to water down the definition of fear as being "reverent awe" or simply "respect" for God. But John, the loved apostle, who literally snuggled with Jesus, was so terrified when he encountered the King of Glory in Revelation 1 that he fell to the ground as though he was dead!

Mankind is actually built with a normal, healthy capacity to fear that must be satisfied. This is why we turn to extreme sports and horror movies and roller coasters. Most people who shun the concept of the fear of the Lord are actually in bondage already to the fear of man. The fear of man is a "snare" the Scriptures say, and to fear man is much more oppressive than to fear God. David said, "Let me fall into the hands of the Lord, for His mercy is very great; but do not let me fall into the hands of men." (2 Sam. 24; 1 Chron. 21).

God is truly a holy terror, but also the kind you can delight in. When we "understand" the fear the Lord (Prov. 2:5), we actually *want* to tremble in His presence. It is not an irrational panic attack. We *desire* to shake in our boots, because it is the immensity of His love that frightens us. It is not a slavish fear. We are terrified by His beauty. And we know that even His judgments are sent merely to drive away every hindrance to intimacy. To become a people who can "stand" when He appears, we should apply ourselves to understanding the fear of God.

The fear of the Lord is simply a tutor to draw us into a deeper communion with Him. This is obvious when one considers the many blessings attached to the fear of the Lord. For one, He "confides in those who fear Him" (Ps. 25:14). The angel of the Lord also encamps around those who fear Him, and He delivers them (Ps. 34:7). Or how about this—"those who fear Him lack nothing" (Ps. 34:9). To fear the Lord is simply to agree with love, and to literally hate evil. Consider these blessings:

> *The fear of the Lord adds length of life, but the years of the wicked are cut short (Proverbs 10:27).*

> *Humility and the fear of the Lord bring wealth and honor and life (Proverbs 22:4).*

To fear God is not masochistic. It is actually to choose life and liberty and blessing. We also find, along the way, that our fear is overtaken by passion and an intoxicating hunger for more of His presence. Fear somehow is transfigured into pleasure, and we begin to "delight in the fear of the Lord" (Isa. 11:3). I tell you that this pleasure is more addictive than <u>crack</u> cocaine.

I have come to the point in my life where I actually want to encounter angels that seize me with fear. I literally want to see the Lord like Moses did, even if it scorches my face off. During such encounters, we regret ever saying those words, because of the sudden grip of holy terror in that instant. But nevertheless, there is an addicting hunger—a passion—that drives us closer to this all-consuming God, even to our own hurt. We are compelled to reach in and touch a level of glory that will knowingly cause us to die.

This type of self death is what will draw some to experience the *exastrapo*, the "glistening," like a flash of lightning, manifest by Jesus on the Mount of Transfiguration. This radiant, manifest glory on Jesus' face and clothing came just after He spoke about denying one's self, taking up your cross daily, and not being ashamed of Him before men.

There is a fiery holiness that is the direct result of God drawing near to us, as He increases and we decrease. While we think we want these intense encounters—always begging God to draw near—it is actually God's mercy that we don't experience them. With such filthy hearts, we would likely die in His presence. Tommy Tenney says, "The more death that God smells, the closer He can come."[4]

Let us continue to press into this love that overcomes fear. This dangerous love that flirts with death to self and compels us toward a greater resurrection. Above all, let us fix our eyes on Christ, so the example of His passion and purity is reproduced in us.

ENDNOTES

1. Tertullian, *Apologeticus*, a.d. 197.

2. The story of Maurice and the Theban Legion is passed to us from Bishop Eucherius of Lyon in the late fifth century in his Passion of the Martyrs of Agaune.

3. Eusebius, *The History of the Church* (London: Penguin, 1965), 337-338.

4. Tommy Tenney, *The God Chasers* (Shippensburg: Destiny Image Publishers, 1998), 60.

CHAPTER 3

Desert Voices

BY the third and fourth centuries, the deserts of Egypt, Palestine, Persia, and Arabia had become filled with a radical wave of hermits and monks, who had chosen solitude apart from a decadent society, in a quest for deeper connection with God. They were not out to form a Christian counterculture, and they were not merely escapists. Theirs was a purposeful life of intercession and spiritual warfare, waging battle from their holes and caves. To them, Christian *society* did not require an overabundance of church services, prayer meetings, and accountability groups. The Body of Christ, and their connection to it, was a mystical identification. Their lives, meanwhile, were spent in continual prayer. They waged war against demonic forces on the very frontiers of the world. And while there are extremes with any movement, these men were not overly negative or bent on withdrawal at the expense of reaching out to society. In fact, society came to them for advice.

Governors, nobles, and church leaders came to the deserts of Scete and the Nile delta for counsel, prayer, deliverance, and healing—even pagan rulers. Traffic increased so dramatically in the desert that many monks mourned their loss of solitude and found even more remote areas to live. Despite their solitary lifestyles, there were still strong elements of community within their ranks. They would occasionally emerge from their small cells for corporate worship. But on the rare occasion that a hermit came to a city or a population base, it was because the area was ripe for a powerful encounter. They did nothing willy nilly. They listened for the Father's voice.

The Desert Fathers were constantly wrestling against territorial demons, combating the deities of the heathen temples and demolishing their strongholds. The intensity of their spiritual warfare was much greater than what we commonly experience today. While we tend to look exclusively to the first century church as our shining example of supernatural exploits, we have largely forgotten the thread of wisdom and divine experience in the Desert Fathers. These men were detached completely from the spirit of their age, that their souls might be illumined in the presence of Christ.

"With the Desert Fathers, you have the characteristic of a clean break with a conventional, accepted social context in order to swim for one's life into an apparently irrational void," writes Thomas Merton in *The Wisdom of the Desert*. "The Desert Fathers were pioneers, with nothing to go on but the example of some of the prophets, like St. John the Baptist, Elias, Eliseus, and the apostles, who also served them as models. For the rest, the life they embraced was 'angelic' and they walked untrodden paths of invisible spirits. Their cells were the furnace of Babylon in which, in the midst of flames, they found themselves with Christ."[1]

St. Antony the Abbot (a.d. 251-356) lived in Upper Egypt, and we have a first hand account of his life written by Athanasius. After selling his possessions and giving the money to the poor, Antony began living the life of a hermit, eating only bread, with a little salt, and drinking only water. Much like John the Baptist, Antony wore animal skins, but with the hair turned to the inside, and he never bathed or washed his feet. He lived a life of strict prayer and fasting, and often would eat only once every three or four days. He slept either on a rush mat or on the bare floor. He lived in solitary places far away from others, usually shutting himself up in a small cell for prayer and meditation. He planted a number of ascetic communities, but would always withdraw, returning only to visit them

St. Antony the Abbot

occasionally. In fact, Antony is considered by many to be the very father of monasticism.

At times, when Antony preached openly, the people flocked to hear him, including pagans, who were all struck by the depth of his character. Many were converted, and he was known for working many miracles. He also had open visions, heard the audible voice of God, cast out devils, commanded animals to do things at times and even caused water to spring up in the desert by his prayer during a drought.

Like other Desert Fathers, Antony's life was filled with constant interaction with angels and demons. Satan was permitted to assault Antony in a visible manner, often terrifying him with gruesome noises, and once beat him almost to the point of death. Such experiences gave Antony tremendous discernment. Demonic beings threatened to burn him alive in his cell with torches, but as Antony began singing the Psalms, they fled. On several occasions, his cell was supernaturally filled with snakes and reptiles, but after commanding them to leave, they also departed. Several times, demons manifested as angels of light. Once, a demon appeared in the form of a monk, telling Antony to rest from his prayers, because he was only a man of flesh and blood. Antony then bowed and asked the Lord to make an end of this devil, and the demon vanished like smoke.

"Let us pray that we may know the hidden things, that we may have power from God to stand against the darts of the evil one. And if we desire to know the hidden things, then we must have our hearts pure, that we may be a habitation for the Holy Spirit and then He will abide and rest in us, and the light that proceeds from Him will enable us to see hidden things; even from remote distances," said Antony.[2] Like other fathers, Antony constantly walked in the Spirit and saw into the spirit realm. "Did not Elisha because of the purity of his heart, see with his spirit that which his natural eyes had never seen. We must then see and make a distinction between the things of God and the things of the congregation of the evil one. ...This fact I have learned from long experience. The visions and revelations of the Holy Spirit are not of tumultuous character, but take place under conditions of peace and restfulness," he said.

A few of the better-known Desert Fathers.

When we approach the lives of ascetics, it is important to keep a proper perspective. If we look only at their outward actions and austerity, we easily misunderstand them. Their outward extremes were only a visible sign that they had discovered an inner paradise. When asceticism is undertaken as a religious ascent to God, rather than a result and response of supernatural hunger, it can be a most twisted exercise in religiosity. If their lives seem stern, severe, or somber, it is only because we do not see the inner joy, peace, and ecstasy that drives their rigorous lifestyles.

What drew them into the desert? The Desert Fathers were not strictly running *away* from an immoral society, but rather, they were running *toward* deeper intimacy with Christ in the wilderness. As for their outward actions, many would eat only once or twice a week. Their lives were filled with prayer and simple work with their hands. They often would make straw mats, selling them and never bickering over the price they were given. They gave away most of the proceeds. The fathers kept watch day and night in prayer. Of the monks of Nitria, a student said, "Some of them never sleep at night—but either sitting or standing they persevered in prayer until the morning light." They often believed that, "One hour of sleep at night was enough for one who was a fighter."[3] At this time, a number of early church doctors and theologians were confronting heresies of the day. The Desert Fathers did not jump into the fray of much controversy, but sought to live humble, quiet lives of devotion. Occasionally, some of the fathers would venture out to preach against heresies. At this time, there were also a considerable number of believers who fled to the desert because they were disillusioned by the Roman Empire's sudden embrace of Christianity and the subsequent governmental control of the church that resulted from this church/state merger.

One of the chief characteristics of the Desert Fathers was that they never assumed to know more than they really did. They were more prone to listen than to speak. Theirs was a violent embrace of humility characterized by James 4:6, "God opposes to the proud, but gives grace to the humble." An elder once said that if a young monk is ever seen climbing into Heaven by his own will, they should "take him by the foot and throw him down to the ground," since it is not good for him to do so. The Desert Fathers applied themselves to meditation, humility, and the fear of God.

Separation from the spirit of the world, combined with perseverance in prayer, will be key to winning cities and nations in this hour and ushering in an awareness of God's presence in the 21st century. We have much to learn from the Desert Fathers. Their stories show us that God's power comes with a price. The coming age will show us a breed of men that will surpass even their holiness. And holiness is not just a matter of outward self-denial, but a matter of bearing the Spirit's fruit. In discussing the last generation, a Desert Father named Squirion once said, "At that time wickedness will overflow and the charity of many will grow cold. And there shall come upon them a terrible testing. Those who shall be found worthy in this testing will be better than we are and better than our fathers. They shall be happier and more perfectly proven in virtue."[4]

"Ours is certainly a time for solitaries and for hermits. But merely to reproduce the simplicity, austerity, and prayer of these primitive souls is not a complete or satisfactory answer. We must transcend them, and transcend all those who, since their time, have gone beyond the limits which they set," says Merton.

Among the Desert Fathers was Abbot Agatho, who supposedly carried a stone in his mouth for three years, until he learned how to be silent. Agatho once said that even if an angry man were to raise someone from the dead, he would not be pleasing to God because of his anger. The fathers understood that good character is greater than miraculous feats. There is a story of one hermit who became angry with a disciple and told him to drop dead. However, the hermit was not aware of how much power dwelt within himself at that moment. Immediately, his disciple fell over dead, and the hermit was filled with grief, praying that the Lord would bring him back to life, promising to be more careful with his words. The disciple was immediately restored to life.

Another, Abbot Theodore of Pherme owned only three books, the reading of which was helpful to him. But after discussing this with an elder, he determined that it was better to possess nothing at all. He sold the books and gave the money to the poor. Another man, Serapion, sold his one book of the gospels, saying, "I have sold the book which told me to sell all that I had and give to the poor."[5]

The Abbot Sisios was so prone to raptures that he had to lower his hands and quickly stop praying at times, unless his mind was carried away to Heaven, never to come back. Whenever he prayed with a brother, he was quick to lower his hands, so as not to be caught up into the heavens and remain there.

Amun was a man known for working many signs and wonders. He was once about to cross the river Lycus during flood season, and he asked his friend Theodorus to stay at a distance, so they would not see one another naked as they swam. After Theodorus left, Amun felt ashamed even to see his own naked body. As he was considering this, suddenly he was translated to the other side. Theodorus, when he approached and saw not a drop of water falling from Amun, wondering how he had got over.[6]

A group of men once hired a woman of ill repute to ruin a very famous hermit. She came to his cell late at night in the desert, weeping and pretending to be lost, in order to seduce him. Having pity on her, he allowed her into the front room of his cell but locked himself away in the inner room, so he wouldn't be tempted. The woman then began to wail, saying she was afraid of wild animals in the exposed outer room he had given her. The hermit became consumed with the fear of God, because temptations began to burn inside him. Nevertheless, he let her in. He lit a lantern and told himself, "Let's see whether you are able to bear the flames of hell." He put his finger in the flame, but could not even feel it because the burning intensity of lust in his bones. The woman was frozen with fear. He kept doing this to himself all night, until the conspiring men came looking for the woman the next morning. The hermit pointed the woman out to them, thinking she was asleep. The men found, however, that she had actually died of fear. Then the hermit showed them his hand. He had burned away all of his fingers to stave off temptation.

After that, the hermit prayed for the woman, and she returned to life. She became a Christian and devoted her life to purity.

An official was once looking for a certain abbot named Moses, because he was considered a great holy man. Hearing that the visitor was coming, Moses fled because of his humility. But on his way, he accidentally ran into this same official and his entourage. Not knowing who he was, they asked Moses for directions, and he replied "What do you want with him? The man is a fool and a heretic!"[7] As the official reached the church at Scete, he told them he had come looking for Moses, but that he had encountered a strange old man along the way. He wondered who would have said such things about the respected abbot. After describing the old man to them, the brothers confirmed that it was Moses himself, not wanting to be seen by the official. The official left, greatly encouraged by the monk's humble character.

One time an abbot came to another and asked what more he should do besides fasting, prayer, meditation, and contemplative silence. The elder stretched out his hands, and his fingers began to glow like ten lamps of fire. "Why not be totally changed to fire?" he asked.[8]

Perhaps one of the most bizarre examples of extreme asceticism is found in the life of fourth-century hermit St. Simeon Stylites. Simeon began living on top of a stone column. He never came down from the top of it for 36 years, and only ate one meal a week.[9] He even inspired an entire movement of *stylites* who followed his example and separated themselves from the world by living atop columns.

SHADES OF GNOSTICISM

As we look at the Desert Fathers, it is easy to be swept away by their devotion and sacrifice. But we must also recognize that lurking behind much of their austerity was the sinister influence of gnosticism—against which the church has had some of its greatest struggles. It is a demonic stronghold that is married ever so closely to the religious spirit and the spirit of antichrist.

Before we discuss gnosticism directly, we should understand that as we near the end of the age, and begin to experience the same signs and wonders as the early church, we will also be fighting many of their same battles. In fact, there were spiritual wars they did not win, that we are still waging now. We cannot afford to simply imitate the first century church. We must go further and complete what they could not finish. There are many ancient heresies that will re-emerge in this hour, and there are many that never went away.

We should not get worked up over minor doctrinal issues; however, it is critical that we do pursue sound doctrine. The Lord will bear with us as we grow in understanding, and we are all in the process of having our minds renewed and filled with truth. But gnosticism is a *major* error that cannot be tolerated. It poses an immediate danger, because of its spreading popularity in this hour. We should not study the enemy's strategies more than we study the Lord's, but it is important to identify our enemy. The church is still battling, at its very foundations, the antichrist spirit. And gnosticism is about as antichrist as you can get. I believe the antichrist will probably come as a literal, individual man. But it is a waste of time to try and figure out who he is, while ignoring its work in our own lives and minds.

Dear children, this is the last hour; and as you have heard that the antichrist is coming, even now many antichrists have come. This is how we know it is the last hour (1 John 2:18).

We should not be intimidated by the antichrist spirit—all of the antichrists combined do not have the power that is found in one Spirit-filled believer. But we must recognize its prevalence because of the hour we are in, and protect ourselves from deception. Satan comes to us not with horns and a pitchfork, but masquerading as an angel of light. This spirit will not simply oppose the deity of Christ, but also the *humanity* of Christ. We must come into a full revelatory understanding that Jesus was fully God and fully man.

> *Many deceivers, who do not acknowledge Jesus Christ as coming in the flesh, have gone out into the world. Any such person is the deceiver and the antichrist* (2 John 7).

Gnostics point blank deny that Jesus came in the flesh. Jesus suddenly becomes a *spiritual* superhero, but no one can imitate Him if He was not flesh and blood like us. This was the root of nearly every major early church heresy, the seed of which has continued to spread throughout history. It has spurned innumerable doctrines of demons, and is still a major stronghold in the church today.

Gnosticism, or *gnostic docetism*, claims that all physical matter is evil, and all spirit is good. It denies that Jesus came in the flesh, professing that He was only a spiritual being. Since the flesh is made of matter, it is therefore "evil." But we know that unless Jesus became a man *like* us, He could not have died *for* us. He had to become like us in every way, yet be without sin, in order to bear our sin and bridge the gap between God and humanity. This is foundational. The apostle John—who preaches against gnosticism more than anyone else in Scripture—makes it clear that "the Word became flesh and made His dwelling among us" (John 1:14). The incarnation of Christ is the very crux of the gospel—God became one of us, in order to save us.

Gnostics also believed that man is saved by attaining a special, *secret knowledge*. This is important to remember, to see how it's tied to the religious spirit. It takes the focus off the cross, and puts it on our own works. Gnosticism comes from the word *gnosis* "to know." By a process of learning and attaining a hidden understanding, gnostics think they can save themselves. This puts the focus on our own attainment and "head knowledge" rather than on Jesus.

How is this relevant to us today? Gnosticism is not just a stronghold behind secular intellectualism. Gnosticism is the main dish served at most seminaries and Bible schools today. It is the Captain Crunch of most Sunday morning services (by *knowing more about* God, or even memorizing the Bible, you are saved—versus knowing God *relationally* or experientially). It is heart belief—not a head trip—that is counted as saving faith.

> ...*if you confess with your mouth, "Jesus is Lord," and* **believe** *in your* **heart** *that God raised Him from the dead, you will be* **saved**. *For it is with your* **heart** *that you* **believe** *and are justified, and it is with your mouth that you confess and are* **saved** (Romans 10:9-10).

The idolatry of godly knowledge can even cause us to worship the Bible, rather than the God of the book. Knowing *about* God is not the same as knowing God. I can know lots of facts about a person, but until I meet him, I do not really know him. An overemphasis on "head knowledge" versus "heart knowledge" is gnostic. This spirit will also cause us to try and figure out all our spiritual problems, without ever actually taking them to the cross. It is a form of godliness that denies the power (2 Tim. 3:5). It produces hearers of the Word, but not doers of the Word.

We recognize this critter most obviously as that unnatural, overpious, uptight religious monkey. That's because it goes against what is normal and natural and human, and calls the contorted result "holy." It tries to make you *ascend* to God, rather than believe Jesus already came to you. It manipulates the exterior, to appear "spiritual." Religion exalts a mode of self-denial, while never dealing a death blow to the root heart issues of pride and fear.

Our embrace of the cross is not just an embrace of death. It is the embrace of hope in a greater resurrection. We have no guarantee that sacrifice will be fun. But the chief end of Christians is not just to make sacrifices. Our objective is to enjoy God, come what may. Religion worships self death. We worship the Lord.

Mahesh Chavda

Mahesh Chavda (1946-present) is a great example of someone in the present day who has undertaken severe ascetic disciplines, not unlike the Desert Fathers, but not in a legalistic way.

Mahesh has literally taken dozens of 40-day and 20-day fasts in his lifetime. But he is still a normal guy. Likes movies. Likes Doritos. He fully understands that God's love for him is not dependent on his own personal discipline. Yet it is Mahesh's *craving* for more of the higher walk that drives him into fasts.

Fasting and ascetic practices, when done properly out of godly desire instead of religious striving, are like a spiritual narcotics. It also opens the door for miracles faster than almost anything else. Mahesh has raised the dead. He heals the sick very regularly. Just about every time Mahesh preaches—and times in between—a supernatural manifestation of gold dust begins to cover his body and come upon those who are listening. Other spontaneous miracles occur in his ministry, such as the appearance of feathers or clouds during meetings. These are becoming common miracles in certain streams of the corporate church body in this day, and are therefore taking its expected criticism. But many occurrences are the outright result of someone paying the price.

God responds to spiritual hunger. When we deny ourselves to make room for Him, He will meet us. We must understand that asceticism is not the enemy. Many in the coming days will fast and pray even more stringently than the Desert Fathers. There will even be a revival of hermits and neo-monastics in the coming days that will blow us out of the water. But they will not be fueled by a religious spirit. They might even look oddly irreligious at times.

There will always be external acts of sacrifice—fasting, giving, extreme discipline, etc.—and we will always be a peculiar people. It's unavoidable. We will always do weird things, because we are aware of a greater reality than the seen world. But there is still a way to interact with the spiritual realm in a natural way that does not vilify our own humanity. We can be natural, yet free from sin, like Jesus. For too long, the church has separated the spiritual from natural. John Wimber always hammered the point that we must learn to become *naturally supernatural*. I believe that's why God moved so powerfully on the hippie Jesus Movement of the '60s and '70s, because they were restoring a natural, organic dynamic to the faith. Jesus, in His humanity, experienced all that we experience in day-to-day living. He was completely bizarre and completely normal—100 percent God and 100 percent man. No half and half. Seeing angels should be a regular part of the natural life of a Christian. Chopping wood or mowing the lawn should be no less holy a task than raising the dead.

Francis of Assisi seemed to walk in this understanding of the interconnectedness of the natural and spiritual realm. He was once cultivating a garden, when someone asked, "What would you be doing right now if you knew this was the last day of your earthly life?" Francis simply said, "I would keep on hoeing this row of beans." Brother Lawrence went so far as to say the presence of God should be no less powerful in your daily activities than it is in the prayer closet.

Jesus showed us how to live with a human nature, but not to be driven by sinful desires. He shows us that physical matter is not evil. He ate, slept, and worked as a carpenter. Wrongly rejecting the natural realm can actually prevent us from attaining the spiritual heights we long for. It is like taking out the lower rungs of Jacob's ladder. Of course, Jesus didn't worship His natural desires. Keep in mind that "flesh and blood cannot inherit the Kingdom of God, nor does the perishable inherit the imperishable" (1 Cor. 15:50). Physical matter is not eternal. It is passing away, and so we do not cater to it excessively. But on the other hand, it is not evil. Evil is a product of what comes out of the heart. A natural thing can be used for good or evil, depending on the outflow of the heart. The *desires* and *lusts* of the flesh, which arise from our inner man—those are what defile us. That is why Jesus said it is not the food and things that go into a man that defiles him, but the evil that comes out of his heart. By vilifying the subject matter that goes into us, along with the physical substances of the world, gnosticism causes us to ignore the true roots of evil in our hearts.

We must be on guard against doctrines of demons in these last days that will move more overtly in this direction. The church has been in bondage to dress codes, cosmetic laws, and countless other silly issues in its exterior strife toward "holiness" over the years. First Timothy is pretty clear on the whole issue:

> *The Spirit clearly says that in later times some will abandon the faith and follow deceiving spirits and things taught by demons. Such teachings come through hypocritical liars, whose consciences have been seared as with a hot iron. They forbid people to marry and order them to abstain from certain foods, which God created to be received with thanksgiving by those who believe and know the truth. For everything God created is good, and nothing is to be rejected if it is received with thanksgiving...* (1 Timothy 4:1-4).

DOCTRINES OF DEMONS

Gnosticism crept into the early church from the very beginning. Here is a good example: Since the pagans used musical instruments in their worship, some early church fathers rejected their use in the church. But their reasons for doing this went beyond a "let's look different than the pagans" mentality (which isn't really a good excuse anyway). Some early church leaders, like Clement of Alexandria, stressed that instruments were *natural* or *external*—implying that they were of no spiritual good, and in fact, evil. See the gnosticism in that? This single demonic doctrine held people in bondage for centuries, unable to freely express their worship to God through sound. We still see the aftereffects of this today, although God is changing it rapidly. The church is even now beginning to release the supernatural sounds of Heaven. Entire new genres of music are about to come out of the church that the world has never before heard. Some of it will be so saturated with God's Spirit, you will literally be able to see the sound. Jason Upton and other pioneering worship leaders have actually captured the voices of angels singing on their albums.

The church fathers were so focused on battling outright paganism in the world that gnosticism slipped right in the back door of the church. While the early fathers did fight against it, the heresy clearly influenced even them. The very fact that they debated the gnostics, rather than simply demonstrating Christianity with miracles, is a sure sign that gnosticism had rubbed off on them. Religion will strip you of power faster than anything else. The gospel was being reduced to talk, knowledge, theory, and argument.

Gnosticism's approach, being more esoteric and intellectual than paganistic—along with the fact that it could embrace certain aspects of Christianity in a *form* of godliness—made it a dangerous counterfeit. Since gnosticism taught that the physical body was of no value—that the body only imprisoned the spirit—it led to two paradoxical extremes: Seeing the body as an enemy of the spirit, many sought to starve away every natural, human desire possible, turning to extreme asceticism. But others thought they already had the secret to eternal life and the evil body didn't matter anymore. So, they indulged their bodies in gluttony and sexual sin.

The Nicolaitans were a type of such gluttonous gnostics. Jesus Himself spoke against the Nicolaitans in the Book of Revelation. "But you have this in your favor: You hate the practices of the Nicolaitans, which I also hate" (Rev. 2:6). The Nicolaitans represented an extreme form of gnosticism that practiced this unrestrained indulgence, feeling they had license to sin with the natural body. Their belief is also connected with *antinomianism*, a belief that recognizes the need for God's mercy for salvation, but it allows man to freely partake in sin because God's law is no longer binding. Sound familiar? Today we call that "cheap grace" or nominal Christianity—Christians "in name only." They call themselves Christians, but never put away sinful practices. I was one of those for many years of my life, and the Bible Belt, where I am from, is full of them. Such a one thinks that a mere intellectual "belief" in God's mercy has saving power. But as we know, "the devils also believe, and tremble" (James 2:19). Salvation is a free gift based on our belief, but our works show evidence that we truly believe in our *hearts*. Repentance from sin brings our inner belief into outward experience and shows proof of our faith.

Nicolaitan comes from the Greek *nikao*, "to conquer," and *laos*, which means "the laity" or "the people." We see how directly this is also tied to the religious spirit. This spirit seeks to overcome, or squelch the laity—it keeps power and authority out of the pews and puts the focus on one man in a pulpit. Most of us are familiar with this political, hierarchical human authority in the church. It is usually marked by spiritual pride, control, manipulation, and rebellion to God's rightful authority.

Gnosticism had many offshoots in the days of the early church. For instance, *monophysism* was a heretical belief meaning "one nature," that also denied Christ's human nature. Monophysism said Christ's human nature existed, but only "as a drop of wine in an ocean." Eventually, the most orthodox theologians began to bear traces of gnosticism in their writings and sermons. Augustine's writings were perhaps the most popular. Understand that the Desert Fathers were not gnostics, nor was Augustine or any of the early church fathers. However, gnostic thought did infiltrate their beliefs severely, if not innocently, as they began to split from the natural world.

St. Augustine of Hippo (a.d. 354-430) is considered a doctor of the church, and he is regarded as a spiritual ancestor of Protestantism. While Augustine surely made remarkable contributions to the Christian faith, he also brought a gnostic influence to mainstream Christianity. Augustine believed the entire world was altogether fallen, to the point that nature itself was basically sinful. His beliefs resurfaced centuries later, influencing reformer John Calvin's teachings that man is completely depraved apart from conversion.

St. Augustine

It is one thing to say all have sinned and fallen short of the glory of God. It is entirely another thing to say everything is utterly corrupted. Surely we can do nothing of positive, eternal consequence apart from Christ, but there is a basic, inherent value in the natural realm that cannot be denied. There is original sin, but there is also a measure of original innocence. Eastern Orthodox theologians respect Augustine, but like many in the West, they do not believe this doctrine of "intrinsic impairment" to be necessary. In Romans 7:18, the apostle Paul says, "I know that nothing good lives in me, that is, in my *sinful nature*." The key term to remember here is "sinful nature"—it is the nature of our wicked hearts, not the natural realm itself, which is evil. We live a paradox as Christians. On one hand, we realize we are utterly worthless apart from Christ, and on the other hand, we carry the full worth of God Himself.

His inability to separate the sinful nature from healthy natural desires probably explains why Augustine was a self-admittedly tortured man in the area of sexuality. Had he acknowledged the inherent good in proper marital relations, it is possible that a foundation would have been laid for future clergy. Augustine burned with lust, but he would not marry, contrary to the apostolic teachings. Legalistic abstinence only opens the door for temptations toward aberrant behavior. Augustine's pivotal role in early Christian theology possibly explains the Catholic church's consistent inability to find balance in areas of sexuality in ministry that remains today. While we should not paint a broad target over our Catholic brothers, it is scripturally clear that abstinence from marriage was never a requirement for ministers in the apostolic writings. And Peter himself, whom Catholics regard as the first Pope, took a wife.

There were other Augustinian faults that have trickled down through the ages. He advocated persecution against fellow Christians—the first time that had ever happened—developing the concept of "just war" against the Donatists. Augustine reasoned that the church had the right to kill the Donatists, a type of fringe holiness movement of his day, because he felt they were leading others astray spiritually. It was not long after this in church history that popes became absolute military dictators. This militant spirit still affects much of the church today in its approach to the world. Many in the world see all Christians as militant abortion clinic bombers, willing to impose their beliefs by force, if necessary. Unfortunately, there has been some truth to this stereotype. But our militancy should never be waged by carnal means.

To top it all off, Augustine diminished the role of natural Israel in God's continuing work in the earth, making room for a replacement theology that would eventually be the basis for outright anti-Semitism. Not only did the Catholic church use Augustine's writings as a means to write off Israel, but so did Martin Luther and other Protestant reformers.

While these things did heap centuries of problems onto the church because of his great influence, Augustine, in most other areas, was a theological champion; and his writings on the whole are impressive. My intent is not to criticize. I only hope to bring balance here, through an awareness of a few gnostic cracks in the church's foundation. It is worth mentioning, on an ironic note, that Augustine also received prophetic visions, although the theological streams that most highly regard him today believe such gifts died out with the apostles before him.

Outright gnosticism appeared to subside after the Patristic period. But it had already infiltrated common thought. It just got a facelift in each subsequent age. Gnosticism saw a great renewal after the Protestant Reformation. The Rosicrucians were a new brand of blatant gnostics that swept Europe and the world at that time, posing as Christians. Their name meant "order of the rosy cross," and they are believed to be the roots of freemasonry. They claimed a secret saving knowledge and denied that Christ came in the flesh. In this way, gnostic influence became a major thrust behind the Age of Reason and Enlightenment. Enlightenment philosopher Immanuel Kant, in the 1700s, purported that man was maturing to a higher state of awareness and throwing off the childhood restraints of God and church. This was in complete contradiction to "trust in the Lord with all your heart and lean not on your own understanding" (Prov. 3:5).

Modernism is chock full of gnostic principles. Gnostic tenets have either directly or indirectly influenced evolution, comparative religions, abortion, the mind sciences, theological liberalism, unitarianism, theosophy, and the new age movement. That may sound like a broad statement, but their roots are all the same. In fact, many in the new age movement today openly embrace gnosticism by name, and it will be one of the biggest pop cults to sweep the nations in the near future. As mentioned in Chapter 1, the *DaVinci Code* book is re-popularizing the stronghold even now. In fact, Hollywood is today flush with professing gnostics.

Since it denies the flesh (yet, in an improper way), gnosticism does have a strong appearance of true spirituality. The antichrist spirit will not just *oppose* the Lord, as much as it will try to *substitute*, or take the place of Christ, the "Anointed One." *Anointing* means to smear, as with oil. The anointing is the smearing of God's Holy Spirit, His presence. The antichrist comes as the "anti-anointed one," or in fact, he poses a false anointing—a substitute, unholy spirituality.

The reason we are focusing so heavily on gnosticism, is because the antichrist in this hour wants to offer this unholy spirit to fill mankind's craving for the Heavenly realm. Overt gnosticism is the source of nearly all counterfeit mysticism, so we must take cautions to avoid it. The early gnostics even incorporated a form of unorthodox Jewish mysticism—the kabbala—giving their heresy an even stronger sense of true spirituality. But in the church today, gnosticism is more subtle. It wrongly elevates knowledge and Greek logic, putting too much focus on the mind—we think of the Greek philosophers Plato, Aristotle, and Socrates, for instance, as the shapers of human reasoning. But Hebraic tradition urges us to have *literal* experience with God, not just logical, doctrinal thoughts about Him. The Hebrew approach is always more literal than symbolic, and its focus is more on faith than analysis.

We can boil down the gnostic influence on the church today into a three-fold cord that we must overcome:

We are saved by "knowing." Knowing lots of Christian information and theology has been a substitute for relationship with God. We even know our problems and are aware of the sin we struggle with, but fail to take it to the cross or actually repent. Our level of knowledge far outweighs our level of obedience. Hearers, but not doers.

Leads to death or indulges the flesh. Our humanity is not evil, although we do have a sin nature that must be dealt with. We are to deny ourselves, but not become masochists. The religious spirit will try to make you kill yourself, versus submitting to the Lord and letting Him purify you. We are called to embrace His refining fire, but not go looking for persecution and death. Religion's end is suicide. The opposite extreme here would be to take grace as a license to sin, and think that sins of the flesh are not important since we have spiritual salvation.

The spirit realm seems out of reach. We feel "chained" in our bodies, because we have an underlying belief that we are evil and sinful. This prevents us from naturally flowing in the supernatural realm. We are unable to see God's glory in the simple things of life, and are more aware of an *uncleanness* around us than we are of God's presence.

It does not take much "discernment" to point out these flaws with the body, but our main task is to build up the church and focus on the Lord—not criticize and focus on the enemy's work. Fortunately, as we become full to the brim with the real anointing, and turn our eyes to the living Christ, these strongholds are going to topple.

Our bent toward the natural realm should be to somehow see the glory of God in all things. Remember that we are made in God's image. Ever wondered what God looks like? You look like Him in a lot of ways. Even the natural realm reflects God. God created matter, and nature is not utterly corrupted. We should have an eye for redeeming even those things which are used for evil. When God created the earth, He saw that it was good. This is because the very earth declared His majesty. And there is a higher purpose in store for the earth that prompted God to redeem it. Although we may not always be aware of it, "the whole earth is full of His glory" (Isa. 6:3). Keep in mind that this verse was written after the fall, yet it is still truth. The Kingdom of God is always just at hand—within fingertip reach even while we are in this world—the problem is, His glory usually goes unnoticed.

Like Elisha's servant, we need our eyes opened to the spirit realm, even amid this earthly reality. Heaven is *already* touching earth, we are just not aware of it. We need to manifest this reality. One day, the earth will also be filled with the *knowledge* of the glory of the Lord, as the waters cover the sea (see Hab. 2:14). That is, one day we will be aware of the omnipresent God who is already in our midst. It is not that the angelic realm will step into our world, but that we will enter more into theirs through a consciousness—an awareness—of God's reality. That, after all, is faith. Believing in the unseen. There will be such an acute consciousness of God's glory that we will see His reflection everywhere we look, even amid our mundane, natural circumstances.

We often pray for God's glory to come. But we should be asking to see and know the glory that is *already at hand*. We are not to pull Heaven down from some hazy, unreachable place. Heaven is already within us—we must learn to release it through simple belief.

Already the Lord is renewing an awareness of the Kingdom at hand, which is the key to miracles in the marketplace in this hour. During the past year, I was praying for an amputee in a wheelchair in an outdoor shopping plaza, asking God to regrow his legs. While this would seem foolish to most people, I set my goals high. No legs popped out of the man, but as I was praying, he began to weep, because the Lord began healing him of a chronic stomach ailment right there on the spot, which I knew nothing about. This kind of thing starts to draw a crowd. And the next thing I know, we are praying for a lady merchant whose foot was wrapped up in bandages. Five minutes later, she had ripped them off and she was walking away back to her store, healed. God's power was displayed to onlookers in the streets. These were "little" healings compared to what I was shooting for. But if I had not set a big goal for a big God, my faith would never have risen high enough to expect even the lesser things.

The Lord is calling us to a radical shift of perspective. The church has long considered "faith" to be a set of mental beliefs and intellectual principles. But living in the realm of the mind—and pursuing a strict knowledge-based spirituality—often causes us to neglect the simplistic childlike expectancy that constitutes true Heavenly wisdom.

GETTING PAST THE MIND

The very word *repentance* implies a change of mind. Repentance, or "metanoia" does not just mean a turning from outward sin. Rather, it means a shift of consciousness from self to God. It is a type of inner transcendence. A change of focus. It is simply a change of mind, or better yet, a change of heart.

We must focus everything within us on Heaven. God does not call us to abandon the mind—far from it! He wants us to redirect it. God does not want a church full of idiots. He wants us use our minds, to be leaders in science, medicine, technology, and other areas. But first come the heart issues. The more intimacy we have with God in our lives, the smarter we will become intellectually.

If we learn anything from the mystics of the desert—from the early fathers of the faith—it is not just their bizarre deeds or theological creeds that set them apart. They possessed humility and character that superseded their miracles, and they possessed a faith that transcended the Platonic logic of their day.

A man's spirit is the seat of his being; the mind is subsidiary. The mind is an important part of our being. It is a fortress to ward off the enemy from our souls, but at times, it can also be a stronghold to ward off God. We should not elevate the mind, or use it to box God into a corner. We want to be led by the Spirit and the Word, and not by human wisdom. Of course, Greek rationalism is important, and even a God-given phenomena. It is no coincidence that nearly half the Scriptures are written in Greek. But did you know there are other ways of using our mind, outside of Hellenistic logic? The reason we only use 10 percent of our brains is because you can only go so far with rationalism. As our spirits are renewed, we can move into forms of sanctified imagination and pattern recognition that are not "delusionary thinking," but actually revelatory inspirations of the Holy Spirit. Rational thinking is good, only incomplete. I believe it is Western elitism and arrogance that paints the more spiritual-thinking societies of the world as unintelligent.

> *Jews demand miraculous signs and Greeks look for wisdom, but we preach Christ crucified: a stumbling block to Jews and foolishness to Gentiles, but to those whom God has called, both Jews and Greeks, Christ is the power of God and the wisdom of God. For the foolishness of God is wiser than man's wisdom, and the weakness of God is stronger than man's strength* (1 Corinthians 1:22-25).

Although we are making a strong case for supernatural encounters and godly wisdom in these chapters, we do not preach a "signs and wonders" gospel anymore than we preach an "intellectual" gospel. We preach Christ crucified. That is our gospel. It is a gospel with signs following, and it also leads to wisdom. But the cross will always be an offense and a stumbling block to many.

One huge block to deeper spiritual encounters is our need to understand a thing before we experience it. But Jesus very often has us experience a thing, before we receive the understanding of it.

Jesus had not been with His disciples for very long before he sent them out and told them to cast out demons and heal the sick. This was all new to them, and it was beyond their understanding or personal capability to perform. It was on-the-job training. It was not until they returned with stories of their exploits that Jesus gave them understanding into what they had been doing.

We want to understand and perfect a thing before we take the necessary risks of obedience. Human wisdom loves to justify disobedience or make excuses to avoid stretching circumstances. Human wisdom says, "If it's not in the Word, don't do it." Jesus says, "Do what I tell you, then I'll show you where it is in the Word."

Sometimes, our greatest sin is settling for a mundane life and not stepping out into the unknown. God is looking for courageous pioneers. He would rather us step out in faith than sit on the sidelines, afraid of operating in presumption. Faith must precede reason. Faith is a cornerstone of the Kingdom of God. Many cloak their unbelief and spiritual inexperience in an unholy rationalism under the guise of a "Berean" study of the Scriptures. They never risk the unknown, even at the Holy Spirit's prompting. "If it's not in the Bible, we won't believe it," they say. Well, cheeseburgers are not in the Bible; do you believe in cheeseburgers?

God does not want to keep our minds darkened about spiritual things. God loves questions, because He loves dialogue. But He despises arrogance and reckless insubordination. Like the fathers, let us embrace the humility to trust God and embrace the unknowns until the answers come in Spirit and in Truth.

The believer will necessarily encounter things for which there seemingly is no biblical precedent—or at least no apparent precedent. If the Christian walk is confined to the limits of our knowledge or mental understanding, our capacity for spiritual experience will not go very far. Many reject certain supernatural activities not because they are unscriptural, but because they don't jive with their personal *interpretation* of the Scriptures. We are often blinded to the truth of Scripture on such matters, not because we are unfamiliar with it, but because we have hardened our hearts in such a way that it becomes incomprehensible.

Even in the most charismatic of circles, there are unspoken "lists" of what type of experiences are appropriate. For instance, when I mention levitation or walking through walls, many people instantly think of the occult. But Jesus did both. This is all rooted in a desire to understand or know about a thing before we are open to experiencing it. And to a degree, this comes from a gnostic dependence on the mind. Did Peter have time to understand the scriptural basis for walking on water? No, but he wanted to jump out of the boat, and so Jesus let him. We need to be eager to step out on the waters of the supernatural with Jesus.

God is beginning to inhabit His church again. We have to be OK with experiencing His glory and watching Him do incredible things that boggle our minds. God is giving us more insight into His character and His ways in this hour, through this present move of His Spirit. But there will always be mysteries and paradox. The Desert Fathers understood this clearly. One of the ways they recognized maturity in a monk is when he stopped assuming to understand everything about God and Scripture, and could honestly say, "I don't know."

Although God is drawing closer than ever, and we can see Him more clearly, we must continue to resist the temptation to formulize His ways. The church must continue to move and flow like a river, lest we stagnate. We must take new ground, occupy that ground, and then take more ground. A sure sign of life is *movement*.

I do not suggest we throw all caution to the wind and abandon sound truth in our spiritual walk. But what we need to do is get rooted and grounded in a wholehearted love for Jesus. Knowing Jesus was the only requirement the disciples needed when He sent them out to perform miracles. And *loving* Jesus was the only thing that kept the disciples from going astray after He was crucified. We can never brace for every bizarre encounter or every theological problem. We will never figure it all out. But falling in love with Jesus—abandoning ourselves to His presence—is the safest, yet most radical thing we can ever do.

Unlike those early disciples, much of the church is so afraid of the demonic, that we won't open up to new ways of spiritual expression with which we are unfamiliar. Yet Jesus purposely sent spiritual babies to cast out demons, despite their obvious immaturity. See, it's not about us—nor about us figuring things out. It's about Him.

We will never step out to face giants without raw faith, because reason will always point to the fact that they are bigger than us. Faith pleases God, not brains. It is faith in the unseen that assures me God is over all. Even His holy angels outnumber the demonic forces of hell two to one, and we are always safe when our hearts are in pursuit of Him. Is your fear of the demonic greater than your hunger for God?

I have found that, as I lay down my mind and my own understanding, God always expands it. When I respond to those urgings from Him that I least understand, I am often most blessed. Much of what I know intellectually was simply handed down to me, but never experienced firsthand. *Knowledge* is no more than a mental collection of facts. But true understanding and wisdom are rooted in a supernatural discernment of what to do with those facts. It comes supernaturally, and is rooted in love.

As a student in school, most of us experienced what I like to call "academic bulimia." We would memorize a bunch of facts until test time, then regurgitate—dump out the mental hard drive and start over again. In the West, we are similarly overstuffed with religious information that would qualify the average pew warmer here to be a full-fledged Bible school teacher in many developing nations. But only a handful have the motivation or heart to actually go and reach the poor and the lost. We think we are rich, but we lack substance.

Unfortunately, we are usually only obedient to a very small percentage of what we know. We are glutted on truth, with a very small margin of obedience to accompany it. Throughout history, many Christians have recognized this and gone overboard. They toss out what they deem "head knowledge" and become senseless fanatics. Being a fanatic is not so bad, but why be a senseless one? We need intellectual Christians in the marketplace—in business and politics—who have amassed great reservoirs of learning, yet who are foremost yielded to the Spirit of God. The world is afraid of an intelligent Christian, because he gives a rational credence to his life of faith. However, the world is more challenged by a fiery Christian. They want you to be either tame and predictable or a complete nutcase, so that they can criticize and classify you. But I think it is possible to break both molds. Why not be a complete genius, yet still wacky enough to cast out demons, heal the sick, and raise the dead?

The false stigma that Christians are idiots is about to dissolve. There is coming a swift manifestation of the "mind of Christ" in the church like never before. That's because we're finally figuring out that the *heart issues* must come first. There will still be critical spirits in the world, which stereotype us as mindless bigots, but Christians are about to display such creative insight that the world will not be able to argue that the church produces the brightest minds. Now that God is raising up a prophetic church, Christians are about to walk in unprecedented areas of innovation in every career field.

Another thing we should take with us from the Desert Fathers, before we move on, is the radical nature in which they wrestled the enemy within.

Many believers do not fully realize that the mind is a spiritual battleground. Negative thoughts are one of the enemy's most powerful tools against us. The mind is in need of renewal, and that comes by applying ourselves to truth. The enemy will constantly assault our thought life with innumerable doubts and temptations until we resist him with the Truth. Many men and women are complacent today, simply because we have bought the enemy's lie that we are in some way limited or incapable of fulfilling our calling. We are constantly hearing lies and being harassed by negative thoughts about ourselves and others. The enemy will repeatedly whisper lies into our ear that we are incompetent; that we will miss our destiny; and that we are incapable of achieving our God-given desires and callings.

It is time to recognize these types of negative thought patterns for what they are: demonic strongholds. There are harassing spirits that try to pull a veil of stupor over our eyes and block us from our purpose by intimidating us and pointing out that we are not worthy or able to step into destiny. There are literally tormenting spirits that can be assigned to you and I, simply to whisper negative thoughts into our ears.

I believe that God gives us mysteries and paradoxes so that we might transcend the mind, and so rise above this warfare. He purposely withholds answers to teach us not to rely on our own understanding, but on His name. In this war, satan will use truth to keep you engaged on the lower realms of spirituality. His goal is to never let you embrace your true authority in God. He will distract you with "lesser truths," issues of good and evil, so you don't turn to the Tree of Life. His first temptation is always to question God's authority and identity, particularly how it relates to you. Satan will point out your flaws, readily pointing to your sin nature. He seeks to lock you into a self-justification cycle—perhaps even locking you into a lifetime of mortifying your flesh like a desert hermit. Satan would love to keep you engaged in battling him, because you are harmless. He wants your attention.

But we no longer identify with the sin nature. We identify with the Lord of Hosts. We are partners with the great Lord of the armies of heaven, with whom our enmity has been cancelled. Satan is not afraid of you, but he is terrified of the One who dwells within you. The Kingdom is close at hand. Walk in the Spirit, and the warfare of the mind vanishes in an instant.

When we appeal to a higher realm of grace, throwing our eyes and hearts toward the Lover of our souls, we transcend the ground warfare, and we are not fooled by the devil's schemes. One of the best ways we can overcome our adversary is to agree with him quickly, before he drags us into court (see Matt. 5:25). Don't try to justify yourself. Forget the denial! We just admit our desperate shortcomings and embrace the power of the cross. Never give satan the benefit of putting you on the defensive. It is true that you and I are incapable of fulfilling our callings alone, but the fact is, Christ within us can accomplish all things. The blood of Jesus makes a way beyond myself. In my weakness and lukewarm struggles, He is strong and fiery. It is Him who saved me; it is Him who is purifying me; and it is Him who will bring His work in me to completion. In Him, nothing can hold me back from walking into my prophetic destiny. The cross is always a stumbling block to the mind, but it is also the greatest key to wisdom and power.

ENDNOTES

1. Thomas Merton, *The Wisdom of the Desert* (New York: New Directions Publishing, 1970), 9-10.

2. Translated by Wallis E.A. Budge, "The Spiritual Warfare of the Desert Fathers in the 3rd-4th Centuries," notes from The Paradise of the Holy Fathers, vol. 1. Accessed 19 Oct. 2004 <http://www.consumingfire.com/desert.htm>.

3. Ibid.

4. Merton, *The Wisdom of the Desert*, 48.

5. Ibid., 33, 37.

6. Athanasius. *The Life of Anthony*, translated by Rev. H. Ellershaw. <http://ccel.org/fathers/NPNF2-04/Athanasius/t95.htm>.

7. Merton, *The Wisdom of the Desert*, 35-36.

8. Ibid., 50.

9. Elesha Coffman, "The Quest." Christian History and Biography (Spring, 2004), 39-40.

CHAPTER 4

Nature Mystics

OVERCOMING gnosticism and religion will bring a release of the *nature mystics*. When mankind is fully and properly in balance with God, he can walk in the same authority as Adam held over nature in the garden—and as Jesus, the second Adam, when He walked the earth.

Whatever new age principles you may associate with the term "nature mystics," let us throw that all out. Let us take back terminology that is ours as believers. Rick Joyner often says we need to take back even the term "new age," because Christians, more than anyone else—more than any utopian philosophy—have the greatest hope for the future. We will surely see a new age, as we dwell in a new Heaven and a new earth. But even before the new earth and millennial reign of Christ, God is going to restore His people to walk in Adamic power over nature.

> *The creation waits in eager expectation for the sons of God to be revealed* (Romans 8:19).

The very earth itself is *longing* for its rightful stewards, mankind, to demonstrate the substance of Heaven. This almost sounds pantheistic—as if inanimate creation has a voice and a desire. As the dynamic of sonship is released in a fuller way in these last days, we will have a deeper understanding of how we are really supposed to relate to nature. Even as God breathed life into inanimate earth to create man, so are we called to breathe the creative substance of God into the world, as reflections of His image.

For starters, let us realize that the sons of God will manifest the Holy Spirit, not a religious spirit. That means they will have to be like Jesus, fully spiritual and fully natural. The world is about to truly see *incarnational* Christianity.

The modernist mind-set has sought to conquer and subjugate even the natural terrain of the land. During the Age of Enlightenment, Europeans began to build elaborate gardens into strict geometric patterns. Anything wild or uncultivated had to be eradicated or confined. Everything had to become domesticated and controlled—put in a box. Creativity diminished. While man has been given control over the earth to cultivate it, we have gone quite overboard, exploiting the earth rather than stewarding it.

This type of thinking has gradually grown into a general disrespect for the ground over the ages. Remember in Genesis 4 that Abel's blood cried out *from the ground*, so that even the soil itself was cursed from sin. Consider how we have defiled the earth with blood ever since that time through murder, wars, holocausts and the horrible reproach of abortion. Yet I believe God's original intent was that not even animals should be harmed. "A righteous man cares for the needs of his animal, but the kindest acts of the wicked are cruel" (Prov. 12:10). In fact, the first place we ever see God even giving permission to eat an animal is after the earth was flooded (see Gen. 9:2-4). Before that, animals did not even fear man, and the earth had a unique type of communion between nature and mankind.

I do not by any means suggest that we all become vegans and start farming communes. Even Jesus ate meat. But I do believe that Christians should be on the vanguard of environmental conservation, although sadly the opposite has been true. Had we stepped up to the plate on this issue decades ago, we would not be criticized today as right-wing, environmentally irresponsible people. Satan will often blind the church to a social need (which is not hard to do, considering the appetites of our flesh), so that the ungodly can find reason to criticize us and justify their own rebellion. Not that the environment should be our focus, but our focus is one that benefits the environment.

The point here is that we lack a balance between our natural circumstances and our spiritual life. Sin not only distances us from God. It even distances us from the land. Remember that one of the first curses was that Adam and Eve were thrown from the garden. To see the Kingdom come, on earth as it is in Heaven, these gaps must be bridged. Remember that Jesus had favor both with God and with man. He had vertical, as well as horizontal balance. That does not mean Jesus succumbed to the "ways of the world" or the spirit of the world, but He did become relatable in a way that even the worst of sinners found a way to connect with Him. Jesus is the link between man and God, between earth and Heaven.

A great example of this kind of mystic is St. Francis. He lived an incarnational Christianity in such a way that even nature itself bowed to his command.

St. Francis of Assisi (1182-1226) dropped his pants in front of a bishop, talked to animals and gave away everything he owned. By most modern standards, he would be considered mentally ill. But Francis is perhaps the best-known apostle of the medieval period, a solid anchor for the church, and his example still shines brightly today.

Born Giovanni "Francesco" Bernadone in Italy to a wealthy cloth merchant, Francis was a fun, exuberant young man, full of life, and a big party animal in his early 20s. Leaving for battle with a neighboring city, Francis was taken captive as a prisoner of war for a year, where he became physically wrecked and spent another year convalescing at home after his escape. It was some time then when God began to break into Francis' life.

Francis was suddenly gripped with a heart for the poor and the lepers, and he began giving away his father's

Artwork by Benjamin C. Boulter

expensive possessions to the needy. His father became livid, and dragged Francis before the magistrates in order to have him reprimanded in some harsh way. But since Francis' acts were spiritually inspired, he had to be carried before the bishop instead. It was there that Francis stripped completely naked, handed his father back the very clothes he was wearing, and proclaimed from that point forward, that his true father was in Heaven.

To the shock of everyone, this wealthy son of Assisi voluntarily and quite joyfully chose a life of poverty, renouncing all his possessions. Francis had a romantic charm and beauty that inspired the very Renaissance. His playfulness and exuberance was unlike the stereotypical ascetics, shunning the world around them. He was known as *God's Juggler*, and he was full of song and poetry. While he demonstrated the simplicity and humility of Christ, Francis showed that it was all an outworking of an inner happiness, not religious misery. He was always moving his feet around and dancing because of a cheerfulness he could not seem to contain.

Francis began hanging out at a dilapidated old church called San Damiano. Then one day, he heard the audible voice of God come from the crucifix hanging there, saying, "Rebuild My church." Francis took this literally, and began begging for stones, which he hauled one at a time up the walls of the old building in backbreaking labor. But God would use Francis for a much larger building campaign, overhauling His entire church body, whose clergy was corrupt with materialism and spiritual pride at the time. I would not suggest we go taking vows of poverty, but Francis' life was a prophetic sign in his day. He restored a voice and a hope for the laity and the poor in his era, portraying the accessibility of God to the common man. He also demonstrated the nature of Christ in a way that was sorely lacking in the church.

Francis left behind his life of drinking, sex and revelry, but his upbeat personality did not diminish; it only increased. The anointing on him was quite contagious. His old friends were drawn to renounce their own wealth and join him. He also inspired a hometown girl, Clare Favone, to lead a similar group of women followers.

Pope Innocent kisses Francis' filthy, humble feet in Paramount Studios' "Brother Sun, Sister Moon," a 1972 film adaptation on the life of Frances

They were the Franciscans and the Little Clares. They performed manual labor or begged, and they initially just lived on the streets. But they truly enjoyed and clung to this lifestyle in a naturally supernatural way. They worked in the fields, slept in haylofts and under eaves, and inspired followers from all walks of life. They traveled from one town to another, preaching in the everyday language of the people with music and singing. Crowds would bring Francis the sick for healing, and would throng him to cut off a piece of his tunic. He healed the blind. Tumors vanished when he prayed. He was once preaching in a small village and the whole congregation was so touched, the entire group asked to be admitted into his monastic order as one corporate body. Such requests prompted him to found a monastic society for families and those who needed a middle-of-the-road order—for people still working in the world but wanting to live a lifestyle of full-time prayer and intercession.

But Francis could not grasp whether it was really possible to live the gospels in such a simple fashion, or if he was just being naïve. So he decided to go directly to the pope and settle the question. Francis basically asked Rome if he could live by a written rule that was no more than the bare words of Jesus found in the gospels. In his simplicity, he did not even have his friars study theology, choosing instead to have them read just the gospels and work with their hands. This doubtlessly intimidated many ecclesiastical authorities. At this time, clergy were filthy rich. They ministered in Latin and many were essentially upper class snobs. And here was Francis putting them to shame. It was during this era that the pope once said to Thomas Aquinas, "Ah, Thomas … the church can no longer say, 'silver and gold have I none.'"

"That is true, your holiness," replied Aquinas, "but then, neither can it now say, 'Arise and walk.'" The church had secular and material power, but no spiritual authority.

When Francis approached Pope Innocent, it is said that the pope had a dream the night before, wherein he saw Francis leaning against a large church building, holding it up before it fell. After that, the pope approved Francis' monastic order.

Another account says that one of the pope's advisors recommended that he bless the growing Franciscan movement so that Rome wouldn't lose the allegiance of the poor or have an uprising. Either way, whether the pope had spiritual or political motives for sanctioning the Franciscans, they were nevertheless allowed to continue as a movement.

Francis' naivety led him not only to waltz right up to the pope. It also led him to walk right through the battlefields of the Crusades, where he intended to approach the Islamic sultan himself, give him the gospel and pursue peace. Francis reached the enemy's camp, where he was taken prisoner and brought before the sultan in 1219, according to the eyewitness testimony of his companions. The sultan was not persuaded to convert, but he was impressed with Francis and agreed to treat his Christian captives in a kindlier manner after that.

Francis saw the Kingdom through the mundane things of life, and though he was mystical, he was balanced and grounded in the natural realm. His was a truly incarnational faith. He did not seek to separate God from nature, but instead, he could see God's glory in everything.

"This element of the supernatural did not separate him from the natural; for it was the whole point of his position that it united him more perfectly to the natural. It did not make him dismal or dehumanized; for it was the whole meaning of his message that such mysticism makes a man cheerful and humane," writes G.K. Chesterton in *Saint Francis of Assisi*.[1]

And so we must turn to the nature miracles associated with Francis. Though the accounts of Francis are better documented than many saints of his era, he is still one whose miraculous deeds scholars would say were embellished by his followers. As Chesterton points out, some of the stories of Francis read like fairy tales. This is especially true of the nature-oriented miracles. But I do not believe we should discount them altogether. Their extremity alone is not sufficient reason to write them off. History is too full of accounts of mystics that lived in harmony with the animal kingdom and took command over the elements to classify them all as bunk. Elijah was fed by ravens; Elisha called bears out of the woods; Balaam's donkey spoke, and Moses worked all manner of miracles through nature and with animals in Egypt. Or consider Noah! After all, the very Bible itself reads like a fairy tale, but we know these things really happened if we take it literally. It is either the utmost deceptive book or the most powerful book in human history. In that light, the question of *believability* is not an issue with Francis' acts. Historical accuracy may prove some to be embellishments, but a thing is not a lie simply because it is fantastic.

It is said that Francis was walking with some companions when he saw a great number of birds. He bolted after them, running right into their midst, yet none of them moved. He asked them if they would listen to the word of God, saying, "My brother and sister birds, you should praise your Creator and always love Him: He gave you feathers for clothes, wings to fly and all other things that you need. It is God who made you noble among all creatures, making your home in thin, pure air. Without sowing or reaping, you receive God's guidance and protection."

Then, when he blessed them to leave, the birds all took to the air in unison. From that point forward, Francis made it a habit to share the gospel with every creature, as well as with men. Numerous stories say that wild animals were even drawn to Francis, coming right up to him or sitting on his lap. We can't deny that Scripture tells us to preach the gospel to every *creature* (see Mark 16:15).

Likely the most famous story is when Francis went to the town of Gubbio, which was being terrorized by a wolf that had killed several people, as well as livestock. The town was holed up, afraid to venture out because of the roving wolf. When Francis arrived, he went right about looking for the animal, taking only a few brave companions, some of which turned back with fear. Suddenly, the animal appeared, charging fiercely from the woods. But Francis called to the animal, saying "Brother Wolf," and commanding him in the name of Jesus to no longer hurt anyone. Francis told the wolf to make peace with Gubbio and that he would be forgiven. As the story goes, the wolf was immediately tamed, following Francis to Gubbio and living from that point on with the townspeople, who fed it scraps.

If such an event took place, it would surely have demonstrated firsthand the power and sovereignty of God to an entire region.

Later in life, Francis was also recorded as the first saint to receive the stigmata—the supernatural appearance of bleeding wounds on his hands, feet, and side like Christ. In his latter years, he was so broken with humility over this that he gave up the reins of his own order, returning to a life of quiet and simple communion with God. He also admitted that his own austere practices were excessive for most people, and did not require others to imitate his asceticism. In the end, he even felt obliged to ask the forgiveness of his own body, "Brother Ass" he called it, for treating it so severely.

Francis was full of life and creativity. Francis' poetry and songs often reflected him speaking to nature, calling the sun his brother, or the moon his sister. This too appears almost pantheistic or animistic. But Jesus Himself spoke to the wind and the waves when He quieted them. He even spoke to a fig tree and cursed it, as a prophetic act. Nature itself, to some degree, will be restored to a level of glory through the mouths of mankind. Like Adam, there will be believers who understand how to walk in dominion over nature. I do not understand this, and like the apostle John, I must say that as children of God, "what we will be has not yet been made known" (1 John 3:2). I believe we are slowly coming into an awareness of that power and identity in this hour. John goes on to say in this verse, "But we know that when He appears, we shall be like Him, for we shall see Him as He is." That is a pretty extreme statement, but it has a blessing attached to it:

*Everyone who has this hope in him purifies himself,
just as He is pure* (1 John 3:3).

To be *like Him* is beyond comprehension, but it is fact. It's going to happen. I believe that as we draw closer to His appearance, some people will get a jump start on this promise. At some point, a mountain will literally move at the command of a son of God. I believe that barren deserts will literally bloom into gardens at believers' faith. This type of extreme creative phenomena will come *suddenly*.

Although we do not have a complete picture, we should be leaning into these areas. We do that by becoming saturated with God's Spirit. It is my personal belief that keys of revelation will come that link spiritual laws to natural, physical laws—not that we will intellectually understand it all—and this will release us to walk in such faith. I believe that many new age strongholds of metaphysics are masking and counterfeiting spiritual truths that the church has not yet pioneered. We should not go studying those counterfeits, but by focusing our gaze on the *Creator*, we cannot help but be transformed into His likeness.

I do not think that God made two sets of law—one to govern the Heavens and another to govern the earth. Now that the law has been fulfilled at the cross, this opens incredible gateways of power. Jesus even suspended the laws of gravity to walk on water. Every creative miracle—like the growth of a new limb—suspends that law of physics which says matter can neither be created nor destroyed. What is the difference in having faith for a new limb at a healing service and faith for a whole mountain range to be moved?

As soon as the church begins moving corporately in this type of authority, the end is just around the corner. As soon as the spotless Bride begins operating in the fullness of her spotless nature, the return of the Lord will likely be imminent. "Then suddenly the Lord you are seeking will come to His temple" (Mal. 3:1). The kind of supernatural power we are talking about here will be too extreme for the world to remain fallen around it. It will evoke complete awe, or it will evoke complete warfare.

Religion came against the church so quickly from the onset, because satan knew that Spirit-filled believers could easily begin calling nature itself into proper alignment with Heaven by the indwelling of the Holy Spirit. Then his temporary reign would end on this planet. The enemy does not want us releasing spiritual authority over the natural domain, and he surely does not want us to know how closely intertwined the two realms are. The Kingdom of Heaven coming to earth spells victory. Religion is perhaps the greatest counterfeit balance between Heaven and earth. That's why Jesus spoke so harshly against the religious people in His day. Prevailing over this confusion will ultimately be no different than winning any other battle. We are learning that the master key to overcome all of these demonic strongholds is simple: intimacy with the Lord. In Jesus we find the source of all our strength, power, authority, and dominion. True contemplation will not only flush away the false mysticism of the new age and occult. Counterfeit mysticism will be laughable and obviously powerless in light of the genuine presence and power of the Lord manifest in His children.

Another powerful example of a nature miracle anointing was demonstrated right in America's backyard, in my own state of Alaska, through the life of St. Herman the Wonderworker.

St. Herman of Alaska (1756-1837) was a Russian-born Orthodox believer who pioneered missionary efforts to Alaska, which had just been discovered by Russian fur traders. Among many miraculous signs, Herman demonstrated authority over tidal waves that threatened to engulf his island, stopping their advances. He also drew a spiritual boundary against a large wildfire that threatened the people, and the fire was unable to pass it.

*St. Herman of Alaska
commanding the sea to stop*

Herman's apostolic work really began on Kodiak Island as a young monk, where he settled and built a church with a handful of other missionaries. Thousands of Aleut Natives were converted and baptized, and the mission flourished. But Herman was eventually left alone to his endeavor, after his fellow monks died or returned home. Herman spent much time alone in deep prayer and manifested a number of revelatory gifts of the Spirit. Herman also demonstrated great compassion, using his gifts to counsel and intercede for the people. He founded an orphanage after an epidemic killed many adults on Kodiak. He was also greatly disturbed by the predatory fur traders who enslaved many Natives. Herman was persecuted by some of the profiteers because he protected the Natives. But it was the demonstrations of God's power that won many over.

Herman literally befriended a number of bears—Kodiak Island brown bears are the largest in the world, by the way. And they would often eat from his hands. Needless to say, traders who witnessed Herman's interaction with these bears often left Herman and his Native friends alone. One of the Russians won over to the faith was the colony governor of Alaska who became Herman's disciple and eventually entered a Russian monastery. Other animals were drawn to Herman. Wild ermine lived near his cell and did not seem to fear him.[2]

We are not all called to befriend bears, but we are all called to shake off religious pretention. When we encounter God, nature and even people are drawn to us. The anointing has an attractive element that all substances—animate and inanimate—are compelled to worship! Even the thieves, junkies, and prostitutes were drawn to Jesus, because they perceived the fragrance of Heaven on Him. But people are repulsed by religion. I have found that people can never be fully natural, until they have also learned to be truly spiritual. The two go hand in hand. Otherwise we are masquerading. One of the greatest *naturally supernatural* men of recent history is Lonnie Frisbee.

Lonnie Frisbee (1950-1993) was about as "natural" as you can get, although he was an extreme miracle worker. Frisbee was the hippie evangelist of the Jesus People Movement who can almost single-handedly be credited for igniting three major moves of God.

Lonnie had long hair, a huge beard, and he preached in blue jeans. Before he helped start the Calvary Chapel movement, Lonnie and his wife had been members of a hippie commune called The House of Acts in California. When the Jesus Movement hit the media, Lonnie was often interviewed and photographed in major national maga-

Lonnie Frisbee baptizing new converts in the Pacific Ocean

zines like Time. When he preached, miracles followed; people were often healed. They would regularly be filled with the Holy Spirit, falling to the floor, shaking, prophesying, speaking in tongues, and seeing visions.

Lonnie baptized people in the ocean. He did not have any religious pretention. He was very "earthy." My in-laws remember seeing him at their hippie church in California, where he wore a clerical collar then ripped it off in the middle of the service to prove a point. Lonnie was a self-described "nudist-vegetarian-hippie when the Lord called me. I was going into the desert, taking off all of my clothes and I'm saying, 'God, if You're really real, reveal Yourself to me.' One afternoon the whole atmosphere of this canyon started to tingle and change. The Lord identified Himself to me and said, 'I'm Jesus. I build nations and I tear them down. It is better for a nation to have never known Me than to have known Me and turned their back from Me.' I thought all roads led to Rome, but He explained to me that He was the only way to know God."[3]

Lonnie first worked alongside Chuck Smith as the primary evangelist to birth Calvary Chapel—today a multi-million dollar international denomination. Once the movement got structured and comfortable, Lonnie's power evangelism was too risqué for Calvary, which distanced itself from him and his strong belief in spiritual gifts. But in the early days of Calvary, Lonnie was bringing in 1,000 converts a month, just in small churches.

Frisbee then moved on with John Wimber to start the Vineyard movement, going so far as to suggest the name "Vineyard." Many would say his influence and the spiritual manifestations that accompanied his preaching were the very catalyst that would later explode into the Toronto Blessing, a year after he died. In 1980, Lonnie said, "come Holy Spirit" on Mother's Day in the Yorba Linda Calvary Chapel—suddenly God stepped into the room and the Vineyard movement began. When you say "come Holy Spirit," you better get ready—He keeps coming and coming, because He never ends! It was later on Father's Day in 1994, just after his death, that Toronto was sparked—also out of the Vineyard. The very phrase "power evangelism" comes from Lonnie's ministry. He would later travel to South Africa with Wimber, where many more healings took place.

My wife was saved in one of Lonnie's altar calls as a child, and later as a teenager, he called her out by a word of knowledge at a home group meeting, where she was filled with the Holy Spirit and fell to the floor with her right hand shaking—a common manifestation in his ministry.

But Lonnie's life was not without error. In the early 1970s, he and his wife divorced. He also struggled with homosexuality, which would later lead to his death from AIDS. Although Lonnie was repentant, the churches he helped establish were quick to snub his name from their histories. He was not the first or the last great power mystic to succumb to gross sin. As we will see, many great men of God made equally great errors. At Frisbee's death, he was portrayed as a Samson figure—one through whom God worked mightily, yet he was snared by his own weaknesses.

Lonnie was clearly ahead of his time, although a number of ministries are now beginning to walk in the level of power that he once did. I believe that, in many ways, Lonnie's very life was a signpost of the available power and the struggles that are now facing our generation. It is interesting that Lonnie believed youth culture would play a powerful part in God's latter day move, as prophesied by Joel.

Some would find it ironic that physical manifestations of the Holy Spirit were a part of Lonnie Frisbee's ministry, and he was a major catalyst for the Calvary Chapel movement and the Vineyard.

But both of these backed away from the supernatural manifestations in the Toronto renewal. Some of the biggest critics of Lonnie's style of power ministry came out of the same churches that he founded. This is why we need to understand our roots.

A friend of our family and a powerful minister, Jonathan Land, was close to Lonnie, and it is amazing how many major prophetic voices today were also influenced by him at some point in their walk—ministers including Marc Dupont, Jill Austin, and others. Land remembers a meeting where two troubled teenagers came in, unsaved and profane, and were sitting in front of him, mocking and laughing. The Lord told Land to pay attention to what was about to happen to these young men.

As Lonnie began to speak, the power of God began to move in the room. Here's Land's account of what happened:

"Just then the boys' heads started slowly wagging, in a few minutes their heads were jerking and slashing back and forth and sideways so fast and so violently that I actually felt some fear that they would be injured or even killed. The speed of the jerking heads was so extreme and so fast as to be impossible. They stood to their feet and their arms and hands started flapping rapidly and violently. It was just a demonstration of the power of God that was extreme. Remember that no one laid hands on these boys. Frisbee had merely asked them to stand when they began manifestations. As they flapped and jerked for what seemed like an eternity, they began to speak with tongues. Really, really loud. They became Christians that night by a direct intervention of the Holy Spirit. From mocking and laughing they began to worship and praise the name of Jesus."

It is said that Lonnie's greatest critics could not deny that God was with him. "I can say that in spite of the stupid things that Frisbee did, he probably impacted the planet more profoundly than is commonly realized. In many ways he was an invisible prophet.

Wherever you see the Holy Spirit moving today, I can almost guarantee that Frisbee had been there," said Land.

SPIRITUAL PARANOIA: SEEING BLACK HELICOPTERS

While we are called to a deeper expression of the supernatural realm, we must also be firmly grounded in the natural world. Not limited by natural confines, but firmly fixed within them. We are dual creatures that live in both realms simultaneously—Heaven and earth. Life is not always jumping from one mystical experience to the next, and we must learn to embrace the reality and nearness of God, even when He seems hidden and we are plugging along in our daily, ordinary lives. When God is silent, we will often turn to a soulish type of hype, in order to twist His arm and wrestle Him back into focus. But there is a much deeper realm of glory, in which we can operate in rest.

God can do a lot more through us if we would just learn to loosen up. When we fully understand our sonship and the grace of God—as well as the latent power of Heaven within us—we can live without the spiritual paranoia that plagues many immature believers. I am not referring to those who are in virtual disbelief of the spiritual realm around us. But those who have had *some* spiritual experience—young prophets, mostly—can often do more damage than those with no experience at all. Often, we put our past experiences with God on a pedestal in such a way that we are constantly trying to live up to them in our own strength. In doing so, we can miss what God is doing right now in the mundane things around us.

I say this not as a deterrent for anyone to step into their calling and test the waters of supernatural experience. There should always be a safe place for beginners to learn to function in prophetic gifts or gifts of healing and deliverance, etc., and we will see many more full-fledged schools of the supernatural being planted in days to come. But it has been a common error in the past that, when a supernatural outpouring has come to the church, the natural paradigm has been neglected in an unhealthy manner. The Heavenly realms are so enticing that, when we taste them, we can actually begin to despise the earthly realm. Paul said that he counted all things as rubbish compared to the surpassing glory of knowing Christ. He wasn't even allowed to discuss all of his third Heaven encounters. In part, this was probably for fear that believers would start literally killing themselves to check out early and go there (2 Cor. 12:2-4).

Just as the reality of the supernatural realm is enticing, it can also lead to extreme paranoia. When believers are first confronted with the fact that angels and demons *really are* behind every bush, it can get a little disconcerting. Many Christians give lip service to their belief in angels and demons—and even in God. But when you first begin to see them, you may wet your pants or lose your breakfast. This is when some turn to extremes. The problem is, we need to balance our spiritual experience with natural reality. We are not of this world, but we are still called to operate in it. Many run off half-baked when they first figure out that this whole thing about angels and spirits and living creatures is legit.

Despite our professed belief, we get startled by the reality of the supernatural when we confront it. Then we go overboard, tackling the spiritual warfare in our lives immaturely, chasing down hell with a water pistol. In our very real discovery of the battle, we often forsake the grace and comfort of the secret place of the Most High. We get spiritually jumpy and trigger happy. That is where we get confused and paranoid. We get stuck in the realm of second Heaven revelation, forgetting our full access to the third Heaven throne room of God's heart and perfect peace.

As for me, I am constantly comforted by the fact that the God of peace will soon crush satan underneath my feet (Rom. 16:20). Peace is a powerful weapon of battle.

Prophetic author John Sandford says that when he gets spiritually worked up and confused—having trouble determining which voice is from God and which is from the devil—he simply settles down, goes outside and starts working in the garden. Gets his hands in the dirt and plants his feet back on the earth. This is good advice.

John says he sets an appointment to talk with God the next day, after the confusion settles, and determines not to listen to any "spiritual stuff" until then. He remembers that God loves him, no matter what.

There is something very humbling about nature. God has us grounded to these bodies for a reason. There's a reason that His glory is poured into jars of clay. It was just after King Nebuchadnezzar arrogantly built a huge statue of himself that God had to humble him. And how did He do it? He sent him outdoors, to feed on the grass like an ox. Sent him right out into nature. Spiritually oriented people, or those with a "prophetic temperament," do well to find natural things to do, to balance out their spiritual antennas. Go for a hike. Wash the dishes. Go fishing. Prophet Bob Jones says, "Whether I'm raising the dead or going fishing, the pay is the same." Without a healthy balance of normal life, we cannot really ascend to the Heavens. And we will always overreact to minor advances of the enemy. We are not called to complacency, but it's good to rest, and let God fight for you every now and then.

I have devoted a great deal of time discussing the need for "natural" balance in the life of the believer. This may seem overly repetitious. But without this vital understanding, it would be difficult to receive the testimonies of some of the fuel-injected, high-octane signs and wonders we will read about in the later chapters. We are building a strong foundation first—getting grounded. Not grounded like a religious weight. Grounded like a lighting rod, because the power is about to strike.

Do not take yourself too seriously. Do not "press in" so hard in prayer to the point of human strife. Be patient with yourself, and always remember that joy is a cornerstone of the Kingdom. He remembers that we are but dust.

For God has not given us a spirit of fear, but of power and of love and of a sound mind (2 Timothy 1:7).

ENDORSEMENTS

1. G.K. Chesterton, *Saint Francis of Assisi* (New York: Image Books, Doubleday, 1990 ed.), 144.

2. Abbess Taisiya, "The Lives of Russian Saints." Accessed 20 Nov. 2004 <http://www.holy-transfiguration.org/library_en/saints_herman..html>.

3. Quote from Lonnie Frisbee's testimony, Anaheim Vineyard Ministry International. A good source of information on Lonnie Frisbee is David DiSabatino's "Frisbee: The Life and Death of a Hippie Preacher." See www.lonniefrisbee.com.

CHAPTER 5

Hidden Streams

THERE are a number of hidden streams throughout church history that receive little notoriety in our day, but which carried lost truths that will be restored. Many were significant movements that were rejected by the corporate church for reasons of politics or expediency. Yet we see a common thread of the Spirit's movement through them all. One river, many streams. Often one generation would reject the hand of the Lord, and He had to hold certain Heavenly deposits in reserve for a future generation.

Montanism (second century) was perhaps the earliest prophetic movement ever to be rejected by the mainstream church. They were marked by ecstatic prophetic experiences and physical manifestations when the spirit of prophecy came upon them. They were unpredictable and uncontained. The group was named after one of its spokesmen, Montanus, who lived in the Phrygian area of Asia Minor. Montanists arose in the second century. Church history defines the movement as an open and shut case of heresy. But was it really that simple?

Montanists were not considered heretics so much as they were labeled *schismatics*, that is, they represented a split from the mainstream. In this hour, God is again calling His people to embrace supernatural Christianity, and to a departure from religious form and shadow. Even Tertullian favored the Montanists and defended them. He tells us that the Holy Spirit was giving new revelation through them, but that there was no new doctrine being proclaimed. Their prophetic utterances only gave direction about matters of church discipline and the like, yet the Montanists remained orthodox in their beliefs. In fact, the Montanists even represented a type of holiness movement in the church during their day, urging believers not to compromise with sin. However, this infringed on the bishops of the church, who were in charge of handling church discipline issues at the time. It is likely that the Montanists were rejected purely due to power struggles and their prophetic unpredictability. By no means should we think the Montanists had developed an extremely mature prophetic gifting. But had the church not rejected them, it is quite likely that the prophetic office could have developed and grown to unprecedented maturity many centuries ago.

Some feel the Montanists were the last flicker of the great apostolic Christianity of the first century. They were condemned by the bishop of Rome, but so were a number of subsequent genuine moves of the Spirit that represented true Kingdom Christianity. Historical accounts are too sketchy to assume very much about the Montanists, but theirs appears to be a sincere move of God that was quenched by religious politics.[1]

As with the Montanists of long ago, the corporate church is struggling with how extensively it wants to embrace the present prophetic movement. Those with ears to hear the Lord in this hour should not be distracted by politics, nor should they operate out of rejection when their words are not accepted. In these days, it is critical to keep pressing into the Lord and receiving Heavenly downloads without getting hung up on those things. Prophetic movements in Scripture and throughout church history have a very high rate of being rejected by God's people. It's par for the course. If God has called you to a prophetic office, you've been issued a ticket to your own crucifixion. Enjoy it. It just means you get more of God in the long run. But you can't embrace a *spirit of rejection*, or you will miss out. These are exciting times in which we live, and we don't want our eyes and ears dulled by prophetic self-righteousness.

"He is releasing secrets that He has reserved from the beginning of the foundation of the earth—secrets and mysteries that even Daniel saw and John saw that were sealed up and held in reserve," says prophetic teacher Paul Keith Davis.[2] This has already begun. We will reclaim ancient mysteries, lost power mantles, and secrets to the Kingdom. This is coming not so much because of our efforts, but because of what our forefathers have sown. We are a generation called to reap what it did not sow. We will be the beneficiaries of all the prayers and promises of Elijah, Isaiah, and Paul that were never fulfilled. We will not only rely on our own prayers, but on theirs. And ultimately, on the Lord's own prayer for us.

I was once praying to the Lord, asking whether to "put my hand to the plow" to begin a particular ministry effort. The Lord responded by saying, "I have not called you to plow. I have called you to reap." Not only will we reap the spiritual benefit of our predecessors, like the Montanists—things we did not even knew they planted—but we will also be the generation to reap the great end-time harvest. God does not want us to keep turning the soil and laying the foundations that have already been laid. Look at all the foundational work that has been done! Just consider the writings and teaching resources that have been passed down to this generation alone! In the age of the Internet, we can access writings from 16th century mystics, or watch live streaming videos of the most anointed ministers in the world. What a blessing! But we are not called to regurgitate the same old stuff or lay the same old foundations again. We are deluged with two millennia of milk and basics. It is time to eat meat and spit out fire. And we are not just to work up to the level of those forerunners, we must enter the throne room, pick up their mantles, and pursue a double portion of what they had.

The Celtic Christians (fourth to sixth century) represented perhaps a more balanced mysticism than that of the Desert Fathers, although in many ways, they very much patterned themselves after those predecessors. They "considered that their revelation of continuous praise and prayer came from the, 'True vine, which came out of Egypt.'"[3]

Art flourished. The Book of Kells, for instance, shows their incorporation of art into worship. The Celts even designed their homes to have aesthetic value and to fit in visually with the land. Their experience bore the incarnational balance of which we discussed earlier.

"The Christianity that evolved around the Celts found a mysticism that remained wholly true to creedal Christianity but was enrapt by the ecstasy of the mystery of God as he reveals himself through his creation and through direct communion with his creatures," writes Celtic scholar David Haggith.[4]

We must also understand that Celtic Christianity represented a flavor of our faith that developed almost entirely on its own, with almost no outside influence from the Roman church. It offers us a completely unique perspective on the Christian life than anything before or after it. It is one of many hidden streams that served as an alternative to mainstream religious tradition in early Christianity.

"Because Celtic Christianity grew on a pristine emerald isle in the ferment of a nature religion, it retained a soul-deep, non-utilitarian appreciation of the earth, whereas the long-civilized Roman Christianity around it rejected the natural world under the influence of Augustine," says Haggith. "The Celts continued to understand nature as self-expression of the Divine, not as 'carnal' in the pejorative sense. Thus, the Celtic saints provide a path back to a world view that is more appreciative of nature as God's gift, artistry and self-expression—a place where we have the assigned role of caretakers, not owners."

As the modern-day resurgence of interest in Druid customs and beliefs becomes prevalent in new age circles, it would serve the church well to revisit the mantle of Celtic apostle St. Patrick. He radically embraced Druid culture to the fullest extent possible, becoming *all things to all men* and redeeming what he could in order to bring the gospel to Ireland. A chief method of his evangelism was to redirect idolatrous devotion over to Christ in any way possible. For instance, he replaced seasonal pagan celebrations with Christian observances that pointed to Jesus. But Patrick's apostolic mantle was also one of signs and wonders.

St. Patrick

St. Patrick (a.d. 386-461) had very little to do with green beer and leprechauns, but he was a great miracle-working apostle. He effected many healings, including raising the dead and worked Mosaic signs and wonders in power confrontations with Druid priests. Born in Britain, Patrick was kidnapped into slavery by Irish raiders at age 16. He was taken to Ireland for six years, where he converted to Christianity and became an intense man of prayer. He later wrote that he prayed up to 100 times throughout each day and night during that time.

Patrick was a product of the independent British or Celtic church—never a Roman Catholic missionary, as some historical accounts would say. Ireland would not be dominated by the Romans for several more centuries. After learning the local language, Patrick miraculously escaped his captors and returned to Britain. He had received an angelic dream that supernaturally directed him to an outgoing ship. But several years later, another dream from the Lord instructed Patrick to return to Ireland to preach. In the dream, an angel held letters from his former captors, saying, "We pray thee, holy youth, to come and walk among us as before." Patrick was led to Ireland by divine inspiration, and not a pope, as some have thought. His was an altogether different breed of Christianity.

Returning to Ireland in a.d. 432 with several companions, Patrick began ministering to the Druids, eventually converting nearly 40 of the island's 150 tribes, planting several hundred churches and ordaining 1,000 native ministers.

The Irish Church grew to be possibly the greatest missionary church in history. Patrick's own sending church in Britain, which bore a greater "civilized" Roman influence, was quite racist toward the "barbaric" Irish. They even resisted his vision for evangelism, but he persevered. We can learn a great lesson through this today, as the Western church faces the need to reach Muslim nations amid similar prejudices. Patrick reached the unreachable. Celtic missionaries would go on to evangelize much of Europe in the fifth and sixth centuries, sending out workers from 24-hour prayer and worship centers like Lindisfarne and Iona, which fueled their worldwide efforts with intense prayer and intercession. The resident anointing that rested on these centers must have been amazing. Many would sleep only two hours a night because their lives were devoted to radical prayer. It was not uncommon for them to stand against a wall or stand waist deep in the ocean all night, so as not to fall asleep during prayer.

The Celts had a wisdom that was far beyond the norm for their era. When Rome fell, they preserved vast amounts of art and literature—both Christian and secular—from the barbaric tribes that swept Europe at the onset of the Dark Ages. In fact, these monks literally preserved civilization as we know it through the medieval period.

We cannot discuss every stream of Christianity throughout church history that has brought a unique impact to the Body of Christ. But we can acknowledge that there are unique streams of the faith today that are drastically different from what we have experienced in the primarily Protestant West. Not just different in form, but different in mind-set. And many of them are widely accommodating to the supernatural. The Eastern Orthodox church, for instance, is highly open to the miraculous and corporately embraces modern signs and wonders far more than most mainline Protestant denominations. Denominational divisions still run deep between Orthodox and non-orthodox believers, but the Holy Spirit will eventually bring unity between us.

While I will avoid contentious doctrinal matters here, I do appreciate the miraculous hagiography that is passed down by our Orthodox brothers. Here's an example of a well-known Orthodox wonderworker:

Seraphim of Sarov

Seraphim of Sarov (1759-1833) was born to a merchant family in Kursk, Russia and had visitations by saints from an early age. He often drew away to pray and at age 18 he became a monk. His life was almost continually in prayer, and he lived a contemplative life for 45 years. He received angelic visitations. He once saw Jesus Himself enter the church where he was praying in the form of the Son of Man, and he was struck mute for some time after seeing this vision.

Over time, Seraphim gradually withdrew to the lifestyle of a hermit, and animals were often supernaturally drawn to him. He was once approached by robbers, and although he was physically strong and holding an axe at the time, he lay it down on the ground, gave himself over to them and was beaten. For a period of time—nearly three years—Seraphim lived on top of a rock in an extreme ascetic manner. Seraphim worked a number of miracles and healed the sick. He was quite prophetic, and could answer people's questions before they had time to ask them.

Despite his withdrawn lifestyle, he opened his cell to visitors the last eight years of his life and thousands came to him for advice. Those who visited him sometimes saw that his face was glowing bright "as that of an angel," yet he was filled with the peace and joy of Christ. One of his disciples saw it glowing like the sun, his eyes flashing like lightning. Seraphim felt that the very purpose of life was to be filled with the Holy Spirit in such a way.[5]

One cannot consider the miracles of Eastern Orthodoxy without discussing the *uncreated light* at the annual Easter celebration in Jerusalem. The Orthodox Easter, or Pascha, is observed each year in Jerusalem, as a priest enters the tomb where Christ is thought to have been buried. Every year, a light flashes from within the tomb, supernaturally, and catches fire to candles or an olive oil lamp without the use of matches or any human instrument. Many Orthodox believers travel there each year for the service, and the flame is used to light candles throughout the congregation. Many people's candles are supernaturally ignited, and the flames are often seen dancing through the air by the entire crowd, from one side of the church to the other. Unlit candles and lamps in other chapels in the city also catch fire at times on their own. Thousands witness this annual miracle. When the flames first appear, they are a bluish color and do not burn. Some people touch the flames, but they cannot feel them. It is often compared to what Moses' burning bush experience may have been like. Why would this happen on a regular, systematic basis? One could ask the same thing about the angels that stirred the waters of the Pool of Bethesda in John 5. It may seem bizarre, but it's a legitimate miracle if it brings glory to God.

I know this sounds weird to some non-Orthodox Christians, but the fact is, there is a lot out there that we aren't clued in on. Last time I checked, He is God and we are not. God is up to a lot of strange things in the world, to which I am not yet privy. What I do know, is that the Lord is about to open up the Eastern and Western church to one another like never before, and we will have to be willing to receive one another, within the proper bounds of discernment. The Lord is also about to spark a mighty revival in Russia like the world has never seen, and many of the young people in that revival will be looking back to their Orthodox roots and reviving old wells of spiritual practice.

There are obviously doctrinal errors in every stream of the church. You obviously think your own stream is closest to perfect, or you wouldn't be swimming in it. But every denominational tributary in the Body of Christ has strengths and weaknesses—strong points and errors. We must stop viewing the church and her denominations as a tiered caste system, ranked in priority of who has the best doctrine. The blood of Christ puts us all on the same, level playing field. We need to see the church more as a river. Every time a new tributary comes into the main stream, there are eddies and turbulence, but unless new waters flow in, the river risks drying up and becoming dead and stagnant. And those splashing in the latest tributary cannot think that they alone are the river.

In the same way, we must acknowledge those streams with which we are least familiar. We often tend to criticize those things we don't understand. With much humility, we have a great deal to learn from the various Christian communions throughout the world. There are a number in the Middle East, for instance, that Westerners do not even acknowledge exist. There are very many strong believers in the Coptic Orthodox church of Egypt, as well as among the Melkite Catholics. If we were in relationship with any of these brothers, we could no longer afford to make rash statements like, "They are not saved." There are unique streams of Christianity throughout the world. In Africa, there are so many denominations you could not begin to count them.

Some of the greatest miracle workers the church has ever seen will come, and are coming, from such places. It will be important for us not to nationalize the coming move of God, any more than we should try to denominationalize it.

THE COPTS

I would like to pick up where we left off in Egypt with the Desert Fathers. I believe the Coptic Church of Egypt still preserves a remnant seed of the faith handed down by those great men, and they will be a critical link to revival in these last days.

The word "Copt" is from the Greek *Aigyptos*, and is usually used to describe Egyptian Christians. Saint Mark is thought to have brought Christianity to Egypt, where some of the church's oldest manuscripts have been preserved. There are monasteries in the Egyptian desert where you can go to find ancient leather-bound manuscripts still preserved from the earliest days of the church. As we discussed, the deserts of Egypt were quickly populated with monks and hermits—monasticism was birthed there—and the nation produced some of the early church's greatest leaders. By the end of the fourth century, literally hundreds of monasteries, along with thousands of caves and hermit cells were carved into the Egyptian hills. Many of these monasteries still flourish and take new vocations today. Isaiah 19:19 says "in that day there will be an altar to the Lord in the midst the land of Egypt, and a pillar to the Lord at its border."

I don't know why, but the Lord always brings deliverers out of Egypt—Moses, Joseph, Jesus. Prophetic teacher Kathie Walters says the destiny of Egypt is to be a refuge. Abraham and Sarah went to Egypt seeking refuge from famine. Joseph was hidden in prison there until the proper time when he was raised up as the provider for the entire lineage of Abraham. And, of course, Mary and Joseph took refuge there to escape Herod until they were free to bring Jesus back to Israel.

In the Old Testament, the Lord even made specific provisions for Egyptians living in Israel—unique from all other foreigners—because the Jews were once aliens in their land as well. Throughout church history, tremendous contributions to the faith were made by Egypt's Coptic Christians. The nation was full of scribes and the Catechetical School of Alexandria, started around a.d. 190, is the oldest in the world, producing the earliest theologians, hosting the likes of Clement, Jerome, and others. The school was re-established in 1893.

It was the Coptic church's refusal to mingle politics with church affairs that got them ostracized from the West in the fifth century. They were falsely labeled as monophysites—a type of gnostic heresy—although they firmly believed in Christ's divinity and humanity. The Copts maintained their own, independent pope, separately from the church of Rome—which they still do to this day. And in recent years, the church has sought to bridge gaps with the worldwide Body of Christ. The Coptic church is a founder of the World Council of Churches and is known today for trying to reconcile minor doctrinal differences in the body.

When the Arabs conquered Egypt, the Copts were allowed to retain their faith. This was primarily because Islam's chief prophet had an Egyptian wife who urged him to be kind to the Copts. To this day, Copts are allowed to remain Christians in a Muslim dominated nation, although they have always experienced some degree of oppression.

Rick Joyner goes so far as to say the entire nation will be won to the Lord:

"As the harvest begins to affect Islamic countries, some will vehemently resist it, but in general the harvest will reap many from Islam. Egypt will be entirely won to the Lord; her devotion and willingness to sacrifice for His purposes will be so great she will actually be called the 'the altar of the Lord.' Some of the greatest apostles, prophets and leaders of the church will come out of Islamic countries. These will rejoice greatly in the truth that sets them free, preaching the gospel with a commitment and abandon which will inspire the entire body of Christ."[6]

The Copts are an oasis of hope in the desert of Islam. Clearly, the nation will be a connector for revival throughout the Muslim world. Isaiah also notes that "there will be a highway for the remnant of His people that is left from Assyria, as there was for Israel when they came up from Egypt" (Isa. 11:16). And also, "in that day there will be a highway from Egypt to Assyria. The Assyrians will go to Egypt and the Egyptians to Assyria. The Egyptians and Assyrians will worship together" (Isa. 19:23). Assyria here speaks of modern-day Iraq. And Iraq also has a remnant stream of pre-Constantinian Christianity that traces its roots back to the first century. We will discuss them later.

Not only will the Coptic church produce some of the fieriest indigenous missionaries in the Islamic world, but we will also see that the Lord is raising up new mystics—a prophetic generation—from all corners of the globe. Joel's Army will not be wearing an American flag or a Canadian maple leaf on its shoulder. Its only standard will be the cross. Its only membership requirement will be the blood of the Lamb. The Lord is telling us to get our eyes outside the box and think of His church as a global entity. The Lord has "sleeper agents" planted throughout the world, who will be called out of their caves at the appointed time of harvest. From the ends of the earth and the most unexpected places will the Lord bring forth His deliverers. Who would have thought that Moses, the very prophet of the Lord, would be raised up right in Pharoah's household! This is the irony of the Lord, and many more surprises are awaiting us just around the corner.

ANCIENT DESTINY

We can't keep our pulse on everything the Lord has done throughout history. But the first step to catching up on the groundwork He has laid for us is simply to draw close to Him. In this day and hour, we are being given the key to open and close gateways of good and evil from the past. We are being given the Key of David, which unlocks doors that no man can close and closes doors no man can open. That key is rooted in intimacy. David was a man of worship—a man after God's own heart. Jesus is the Son of David. The fruit of one who walks intimately with the Lord will always be Jesus. The church, like Mary, is called to *give birth* to an expression of Jesus on the earth. We are a womb to release the invisible into the realm of the visible. To do so, requires intimate union with the Holy Spirit.

Restoration of these ancient streams is our legal due in this hour, but moreover, it is God's loving desire for us. Above all, He wants to restore intimacy. How is this divine passion being revived in our day? The Lord's hand has been restoring the Tabernacle of David (Amos 9:11) through the worship and intercession movement of recent decades. David's Tabernacle was a place of 24-hour praise and worship, where one could have open and intimate access to the presence of God before the Ark of the Covenant, without going through the Mosaic rituals. Worship is a powerful place of intimacy which engages our hearts (in Isaiah 6, we read that a hardened heart is the first step in blinding our spiritual eyes and ears). Out of this intimacy, we learn to hear God, and prophecy is born. Out of prophecy, we learn to obey God's specific directives that release miracles, healings, signs, and wonders. And out of the miraculous, evangelism and harvest are released. Revival starts with worship. The harvest boils down to intimacy. Why does God want souls saved anyway, except to draw hearts back to Him?

It is beyond belief what is coming to the face of the earth. Beyond articulation. The intensity of spiritual activity will make us either great men or crazy men. By the end of the age, men will be fully possessed by God or they will be fully possessed by the devil. But it will be impossible to live in those days without being possessed. We are designed to be consumed by God's love. We have a choice to be fully consumed by Heaven or hell, but we will be consumed.

With this full consummation of love, we are about to see the reproduction of every Spirit-filled ministry from the time of creation poured out in one lump sum. God is redigging old wells because the destiny of many ministries were cut short. When God plants a ministry, His chief intent is to see it multiply and reproduce. The work of a minister is not just to evangelize, prophesy, pastor, or teach. The work of a minister is to duplicate himself—to raise up other evangelists, prophets, pastors, teachers, and apostles. In fact, such reproduction is specifically a chief focus of *apostolic* ministries, since apostles are called as fathers, who raise up children and establish churches as "wise master builders." But all of these fivefold office gifts were given "until we all reach unity in the faith and in the knowledge of the Son of God and become mature, attaining to the whole measure of the fullness of Christ" (Eph. 4:13). Surely, countless ministers have gone on before us without reaching this ultimate level of success: Bringing unity and maturity to *all*, and causing *all* to attain to complete fullness of Christ. Not all have fully reproduced.

Of course, the success of a ministry is not measured by how many people we have in our services—not even necessarily by how many people we have raised up to function at our own level of gifting. True success comes when the baton is passed on to the next generation and they *exceed* our level of ministry and gifting. The true test of adequate equipping is when the successive generation takes more ground than we did. The children must reach further than the fathers. They must go farther—build higher—on the foundations we have laid.

But whenever satan cuts off a movement or an individual calling in a minister's life, we can step in and reclaim those promises and destinies that were stolen. Destinies and callings that go unfulfilled do not disappear. They can actually lie dormant in a state of limbo in the Spirit, until someone else picks them up. Did you know that the roots of an olive tree can sprout again many years after the tree has been cut down? I am no botanist, but some say these trees could considerably lie dormant for hundreds of years before sprouting again. Olive trees represent anointed ministries—producers of the oil of the Holy Spirit. In the same way, ministries whose destinies had been short circuited long ago left behind destinies that we can pick up.

Many of these were destinies for particular geographic regions. On this note, I want to look at another hidden stream of Christianity that covered all of Asia many centuries ago. There are destinies that were lost and cut short for the ancient Eastern church—much to the fault of their Western brothers—that the Lord wants to revive in these last days.

The Nestorians (first to ninth century) were part of another movement that church history writes off as heretics. But in actuality, they represented the Eastern church. This was a group that evangelized Persia, China, Mongolia, and central Asia—even Korea and Japan—for nearly 1,000 years since the time of Jesus! That is the "10-40 window" region—10 degrees to 40 degrees North of the Equator—some of the most unreached places and people on earth. So why do we never hear about them? Let me first tell you about their origins, then how they were cut off from the Western church. The blood of the Nestorian martyrs is spiritual dynamite that is going to fuel the harvest in the Far East in our day. Their blood is a seed planted to facilitate the salvation of their descendants by the Lord's own blood in our day.

The Nestorians lived about 400 years before the man Nestorius came on the scene—the man after whom they were named. Nestorius was not one of them, he was a political appointee. The Nestorians actually held to better doctrine than the Roman church of the West in many ways. And keep in mind that the Nestorians are not the same as the Eastern Orthodox Church. They are entirely different. This is how they began:

There was a small kingdom called Edessa which lay between the Roman and Persian Empire, whose king, Agbar, supposedly wrote a letter to Jesus during His ministry on earth. Agbar told Jesus that he had heard of His miraculous works and requested that Jesus visit him. Understand that the fame of Jesus went beyond Israel in His day, so this is very well possible. Jesus did not just associate with sick peasants—remember the rich young ruler? There were also many things Jesus did that were not recorded, so we shouldn't discount this just because it's not in the gospels. Eusebius, in the fourth century, saw a copy of Agbar's letter to Jesus in the Edessa archives, which he translated. It really could be legitimate.

Jesus, of course, in His earthly ministry, was sent to the lost sheep of Israel, not the Gentiles (see Matt. 15:24), and so historical accounts say that Jude was sent to Agbar instead. Agbar supposedly was converted, and thus began the church of the East. Jude is traditionally thought to have been martyred in Edessa as well. These events may or may not be authentic, and are not really important to our history lesson here except to reveal that the gospel did spread quickly to Persia.[7]

The Eastern church saw serious growth. Like the Roman Christians, they also faced intense persecution at times. What is interesting, however, is that they were not directly affected by Emperor Constantine's merger of church and state in the West. They perhaps envied the West for having a Christian ruler who ended persecution, since the Persian church was still under a pagan king. But in reality, they were spared from a lot of spiritual abuses from a government church. The Eastern church never merged with a military force, and they never persecuted other sects of Christians like the

Romans did. The state never got a chance to water down their doctrine, either.

The East sent its own delegates to the Council of Nicea, which settled issues on the divinity of Christ and also established a world-wide church government. This model, by the way, was actually based on the Roman political system of hierarchy. It was at this council that the Eastern bishops from Persia agreed to come under the bishop of Antioch.

Nestorius

Life was not easy for the Eastern church in those days. The Persian authorities began persecuting Christians all the more after Constantine embraced the church, thinking they would join forces with Rome. A number of Persian Christians fled to India, joining with a church planted there by the apostle Thomas in the first century.

Before long, bishops were jockeying for power in the West and doing downright evil things to get it. Amid all the factions, the Roman emperor appointed an abbot named Nestorius to become a bishop around a.d. 427.

Nestorius was placed over the Eastern church, but he had no real connection with them except that he was from Antioch. He did not even speak their language. Nestorius soon realized, however, that his congregation referred to Mary as the Theotokis, or "Mother of God." He immediately began preaching against this, and said they should refer to her as the "Mother of Christ," since they were close to deifying her. Competing bishops used this against Nestorius—claiming he didn't believe in the divinity of Jesus. But the real issue with Nestorius had to do with Mary.

Nestorius believed the same thing about Christ as the Western bishops. He even agreed that yes, technically Mary can be called the Mother of God since Christ is divine, but he added that this kind of language can lead to misconception. Nestorius' opponents were not interested in working through the language barriers of semantics, however, they just wanted power.

A sham council was set up at Ephesus, and, long story short, everybody started excommunicating one another. This marked end of the Eastern church trying to work under the authority of Western bishops. They basically went independent, and were labeled "Nestorians" because they supported their homie, Nestorius.

To sum it up, it was the emperor who chose to boot Nestorius. So, we see a secular politician affecting the largest church split in history to that date. The worldwide church was split in half. The Ephesian Council subsequently opened a gateway of devotion to Mary that still continues today. In the end, Nestorius was proven right about the Theotokis. I will point out that the East never venerated icons or Mary either. On many points, they remained undefiled by what I believe to be Western errors.

The Romans began persecuting the Nestorians severely—fellow Christians waging war on one another over doctrinal confusion—but this only seemed to drive the Nestorians further into the East where they continued to plant churches. They opened schools and continued to send missionaries to unreached areas. Missionaries would often go out with only a basket and a few provisions, along with a copy of the Scriptures. They had no financial support or "sending church" that could reach them with aide. And to make it harder, the Persian believers were going into the Orient, trying to convert a culture that was much more advanced than their own. Mission work for the Eastern church was often an uphill battle. The Western church, meanwhile, had the backing of the Roman Empire, and its missionaries were usually being sent to less sophisticated barbarian tribes in northern Europe. Western missionaries offered cultural and economic benefits to those barbaric tribes who chose to convert. Roman missionaries had it a lot easier than the Eastern church.

By the ninth century, nearly all of Asia was being reached by the Eastern church, but the West did not acknowledge them as Christians. They experienced severe persecution in many of the pagan nations of East Asia, and were essentially persecuted out of existence by the ninth century. It was about that time that China's

Ming Dynasty wiped out most of them. However, there was always a remnant. In the 14th century, Muslim armies came through India and destroyed many Christian communities, cutting them off from most of their outlying mission work, never to be heard from again. That was the most devastating blow.

Even today, there remains a small remnant of the Eastern church centered in Iraq and Iran, which has developed almost entirely separate from the West. In 1994, Pope John Paul II held a meeting with the patriarch of the church of the East and cleared up many centuries of misunderstanding. The two issued a joint statement, *a Common Christological Declaration*, on the person and divinity of Christ. In fact, history goes to show that the Nestorians never at all held a heretical belief to the contrary. So why all the needless division? Because of this ridiculous church split there are untold billions who have not heard the gospel today.

I believe the work of the Nestorians was not in vain.

> *For there is hope for a tree, if it be cut down, that it will sprout again, and that its shoots will not cease. Though its root grow old in the earth, and its stump die in the soil, yet at the scent of water it will bud and put out branches like a young plant* (Job 14:7-9).

Who will contend for those ancient wells in the Far East? Remember the highway promised between Egypt and the remnant people of Iraq and Iran? There is great purpose that remains for this hidden stream.

Our goal here is not to line out every move of God throughout history. I only hope to illustrate the fact that entire groups of believers experienced tremendous and exotic outpourings in the remote four corners of the earth. Many have been forgotten. But the seeds they planted, both in the nature of their callings and the geographical regions in which they lived, were a foretaste of things to come in greater measure. Throughout history, we have seen numerous ministries reproduce spiritual children that exceeded their own level of anointing. When David passed the torch to Solomon, the glory filled the temple, increasing from one generation to the next. But Solomon subsequently failed to do the same for the following generation. Dozens of healing ministries were birthed through John Alexander Dowie in the late 1800s, including that of John G. Lake and others. Though Dowie saw tremendous, unparalleled success in his day, Lake is considered to have gone even higher in many ways.

Sometimes, the baton is passed directly from one ministry to the next in this way, but at other times, an anointing can be cut off. It can skip generations for many decades or be held in reserve for a time. We are beginning to realize that even if a stream appears to have died out, all will be restored in the last days. There will be a generation that walks in the fullness of God's river. For instance, Lake's healing rooms—a concept he picked up from Dowie—did not continue far beyond Lake's death. Lake did not reproduce the ministry as Dowie did. However, the present-day ministry of Cal Pierce has reopened those wells nearly a century later. Today, Healing Rooms are being planted around the world, in the same vision and power of Lake.

The apostolic reproduction of streams and movements in the church are sometimes immediate and sometimes left on the shelf for centuries. Imperfections in ministry, or lack of receptivity among the people, sometimes hinders a generational transfer. There are numerous reasons. Sometimes God's times and seasons must simply be played out to their fullest. On this point, it is interesting that today we are seeing the birth of another great healing revival in the power of Dowie, Lake, and the healing evangelists of the mid-20th century. It would serve us well to look back at John Dowie.

John Alexander Dowie (1847-1907) was one of the most anointed and colorful characters in recent church history. He founded an entire Christian city based on miracles! His truly apostolic ministry can be credited for pioneering modern healing ministry as we know it. He is credited for literally millions of conversions, untold thousands of healings, and he founded an entire Christian city outside of Chicago, always facing intense persecution from religious leaders, civil authorities and slanderous newspapers. Dowie has been called the father of healing revivalism. A number of influential leaders of the Pentecostal movement were birthed from his ministry such as F.F. Bosworth, John Lake, Gordon Lindsay, Raymond Richey, and many others. In fact, he prepared the way for Charles Parham and Pentecostalism itself.

John Alexander Dowie

Born in Edinburgh, Scotland, Dowie had read the entire Bible by age 6. His ministry began like many other great men of God—with intense failure. He was pastoring a church in Newton, Australia, when a severe plague swept through, and Dowie presided over more than 40 funerals in a short period of time. He began digging through the Scriptures looking for answers. Having some medical background, he knew there was no natural solution to the plague. However, as a young man, he had been miraculously healed of an illness by God. One day, after much prayer, he was suddenly inspired by reading of "how God anointed Jesus of Nazareth with the Holy Ghost and with power: He went about doing good, and healing all that were oppressed of the devil; for God was with Him" (Acts 10:38).

Dowie suddenly realized that the devil was actually responsible for sickness—not God—and that he had authority over the devil. He was awakened to a tremendous spiritual reality. He was immediately called to a parishioner's house, moments after this revelation, and healed her on her death bed. He thus began to move with great faith, healing the remaining members of his congregation, and not another died of the plague. Frustrated with denominationalism, however, he left the ministry for a short time after that to run for secular Parliament. We see that throughout history, great outpourings of supernatural power are often forfeited for some type of governmental authority.

Nevertheless, Dowie soon returned to his calling and went to America in 1888. He first came as an itinerant minister, touting the theme, "salvation, healing and holy living." Settling in Chicago, he opened healing meetings across the street from the Chicago World's Fair, and his ministry exploded. Thousands came for divine healing and to sit under his ministry. No one had ever heard of such miracles. In 1896, Dowie's headquarters was a seven-story building in Chicago, and by 1900, he founded Zion City on 6,800 acres of nearby farmland that he purchased. Though Dowie was barely known when he arrived in America, his ministry would reach international proportions. Many started small meetings in their own communities after attending his meetings, and small churches developed around the world.

Some people absolutely despised Dowie—a very common reaction for miracle workers. But Dowie seemed to feed on persecution, and it only made him stronger. He was hated by religious clergy of the day. Newspapers tore him to shreds. A street riot nearly mobbed him in England. Once when he was sitting at his desk, he heard an audible voice tell him to leave his office. At first he did not respond, but after hearing the voice again, he left the office, whereupon it immediately exploded. Someone had planted a bomb there intending to kill him.

Because Dowie refused to buy a meager $20 certificate that said he was practicing medicine, he was arrested 100 times by the city

"Sholob," John Dowie's Zion Tabernacle healing center seated thousands. Its walls were lined with crutches and other trophies of miraculous healing.

of Chicago in a single year and raked up $20,000 in legal fees for practicing medicine without a license. But Dowie adamantly refused getting the license, saying he was not practicing medicine. Instead he was laying hands on the sick and seeing them recover. Dowie was bold, straightforward, and he battled sin and compromise.

Dowie started a magazine titled *Leaves of Healing*, and began to open "Healing Homes," where the sick would come and stay, receiving ministry over and over until their healing was complete. This was the inspiration for John Lake's Healing Rooms ministry which followed. Lake brought several family members to Dowie's Healing Homes and they were cured of terminal illnesses. Dowie's Healing Homes were similar to convalescence houses where people received continual prayer until they were healed.

Dowie taught clean living, perhaps to an extreme. Though coming out of the holiness movement, one might understand the legalism of the day. He preached against the use of tobacco, pork, alcohol, pharmaceuticals, and "medical quackery." This did not help his reputation among the medical community. Dowie was so opposed to the use of medicine, that he allegedly banished a Zion resident for giving his own daughter Vaseline after she was burned with an oil lamp, and she apparently died of the condition sometime later. He rightly taught that healing is promised in the atonement, but insisted that anyone who sought faith healing should abandon all medical care. He felt that doctors were instruments of the devil. We must understand, however, that Dowie was a pioneer and that divine healing was a new concept in his day. We should gracefully overlook some of these extremes.

Despite such tough views, Dowie's ministry bore tremendous fruit. He launched a great evangelism effort that brought the gospel to almost every single resident of Chicago. His writings were featured in newspapers across the nation. With his huge following, Dowie began the Christian Catholic Apostolic Church, and by the time Zion Tabernacle was opened, he filled 6,000 seats each service. The walls of the tabernacle were lined with hundreds of canes, crutches, braces, and other examples of the thousands who had been healed by the Lord in his meetings. It was reported that Dowie prayed for 70,000 sick persons a year.

During his ministry, Dowie prophesied the coming of radio and television, as well as the assassination of a U.S. President. He met several presidents as well.

Founded in 1900, Dowie's "city of God," was constructed as a place for believers to work and play, distanced from the distractions of the world. Its initial settlers came from around the world on wagons, selling their homes and possessions to start a new life in Zion. He recruited the best minds in Chicago to plan and manage development of the city. They planned streets, parks, a golf course and a marina. Contributions came pouring in, and Dowie established industries to supply work to the new residents. He moved the entire Zion Lace Factory from England, built the Zion Cookie Factory and established a brick kiln factory, lumber mill, electric plant, retail stores, and even Zion's own postal stamps. There was also a school system and a four-year college. Land was leased to settlers, but held in trust by the church. All social, political, and economic efforts were run through the church.

Then he snapped. In 1901, Dowie publicly announced that he was Elijah the Restorer. He began dressing in high priestly robes, considering himself to be the Old Testament prophet. He dropped his last name, calling himself "John Alexander, First Apostle." He was quickly denounced by every religious leader of the day, and all of his great accomplishments were utterly discredited. He died only a few years later in ignominy, having been voted out of his position, bankrupted, and surrounded by continued controversy and lawsuits. He was also struck with paralysis and severe despondency.

Some have blamed Dowie's focus on building Zion for distracting him from the healing ministry and bringing his bizarre and tragic end. Others have pointed to the absolute power he seemed to wield in church and social matters there—as well as his continual pursuit of power in secular arenas. Perhaps the greatest contributing factor was the adoration Dowie received from his flock. While

Dowie was able to stand strong and even thrive amid persecution and hatred from his enemies, his weakness surfaced when people began to idolize him.

A group of ministers once told him that he must be Elijah, foretold to come in the Bible. At the time, he rebuked them severely and sent them away, telling them not to say such things. Nevertheless, the words kept "ringing in his ears," and by his own admission, the thought never left, until one day an intense conviction came over him that he was indeed Elijah, spoken of by the prophets, sent to restore all things.[8]

In later chapters we will examine more of the 19th and 20th century healing revivalists like Dowie in greater detail. Dowie is a wonderful illustration of the power we are invited to walk in to demonstrate the Kingdom of God. We should desperately desire to take up his anointing, and by looking at his life, hind sight shows us several pitfalls we can avoid. By observing his errors, we are graced with the opportunity to move even beyond Dowie in gifting and calling. And we can take solace, for Dowie's sake, in that his deception was not a Christological error, and he never denied his faith. While his confusion was drastic, at least he was only confused about *himself* and his personal identity, not the Lord. It is also reported by those closest to him, that he returned to his original faith in his final year of life.

Did Dowie step outside of his anointing by building Zion City? I think that Dowie surely struggled with power and control issues, and we always have to be careful to remember the words of Jesus, that His Kingdom is not of this world. But our influence on the kingdoms of this world should be an immediate byproduct of emanating the Kingdom of Heaven. His Kingdom come, His will be done, on earth as it is in Heaven. As we seek first God's Kingdom, restoration simply begins to happen in the natural, earthly systems around us. Eventually, the kingdoms of this world will become the kingdoms of our God (Rev. 11:15).

Dowie's merger of church and state was surely not a forced hybrid like some of the cases we will read about. No, Dowie's was more of a spiritual community, I believe, in which a holistic gospel was preached as the needs of the church were provided for, spirit, soul, and body. In this sense, Dowie surely was moving in the *spirit* of Elijah. It is certainly clear, therefore, with such tremendous success, how he could have been deceived. There was surely a thread of truth to his "Elijah" identity, which gave the delusion power in his mind. An entire generation has been called to walk in the spirit of Elijah.

ENDNOTES

1. Peter Davids, "What Went Wrong With Montanism," Tertullian, Apologeticas, a.d. 197.

2. Paul Keith Davis, "From Preparation to Demonstration," conference audio recording.

3. Wallis E.A. Budge, "The Spiritual Warfare of the Desert Fathers in the 3rd-4th Centuries," notes from The Paradise of the Holy Fathers, vol. 1. Accessed 19 Oct. 2004 <http://www.consumingfire.com/desert.htm>.

4. David Haggith, "What the Celts Have to Offer Christianity Today." (2001).

5. Bishop Alexander (Mileant). "St. Seraphim of Sarov Life and Teachings," translated by Nicholas and Natalia Semyanko.

6. Rick Joyner, The Harvest (Charlotte: Morningstar Publications, 1993), 171.

7. David Bercot, "The Nestorians." From Kingdom Christians Through the Centuries Series No. 3 (Amberson: Scroll Publishing, Co.) audio.

8. John Alexander Dowie sources:

   i. Gordon Lindsay, The Life of John Alexander Dowie (Dallas: The Voice of Healing Publishing Co., 1951).

ii. Roberts Liardon, "John Alexander Dowie." Chapter 1, God's Generals (Whitaker House, 1996).

iii. Alice Marshall, "John Alexander Dowie." The News-Sun (Aug. 28, 1996). Accessed 18 June 2004 <http://www.dowie.org/john_alexander_dowie.htm>.

iv. William Schwager, "Alexander Dowie's Dream." (1979). Accessed 18 June 2004 <http://www.ourzion.com/history/dreams.html>.

v. William Schwager, "In The Beginning." (1979). Accessed 18 June 2004. <http://www.ourzion.com/history/beginning.html>.

vi. Andrew Strom, "John Alexander Dowie–A Sign." (Storm Harvest, Inc., 2004). Accessed 18 June, 2004. <http://www.storm-harvest.asn.au/articles/johndowie.txt>.

CHAPTER 6

Power Missions

CHRISTIANS can no longer expect to evangelize the world by developing new strategies and programs. There is an over-abundance of new methods, church-planting techniques, and books on the market touting the latest trend. We are infatuated with all that is *new*. But the basic, biblical approach of Jesus still gets the job done—preach the gospel, work miracles. I have heard it estimated that Jesus spent 60 percent of His time healing the sick and working miracles during His ministry years. Whenever there are miracles, revival accelerates at a phenomenal pace. There must be signs following the gospel (see Mark 16:15-18).

A friend who works among Muslims in Qatar says he spent six years trying new approaches to evangelism. On one extreme, he attempted outright theological debates in the open, with a dozen bloodthirsty Muslims right in his face, as he spouted apologetics. On the opposite extreme, he tried a radical contextual approach where he would wear a turban and even pray with them in the mosques. He attempted every new strategy before the answer became clear. The only thing that is ever going to work is the basic approach of Jesus, a demonstration of raw power. We must realize that this is how the gospel has made its every significant advance to date. The biblical outline was never linear and programmatic. It was always experiential and supernatural.

"I studied Arabic for 10 years. It was a waste of time. I should have been pursuing the power," he said, adding that language studies should have been only a side dish to his chase for the anointing. This is not to say we ignore all strategy and methodology—especially in pastoral work. And the spoken word carries a power of its own. But the gospel must be preached with signs following. We shouldn't be going about doing God's work without His presence and power pouring out from our lives.

In the first centuries following Christ, the gospel spread like wildfire through North Africa, the Levant, Turkey and Europe. We long to see it take root in these same areas again today—especially in a world dominated by the satanic stronghold of Islam. Even secular historians, such as Ramsay MacMullen in *Christianizing the Roman Empire*, point to signs and wonders as the driving force behind the spread of Christianity, prior to its legalization by Constantine in a.d. 312.

MacMullen, a Yale historian, does not believe in miracles—he says they were perceived to be real by the people of the day. Nevertheless, he says the primary reason for the conversion of entire people groups was exorcisms, signs and wonders. He even goes on to say these exorcisms were not just individual in nature, but that regional principalities that posed as gods were cast down.

It was not poetic theology or sound arguments, but power confrontations that were winning the world to Christ. In fact, the exorcist was given an office early on in the church, and by a.d. 500, Rome still had 22 official exorcists. There are still remains of ancient church buildings throughout the modern Muslim world. If it took supernatural power to win these areas in those days, how can we think anything less will suffice for today? Revival will again sweep through the heart of the Islamic world, as it did before, through a gospel backed by power. The former wells will again bring forth water.

St. Francis Xavier (1506-1552) pioneered power missions with astonishing success in the least suspecting location, denomination, and time period in history.

Xavier raises the dead and works miracles in Peter Paul Rubens' "The Miracles of St. Francis Xavier" (c. 1616).

In the early 1500s, Protestants were objecting to the rampant abuses of the church. Likewise, conquistadors were roving the world at the time, imposing cruel and abortive "missionary" efforts toward the indigenous peoples of the world. But it was during this time that a young Spanish nobleman undertook an apostolic endeavor that resulted in thousands of conversions and miracles. While we still consider the nations of India and Japan as largely unreached with the gospel, Francis Xavier was there 500 years ago working wonders. Protestant reformers took the spotlight in his day, and missionaries had a bad reputation. Xavier was both a Catholic and a missionary and he moved in compassion and preached a gospel with signs following.

Having been discipled under the renowned Ignatius Loyola—himself a miracle worker—Xavier set off for India, arriving first at Goa, the capital Portuguese possession. In six months, he had shaken the entire city with the gospel, beginning 10 years of apostolic work. In a single month, Xavier baptized 10,000 converts. Everywhere he traveled, Xavier left a healthy church behind him. He is credited with hundreds of thousands of conversions. He had no great learning, and he knew little about the people to whom he was being sent. And while Xavier was not a social or religious critic, he did object to the abuse of power by the Portuguese in India. Xavier was constantly looking out for the poor and the sick.

Most interesting are the miracles. In the 1500s, Xavier had the gift of tongues. He prophesied, healed the sick, and raised the dead. And his miracles are very well documented. Before Xavier was canonized by the church, literally hundreds of witnesses testified to seeing or experiencing the extraordinary under his ministry—in fact, there are more than 500 pages of sworn testimony. The serious Xavier scholar can study these statements in the *Monumenta Xaveriana*. Among these miracles recorded: A merchant who knew Xavier testified that he was sailing together with him, when for three weeks the ship was unable to find fresh water and all were about to die of thirst. "Francis ordered a quantity of sea water to be brought up, blessed it, and gave them to drink. The water was perfectly fresh."

Limbs were restored that were withered since birth; a dead child was

Xavier lifts from the ground

raised who had already been buried; blind, leprous, cancerous, and paralyzed persons were all healed. A woman testified that a plague had been sweeping her town, but the day Xavier pulled into port, the disease disappeared and no one else died. People apparently took notice.

"At Comorin, when the pagans were not moved by his words, Xavier asked that a tomb which had been sealed the day before should be opened. Then indicating that this would be a sign of God's approval of Christianity, he called to the body to rise. The dead man came to life, with hundreds of natives embracing the faith as a consequence," writes researcher Fr. John A. Hardon, S.J.[1] There were several other resurrections.

A pagan mob was once about to attack a native Christian village, bent on killing the townspeople. Xavier went out to meet them, along with a "mysterious figure whose majesty and splendor terrified the assailants," and they left Xavier alone, fleeing. And another time, a small landing boat which was lost at sea miraculously returned three days later, after Xavier prayed. It was found floating alongside the hull of the main ship, untied, though no one had searched for it. Where Xavier went, miracles followed.

Shortly after his death, the number of Christians in Japan had rapidly grown to 200,000. The only reason Japan is not predominantly Christian today is because of a 50-year persecution that began under the Emperor Taikosama in the late 1500s. To keep Christian merchants from coming into the country, they required visitors to trample a crucifix underfoot. Most Christians were eradicated. But a small remnant quietly passed the faith handed down from Xavier until the next round of missionaries arrived some 200 years later.

Xavier's influence also impacted Spain and Portugal tremendously, simply through his passionate letters from the field. Xavier often experienced raptures and ecstasies in prayer, and people often had difficulty pulling him back to sobriety. At times, he was seen floating a few feet off the ground during communion.

We must add, however, that while Xavier personally demonstrated compassion, he was still influenced by the Inquisition/conquistador mentality of his day. Thus his missionary efforts have been questioned. He requested an Inquisition by the Portuguese king in Goa, and he also used government pressure as a proselytizing tactic. While this, of course, is horrific in retrospect, we must also understand the mind-set of Xavier's day, in which the world was erupt with religious wars and persecutions. Despite some of his darker choices and tactics, Xavier's work accounted for approximately 700,000 conversions. We cannot call into question his compassion, desire to save souls, and miraculous lifestyle.

> *Lord, I have heard of Your great fame; I stand in awe of Your deeds, O Lord. Renew them in our day, in our time make them known...*(Habakkuk 3:2).

Indeed, such feats are already being renewed in our day. Lands that were formerly taken for the gospel through miraculous demonstration will again require the power of God to move in our time. With few exceptions, it has always taken miracles to spark revival. The secular historian MacMullen states that "in religious usage, a miracle is an event in which one knows one is dealing with God."

Got that right. Droughts were quenched in north Africa after saints prayed for rain, bringing in droves of converts. In many cases, temples of idolatry were torn open with a mere word. Early church historians, beyond the first century, recorded extensive miracles that brought salvation far and wide. Often, entire people groups would convert en masse after demonic strongholds were humiliated. Some accounts were more supernatural than others, but all required the risk of faith.

For instance, St. Boniface, apostle to the Germans, worked no great miracle when he took an axe to a sacred oak tree dedicated to Thor at Geismar. This was a tree which was revered throughout the region, and a huge crowd of pagans gathered to watch Boniface get zapped by a thunderbolt when he swung the axe. But when he chopped down their sacred tree (and later carved it into a pulpit), no harm came to him, and the entire countryside began to worship the Christian God.

In a similar story, St. Martin of Tours, a well-documented fourth century bishop, tried to convince townspeople to cut down a tree that they venerated. They agreed, but only if Martin would consent to sit in the path of the falling tree. He sat right under the leaning tree, as they chopped away at the other side. Just before it fell, the tree suddenly shifted in the other direction, in mid-air, without striking anyone. Many were converted that day. Martin ripped down many pagan temples and built churches in their place. He once ordered a huge tower to be torn down. When it was not immediately destroyed, he prayed, and a bolt of lightning shattered it.

God loves to show His power, but he requires bold faith on the part of His ministers. It is written in the apocryphal *Acts of John* that the apostle won over a number of believers with numerous healings at Ephesus. And going into the temple of Artemis, he prayed "O God…at whose name every idol takes flight and every demon and unclean power: now let the demon that is here take flight at thy name." During this prayer, the altar of Artemis ripped to pieces, causing the Ephesians to fall to their knees, tear their clothing and cry out to the one living God.

Apostolic power hitters always confronted the enemy head on, making a public display of God's might and superiority over every regional stronghold. Signs and wonders were truly the *chief instrument* of evangelism.

"The most effective evangelism in today's world is accompanied by manifestations of supernatural power," said Peter Wagner, who has been beating the power evangelism drum for years.[2] But the problem is, far too many charismatic Christians agree with these principles in theory only. It is an altogether different thing to actually step out on the waters and begin "doing the stuff" where it counts.

"Power evangelism takes place when an unbeliever sees and experiences the power of God in a mighty way—such as through miracles or healings, along with a rational presentation of the gospel," explains renewal leader Che Ahn in his book *Into the Fire*.[3] When first stepping out into power evangelism, Ahn began to discover that he simply had to ask the Holy Spirit to touch a person, or to reveal Jesus to them, and the anointing did the rest. He explains this simple, beginner approach to allowing someone to feel the presence of God.

"My theory is that such a power encounter with the Lord pulls down the spiritual forces that are hindering the person from coming to Christ, and the love of God is revealed. Paul states that 'the kindness of God leads us to repentance.' What better way to experience the kindness of God than to feel it! Surely it is better felt than taught!" continues Ahn. "Without the power of the Holy Spirit, we can in no way reach the three billion people who have never heard the gospel. Around the world, power evangelism is getting the job done."[4]

Whether it's a lightning bolt or the simple feeling of the Holy Spirit's peace coming over a person, the size of the miracle is not always that important. With a simple word of knowledge for the Samaritan woman at the well, Jesus evangelized an entire town. It doesn't take much on our part. It only takes God. Ninety percent of my responsibility is just being willing to be used by God.

Mission work—whether overseas or in your own back yard—requires a radical departure from apathy. Willingness is the first step toward faith. If not for apathy alone, the entire world would be evangelized already. In 2004, the world's population was 6.3 billion. According to the Center for the Study of Global Christianity, there were 682 million "Great Commission" Christians. In other words, if every evangelism-minded Christian recruited eight converts, the world would be completely won to Christ. And that is a conservative figure; the workload could be even lighter. The Center reports that 33 percent of the world claims to be Christian. If every so-called Christian won two souls, the whole thing would be wrapped up and we could go home.

If more Christians would get off their couches and simply "go" as we are all instructed to do in Matthew 28, they would be surprised at the power God is willing to pour through their own fingertips.

David Hogan, an edgy, gunslinger-type minister in the jungles of Mexico, has been used to raise more than 20 people from the dead. He is a new, current-day mystic.

Hogan's apostolic network of ministers has raised upward of 300 dead bodies. Like most Christians walking in high levels of supernatural activity today, Hogan is a highly controversial character. He holds spiritual "boot camps," where visiting missionaries are often sent home if they cannot hack the rigorous conditions he imposes by necessity. The entire camp, including children and animals, fasts every other day. They are also constantly confronting armed rebels and guerrillas, with church members sometimes facing assaults. Some of his itinerants have been hacked up by machetes, yet after he laid hands on them, they recovered.

Hogan is blunt and considered caustic by some, but usually just to those who like to wear fake smiles to church on Sunday. There is no religious pretense, only the reality of raw spiritual encounters in his everyday life. He is also regularly taken into intense prophetic encounters and head-on collisions with witchdoctors and demonic powers. At times, his family members have been seized by sudden

David Hogan

ailments, only to look out the window to see a witchdoctor sending curses on them from across the street. The warfare is intense, but the fruit of his work is amazing.

I once attended a meeting where Hogan spoke in a very affluent metropolitan area. Honest and to the point, Hogan called the audience a bunch of spoiled brats. At the meeting, he said the main reason Americans do not see many extreme power encounters, is because we fail to go. We, in our selfish bubbles, avoid the poor, the sick, and the lost. Hogan says he is no different from anyone else, except that he is willing to go into the thatched huts of the poor and peel away the banana leaves from their sick and wounded bodies. How can we expect to heal the sick, he asked, if we are unwilling to search them out and peel away the banana leaves? Our simple initiative to step out onto the harvest fields is the first key to unlocking God's provision of power.

Let us again consider Islam. With one billion followers, or one-fifth of the planet's population, more than 80 percent of Muslims have never heard the gospel. Unfortunately, the church does not seem to care. Less than 1 percent of the Christian missionary force reportedly works among Muslims. In fact, the church has never made a serious effort to reach them.

Pioneering missionary to Islam, Samuel Zwemer said, "One might suppose that the church thought the Great Commission did not apply to Muslims." Some estimates show only one Christian missionary working among every one million Muslims! Islam is growing rapidly, but according to current statistics, less that 2 percent of Western contributions toward mission work go to those working among Muslims. I was personally convicted when I read that more missionaries work with Alaska's 400,000 residents (my home state) than in all of the Muslim world combined. The root of the problem is that we do not care. There is an overt racism, which promotes undue fear and a clear lack of love toward Muslims among Western

Christians. This is partly due to politics and demands repentance on behalf of the church, or we are bound to reap the wages of our sin.

One of the worst failures the West could ever make is to turn its back on Israel. Only those who bless Israel will be blessed. We must stand with her at all costs. Nevertheless, Islam's encroaching attacks, even against the apple of God's eye, should never excuse us from loving its adherents on a personal level. Despite the controversial political issues of recent years, the individual Christian is called to a wholehearted, unconditional love of the Muslim people.

"We have allowed our false perceptions and lack of understanding to result in wrong attitudes and a lack of compassion for Muslim peoples and, therefore, not sought to alleviate suffering among them," states a bulletin from the Frontiers mission agency, one of the few parachurch organizations actively pounding the Islamic world with missionaries today. "We are guilty of believing and perpetuating misconceptions, prejudice and, in some instances, hostility and outright hatred toward Muslim peoples."

Despite our own fears toward Muslims, Jesus loves them enough to lay his life down for them. It is truly the church's task to earnestly pray for reconciliation that opens doors for the gospel. Yes, power ministry will be revived in the Islamic world, and some of the earth's greatest prophets and apostles will come from her ranks. But the flood of power is going to come forth foremost through the gateways of mercy and forgiveness. Love is the greatest demonstration of power. When the church learns to love the Muslim, revival cannot be stopped.

My Qatar friend recently reported that in Algeria today, there are few pockets of Christian missionaries. But for those who are willing to step into the supernatural, they are seeing a 100 percent healing rate for every Muslim they pray for. Yes, Muslims, like the Jews, demand signs to believe (see 1 Cor. 1:22), as do strong adherents of most major world religions. But how will miracles be wrought if there is no one compassionate enough to reach out and perform them?

How, then, can they call on the one they have not believed in? And how can they believe in the one of whom they have not heard? And how can they hear without someone preaching to them? And how can they preach unless they are sent? (Romans 10:14-15).

The harvest is ripe, and it is amazing what God can do with our simple willingness to go. It is even more amazing to see what He can do with our willingness to trust Him in His supernatural power, rather than leaning on our own programs and human wisdom.

Heidi Baker

Heidi Baker and her husband, Rolland, are missionaries to Mozambique. Arriving in the country just after an exhaustive civil war in the early 1990s, the Bakers faced conditions of famine, drought, poverty, abuse, and degradation. Despite her Ph.D. in systematic theology and a history of mission work in other countries, Heidi says she struggled just to plant two small churches and an orphanage there. But after a trip to Toronto Airport Christian Fellowship in 1996, Heidi was struck so powerfully by the presence of God that she could not move for seven days. She was carried around in a wheelchair and thought she had lost her mind. After the experience, she was so infused with the love and power of God, that today she has planted nearly 7,000 churches. The doors of her orphanage were opened completely and she never turned another child away. Today she houses hundreds who all call her Mama Aida. Baker was given a vision that "there is always enough," and since that time, the orphanage has seen food multiply numerous times, not to mention scores of miraculous healings (blind, deaf, and lame), supernatural provision and protection, and many raised from the dead.

Heidi has no formula for raising the dead, except that she literally *loves* people back to life. She has held the dead bodies of babies and others, weeping over them for hours, until warmth came back into them and they were supernaturally revived. Since returning from

Toronto, the Bakers' church planting work exploded, as the power of God was displayed in their midst. As their church planting has exploded, it is a far cry from the two shaky churches they had built before her power encounter. And the Bakers also have the ear of Mozambique's president. Heidi says her favorite church is one they planted in the garbage dump, where the presence of God outweighs the flies and the stench, as they reach out to the poorest of poor. She has had a price put on her head—$20—and has had her life

Heidi baptizes someone under the glory.

threatened numerous times. She has been robbed, machine gun fire has, at times, been a regular sound outside the orphanage's walls. But her life is marked by hours a day lying prostrate before the presence of God, often unable to move because of the heavy weight of His glory. And in this posture of lying down in His love and joy, the Bakers are taking a nation. Heidi Baker is a new mystic.

Who will ask the Lord for a nation? Can the Lord not give over a nation in a day? It all begins from a posture of lying intimately still in His presence. And then it takes love for the lost and dying. Power giftings are needed to usher in this harvest, but laborers are still needed in the fields. Many are simply restrained from going because of fear. In his book, *Call for Christian Risk*, John Piper says, "By removing eternal risk, Christ calls His people to continual temporal risk. For followers of Jesus, the final risk is gone." Piper reminds us, therefore, that taking temporal risks in this life should be the norm for Christians while in pursuit of Kingdom purposes. For satan no longer grips us with the fear of death.

"In America and around the world, the price of being a real Christian is rising. Things are getting back to normal in 'this present evil age.'...'All who desire to live a godly life in Christ Jesus will be persecuted,'" says Piper. "Those who've made gospel-risk a voluntary lifestyle will be most ready when we have no choice."

In the same way, all who begin to tap into the supernatural dynamic of Kingdom power that is available to us can expect persecution.

At present, we are seeing more Christian martyrs than ever before—about 167,000 each year around the world. Consider this amount in comparison to the 2004 tsunami deaths around the Indian Ocean! This is 33 times the amount of people killed in the World Trade Center on September 11, 2001. Also, with population growth increasing, there have been more Christians alive in the latter half of this century than ever before in the history of the church. The spiritual climate is truly escalating in the earth today, and we do not want to miss out on the great end-time harvest that is happening around us. More people are coming to Christ than ever before since the dawn of time. This is the hour for the faint of heart to take courage, for there is no sacrifice which does not offer a greater reward. As the famous 20th century missionary and martyr Jim Elliot said, "He is no fool who gives what he cannot keep to gain what he cannot lose." I believe that the Great Commission is a sacrificial call to *every* believer. Everyone may not be called to full-time overseas ministry, but short-term trips and cross-cultural ministry should be the norm for all of us. At the very least, we are all called to donate financially to reach the nations. And there is a very biblical principal that those who remain in camp to stand watch over the provisions will always earn the same reward as those who go out to battle. As for myself, life is far too boring to flip channels at camp all day. I want to be on the front lines, seizing ground for the Kingdom.

Perhaps Samuel Zwemer resounded one of the clearest battle cries for reaching the nations. And he paid one of the greatest prices. Launching into the heart of Islam at the turn of the century, Zwemer's younger brother Peter died. In Arabia his first two daughters died of disease as well. Unwavering, Zwemer wrote on their tomb stones a simple verse: *Worthy is the Lamb to receive riches*.

Consider this passage from Zwemer:

The challenge of the unoccupied fields of the world is one to great faith and, therefore to great sacrifice. Our willingness to sacrifice for an enterprise is always in proportion to our faith in that enterprise. Faith has the genius of transforming the barely possible into actuality. Once men are dominated by the conviction that a thing must be done, they will stop at nothing until it is accomplished. Frequent set-backs and apparent failure never dishearten the real pioneer. Occasional martyrdoms are only a fresh incentive. Opposition is a stimulus to greater activity. Great victory has never been possible without great sacrifice. Does it really matter how many die or how much money we spend in opening closed doors, and in occupying the different fields, if we really believe that missions are warfare and that the King's Glory is at stake? War always means blood and treasure. Our only concern should be to keep the fight aggressive and to win victory regardless of cost or sacrifice.[5]

It is clear that we have a true charge to take the nations. But we can also push ourselves to make a number of great sacrifices, while missing the big picture entirely.

If I give all I possess to the poor and surrender my body to the flames, but have not love, I gain nothing (1Corinthians 13:3).

The beauty of Heidi Baker's story, is that she is not a stale, iron-fisted missionary wife pounding out her duty to the Lord. Yes, her perspective was different prior to her visitation with the Lord in Toronto. She was so burned out with the religious duties of ministry and missions that she wanted to work at Kmart instead. But like many, she has been radically transformed by the revelation of God's love for her.

Intimacy with Jesus is the new wineskin that will carry the Kingdom to the nations. As we bask in the love and presence of

God, He does a deep work in us. And we are often not consciously aware of what He is doing until we see the fruit. Heidi "wastes" half of her day enjoying the Lord in pleasurable prayer, and the fruit is nearly 7,000 churches. Heidi stays so drunk in God's love that she usually cannot stand up at a pulpit. She usually just preaches from the floor. She waits for God before she yaks about something. We simply have to trust God's presence enough to lean into it—to wait in His presence until we are clothed with power from on high (see Luke 24:49). The more we gaze upon His beauty and goodness—and His joy toward us—the more our hearts are awakened to our own fears and insecurities that keep us locked away in prisons of self-protection. Soaking in God's love, versus just working for God, gives us a taste of freedom and imparts to us a boldness to take the nations.

The thrust for international missions will be totally revolutionized over the next decade, as intimacy with Jesus becomes priority in the life of the believer over evangelism itself. Ministry to the Lord will take priority over ministry to others, and thus *empower* our ministry to others. The love of God will be restored to its rightful place as the chief commandment, thus enabling us to carry out the second commandment—to love our neighbors as ourselves. A revelation of Jesus as our Bridegroom Lover is the key to unlock this end time harvest. Even in recent years, the International House of Prayer model of worship—based entirely on this intimacy perspective— has been connecting with the missionary model of groups such as Youth With a Mission. The Kansas City IHOP has just officially merged with YWAM, to take this presence-based perspective to the harvest fields.

A new generation of missionaries is being raised up, whose hearts are captivated by the Lover of their souls. The Lord is releasing new wineskins to handle this intense paradigm shift in our approach to missions. Prayer and fasting will multiply on the field, breaking down walls, but such devotion will be based *out of* intimacy, rather than *for* intimacy. The very presence and power of God will not be able to squeeze into our old approach to doing things.

Powerless, faithless doctrines will be flushed away as we begin to see the supernatural with our own eyes. New wineskins have an elasticity allowing them to stretch and hold the expanding wine. But the old wineskin can no longer stretch. It becomes brittle, dry, and cracks under pressure.

The new wine is His presence. Many who are currently serving God, either domestically or on the mission field, still have tasted very little of this sweet wine. Sheer determination won't cut it. None of us has tasted more than a drop of His eternal ocean of love. Many still carry a broken shell of emotional trauma, unforgiveness, bitterness and disappointment into their ministry, which blocks the living, moving, loving rhythm of His presence.

In the place of His presence, God does an accelerated work. God is going to place a rapid maturity in an upcoming generation, who are not so consumed with the battlefield that they forget their commander in chief. For those willing to pull aside and wait in His presence—though the storms blow around them—He will promote them above the ground warfare. The key is to dwell in the *secret place of the Most High* (Ps. 91). He will take them to the heights. They will soar over the battle like eagles, receiving strategy and revelation for swift victory.

This new generation will set aside time to soak and heal and receive empowerment. Spiritual growth is accelerated when we take the time to soak in God's presence. It is like a rapid-maturation incubator. Suddenly, from the place of His presence, the Scriptures make sense in ways that decades of Bible study alone could not unfold. And this shift of focus toward intimacy unlocks fiery continual prayer and stifles burnout. Prayer becomes less of a place of trench warfare, and more of a party. Bob Sorge, in *Secrets of the Secret Place*, writes that, "One of the most violent things you'll ever do is wrestle down all the competing elements in your calendar and consistently carve out the time to shut yourself into the Secret Place...."

The most effective ministries in this hour will be returning to a place of contemplative stillness, of soaking in the presence of God.

It is here—in a place of waiting, or tarrying—that we are equipped for the miraculous. It is in the place of rest and laying our head upon His breast that we realize God truly enjoys weak humans. He is not looking for perfection—He is looking for relationship. With this understanding of God's enjoyment of us, we will have the endurance to tackle the most intense situations and disappointments that are always prerequisites to major victories and success. Simply stated, time spent with Jesus is never wasted. There will be a generation whose classroom time has been reduced, so that they can "come aside" and allow the Living Word to penetrate their hearts.

Intimacy is the true source of all supernatural power. Out of intimacy comes the anointing of the Lord's favor. We must first realize that it is *the anointing that breaks the yoke* (Isa. 10:27). It is Holy Spirit Himself who will bring about worldwide revival—not even our miracle working or zeal. It is "'not by might nor by power, but by My Spirit,' says the Lord Almighty" (Zech. 4:6). When the Spirit of God anoints a man to preach the gospel, he will be effective with or without miracles. God Himself is power enough, and the word itself carries an inherent anointing without any other fireworks attached. John the Baptist and the prophet Jonah are perfect examples of highly effective ministries with no recorded miracles. Yet their words carried great power, because they carried a tremendous anointing for repentance.

We are desperately called to the nations. But God is calling us to keep the priority of divine intimacy over evangelism. God wants friends and lovers before He wants laborers and harvesters. Many in the Muslim world and the Far East will be converted after seeing the Lord in visions or dreams, without the aid of any man or ministry. The Lord will sometimes do this just to show us that He does not *need us*, although He wants to use us for the harvest. This perspective should not lead us to evangelistic complacency. But we must remember that our own works have little to do in the grand scheme of things. God wants to find someone who is available to do things His way. That means seeking Him first.

EVERY NATION

On the world mission front, every nation and all flesh will experience an outpouring of the Holy Spirit. As we read in Acts, all nations were present at Pentecost:

> *And there were dwelling in Jerusalem Jews, devout men, from every nation under heaven.....And it shall come to pass in the last days, says God, that I will pour out of My Spirit on all flesh* (Acts 2:5,17).

The church age began with every nation—and every race, every tribe, and every tongue on the globe will see worldwide awakening, with the gospel reaching the ends of the earth before the Lord's return.

Few Christians deny the immediate need for saving souls through international missions. But many younger people, in my own generation, have been soured by the abuses and exploitation of developing nations by Western missionaries throughout history. A lot of this disillusionment comes from the liberal education system, which paints Christianity as the root of all evil. Surely Christianity has gotten a bad rap from many modern thinkers, but there truly has been a lot of war and trading on the name of Christ. And true Christianity is not God's stamp of approval on Western culture. It is not a cultural or religious phenomenon at all. Christianity is about relationship with the God who created all of humanity.

The very colonization of many nations, under the auspices of Christian charity, has resulted in the rape and pillage of their natural resources and the stripping of their dignity in centuries past. American Natives, in many ways, were annihilated under the guise of "Christian values." Slave labor essentially continues today, as Western nations still feed off the sweatshop practices that fill our Wal-Marts and clothing stores, accelerating prostitution and drug use throughout the Third World. It all began with European "mission work" and the colonialization of the Third World.

I do not mean to get political here, but the Lord is calling His church to be pure, irregardless of nationality. Racism must go from the church. And the Lord wants a pure gospel reaching the nations, not a cultural imposition. It is true that the past and present idolatry and sins of many pagan nations has led to their spiritual and economic bondage today. But that does not excuse the Western church for feeding off their poverty; we should be about setting them free, not oppressing them further. I will acknowledge that the West has contributed significantly each year in international aid to the Third World over the years. But nevertheless, this is just a Band-Aid.

Apathy is lethal. Much has been given to us, and we bear a greater responsibility to bless and care for the world. We are our brother's keeper. It is time the church takes responsibility for its own part in the state of international affairs. I am convinced that, if there is suffering in the world, it is only because the church is not walking in her rightful authority to destroy the works of the devil and establish God's Kingdom here on earth. Not a political kingdom, but a spiritual one. Not an American kingdom, or a British one. It is time we pursue serious repentance for the spread of a cultural gospel, if we ever want to see the gospel of the Kingdom take root in our midst. When the church steps up to her task, poverty and disease will be eliminated in unprecedented ways throughout the world.

Will we see a utopian world without poverty and sickness before the return of the Lord? Surely the entire curse of the earth will not be lifted until it is made new. But the worldwide church will walk in unprecedented freedom from that curse through the work of the cross as the day of the Lord draws nearer. The restoration of all things will surely be beyond our expectations.

RELEVANCE AND EXPLOITATION

God wants to release a people who enter the harvest fields, doing ministry the way Jesus told us: Preach the gospel, heal the sick, raise the dead, cleanse the leper, drive out demons. Freely you have received, freely give (Matt. 10:7-8). One of the primary things holding back this release of power on a corporate level, is our own selfish desires to build our own kingdoms, instead of His.

As the church begins to move in power again, we cannot view miracles alone as God's endorsement of a person's ministry or one cultural method of worship. God will not give us power just so we can begin marketing our own way of doing things. Miracles are for the glory of God. A dangerous temptation with all power—whether natural or spiritual—is to use it for control and manipulation. We need only look at the Crusades, the Inquisition, and the genocide at the hands of the conquistadors—all done in the name of Christ—to see power abused.

It is every believer's right to walk in miracles, signs, and wonders. But that does not mean the Lord advocates all our character flaws and bad doctrines. The Lord will bless a lot of ministries He did not initiate. He will even bless a lot of ministries He doesn't fully agree with. But we want something more than a blessing, a few miracles, or a one-time visitation. We want long-term *habitation* with the Lord.

We often take a few divine experiences or miracles as God's ultimate approval of a ministry style or cultural form. This is dangerous. I have seen a number of Messianic Jewish ministries, for instance, begin preaching legalistic food preferences and cultural agendas on the authority of a few miracles. We must always guard against the twisting of our power or giftings in a way that advocates a gospel of personal preference. Furthermore, we do not preach a gospel of signs and wonders. We preach a gospel of Christ and Him crucified—signs and wonders merely follow this message.

This is especially apparent in the subtleties of today's mission field. To this day, you cannot preach in the heat of Africa without wearing a suit and tie, because of the advent of European legalism many long years ago. There is a certain Indonesian tribe, whose only attire is a long, wooden spoon-like contraption that hangs down from the neck and scantily covers the genitalia. The tribe has received the gospel, and churches have been established. But while tribe members still wear this spoon thingy now as Christians, they actually hang a tie over the top of it on Sundays—as per missionary influence. True irony.

I believe it is possible to defile the inherent image of God found in the diversity of a people group, by arrogantly imposing one's own culture. We have a lot to learn about the Lord through other cultures, even those who have not received Him yet! We are supposed to be sharing the gospel, but instead we have sought to destroy innocent customs. We must realize that crucial aspects of all cultures are permissible, if not directly inspired by God, although every culture can bear influence from both the kingdoms of darkness and of light. For the most part, a culture itself is primarily amoral. The apostolic mandate was never to defy other cultures, but rather to use their standards as a vehicle to promote the gospel. All things, in some way, can point to Christ in shadow and type. Christ can use even the worst things to bring glory to Himself. With prophetic insight and revelation, we can see and use the signposts embedded in every people group which point to Jesus.

Joel's Army will not just be a Western phenomenon. Neither will Western culture be the standard fare for Christians throughout the world. Western culture, in fact, is full of its own defilements being spread throughout the world today. We pump out so much pornography, glorified violence, and filth, it is no wonder African nations and other countries are beginning to send missionaries to our own shores.

The church must be multicultural. That does not mean watering down the definition of sin, but it does mean overcoming racism, elitism, and religious form. Like Paul, we must learn to be all things to all men. It is one thing to despise a cultural "practice" that is lawless. It is another thing to stereotype an entire people group. These lines must become very clear in the church today. Hatred of practices cannot equate hatred of people, or we will lose our authority to preach in certain circles.

The apostle Paul, when approaching the Greeks on Mars Hill, gave us a foundational approach to culturally relevant evangelism.

He did not come in with guns blazing, criticizing the pagan Greeks. He pointed out that the Athenians worshiped at an altar which bore the inscription "to the unknown god." "Now what you worship as something unknown I am going to proclaim to you," said Paul (Acts 17:22-23). Paul used the height of the Athenians' idolatrous confusion to point to Christ. Rather than rejecting Greek culture, he *fulfilled* it. Just as Christ did not come to do away with the Mosaic law, but rather He fulfilled it. Christ is the fulfillment of every need and the release to every tension.

Jesus gives us the ultimate example of cultural relevance. He stepped out of Heaven, laying aside all of His power and glory, and came into our world to become one of us. We cannot, in our greatest imagination, comprehend the extreme distance He traveled in order to reach us on our own terms. He stripped and humbled Himself entirely, stepping completely into the realm of mankind. And He didn't come to exploit us, but to redeem us.

There is an inherent respect the Lord wants us to have for those operating in different cultures, different streams of the church, and even and especially for non-believers. There is a coming generation that will not get hung up on the external forms and practices, but will pursue deep and inner change of heart for those they seek to reach with the gospel.

For too long, the church has said to stay away from the bars, stay away from the drug alleys, stay away from the new age circles. But these are the very places Jesus wants us to infiltrate. These are mission fields. And if we do it the right way, people will be drawn to the light of Christ within us. After all, did Jesus not hang out with the drunks, the tax collectors, and the prostitutes? They saw something in Him that they liked. And He saw potential in them, despite their obvious sins. It is much easier to see sin in someone than to see their prophetic potential. It is easy to point out problems with other cultures, rather than to see their strengths. A lot of what we call "discernment" is really just criticism. As the coming generation throws off religiosity and judgmentalism, they will stop cursing the darkness and simply light a candle.

Jesus was so full of light that darkness was immediately exposed in His presence. If we are always focused on the evil of the world, we obviously have our eyes in the wrong place. Jesus said that if our eyes are full of light, our whole body will be full of light. This is the key to evangelism. Focus on Jesus—see Him in the midst of a situation—and you will become a shining lamp. We must see hope and redeemable value in even the "worst of sinners." We must see God formed in them, before they can even picture it themselves. This applies not only to individuals, but to entire cultures. We must see the destiny God has for the nations.

Even false religions have practices and world views with some redeemable value. To say that Buddhism is completely void of truth is insane. There is plenty of wisdom and redeemable spiritual exercise there. The problem is, there can often be 99 percent truth and 1 percent poison, which defiles the whole thing. I do not suggest that believers turn to Buddhism in their search for truth. All truth has been revealed to us in Christ. Nevertheless, Buddhism would not be such a powerful stronghold if there were not plenty of legitimate practices involved. What would the world look like if the Christian norm was to invest hours a day in prayer and meditation before the Lord, just as Buddhist monks devote to their own meditations? What if our *society* was centered on Christian meditation, as Tibet is centered on Buddhist meditation? Buddhists, in their devotion to prayer, put most Christians to shame. This is their draw as a counterfeit system of spirituality. We need to take back this ground. There are a number of non-Christian cultures that live lives of simplicity with strong family orientation that we in our supposedly "Christian nations" could learn tons from. The opening of an R-rated movie is what sparked the Iranian revolution. Divorce is unheard of in many non-Christian countries. And many cultures outside the West are extremely open to issues of spirituality, whereas our belief in the supernatural is often blocked by reason and logic.

It will be those believers who arise from non-Christian cultures that will offer some of the most breathtaking new perspectives on the faith. There is no doubt a fine line between taking back spiritual ground and adopting an approach of syncretism—that is, trying to reconcile Christianity with other religions. The problem is, we have tried to reconcile Christ with the *Christian religion* which is just about as dangerous. Any system that replaces relationship with God is an idol. Christ has no fellowship with evil. But a breed of new Christian mystics is coming whose devotion and supernatural experiences will put to shame the most powerful lamas, shamans, yogis, and spiritists of the Eastern world and the new age movement. The same cannot be said of most Christians today. While we all have access to God's power through the blood of Jesus, few of us have actively opened ourselves to His presence in our daily lives, to the same extent that many pagan spiritists have conversely opened themselves to demonic influence.

Remember Sundar Singh, the Indian Christian who lived as a sadhu? Such is a shining model of extreme cultural relevance, merged with extreme supernatural power and experience. While I am a strong pundit of contextualization and the Mars Hill approach to evangelism—meeting people where they are, rather than imposing religious formula and Bible Belt lifestyles—it is important to remember that the relevance approach to evangelism, by itself, will always be slow and tedious while dangerously flirting with syncretism. We must have relevance mixed with power.

As a postmodern church, we are beginning to recognize that the outward forms and practices of religion are impotent to effect true spiritual change in a society far removed from pop Christian subculture. But is the answer to strictly adopt the forms and practices of secular society in an effort to build bridges? Cultural relevance is needed, but without supernatural power we have a nicely wrapped package with no punch at the bottom line.

This is why miracle crusades—while despised as old-fashioned or ineffective in Western circles—are still having tremendous impact overseas, literally accounting for the salvation of millions today. They demonstrate God's power.

Let us consider the mission fields of America. There are many subcultures in our own society which may have heard the Gospel in Christian terminology, but they have never heard it in their own language. Fortunately, there is a new breed of interpreters on the rise who are not bound by dead tradition—who are able to take the truths of the fathers, strip away the King James, and offer it to the sons in street talk. There are a number of profound Generation X ministries being birthed today, which are offering the gospel in a language not masked by religious metaphor. They are reaching the emerging culture on its own terms. They draw analogies from movies and popular secular songs that old-school Christians would not even watch or listen to. The dress and attitude is not smack full of dead church culture. There are churches today that meet in bars, whose services are laden with punk rock—ministries that are fiery, raw, and honest. They are attempting radical and innovative approaches never before seen in the church. Legalism and religion only breed rebellion and distaste. The emerging church wants nothing to do with formalized religion. It is truly looking for relationship. It is looking for heartfelt interaction with a living God. The earliest apostles held this as the crux of their message. While Paul's letters were quick to establish doctrinal matters and practical order for the churches, the apostles' goal was never to form a secondary system of law beyond the Old Testament. They never wanted a separate "church culture." The goal was always to bring freedom through relationship and intimacy with God.

This generation may be covered in dreadlocks, piercings, and tattoos. They may not be quiet in church, and they may not seem the tame, meek little kitten Christians we are used to encountering. But they will put darkness to shame with the power and authority of the gospel they demonstrate, as well as the tremendous fruit they bear. They will be violent, John the Baptist types who take the Kingdom by force.

An evangelist friend of mine, Shawn Gabie, is one of these young dreadlocked warriors. He goes regularly to satanic coffee shops, ministers on the streets of Mardis Gras and other dark places. Not only does he minister with relevance—throwing religious spirits off guard by his appearance and style—he also operates in power. He often gets accurate words of knowledge in the streets and in the bars, discerning people's names, facts about their background, and other bits of revelation that give miraculous credence to the gospel he preaches.

Or consider Bill Johnson's church in Redding, California. Their city is being taken for the Kingdom of God with signs, wonders, and healings. But it's not happening in the church. It's happening in the local malls and in the streets. Meeting people where they are and operating in power.

Cultural issues aside, it is interesting that the apostle James, when confronted by the miraculous exploits of Paul and Barnabas among the very first Gentile believers, said, "It is my judgment, therefore, that we should not make it difficult for the Gentiles who are turning to God." (Acts 15:19). He suggested that, in approaching new believers, they not heap a bunch of rules and regulations on them. They gave these new believers four basic guidelines—regarding sexual immorality, food sacrificed to idols and other simple food requirements (don't eat strangled stuff or drink blood). In summary, he said, "Let's meet them where they are. It's all about Jesus anyway. They have always been told what is good and bad—the do's and the don'ts. There's a synagogue on every corner where they can hear God's law, anyway. But even the law itself points to Jesus. Don't hold them back from Jesus."

Praise God for the law that convicts us of sin, but the reason God sent His Son was to bridge the sin gap to restore relationship with us. If legalisms and cultural rules are getting in the way of our relationship with God, we are missing the point. Religiosity is not just the offspring of the old mainline denominations. Even post-renewal movements can get lodged in their ways of worship, lifestyles, and perceptions of God that hinders Him from doing a new thing. In fact, many who have truly tasted God's power have become some of the most religiously deluded people I know. Because of their experiences, some feel they are on the *cutting edge* of what God is doing—a sure sign of spiritual pride. Another good indicator of the religious spirit is when you are able to quickly point it out in others, but are unable to see it in yourself.

Clearly, there is only one way to worship God. Deuteronomy 12:4 says of the pagan nations "You must not worship the Lord your God in their way." But what is their way? Primarily, it is through form, and outward exercise, and ritualistic practice. The Christian worships his God not through systematic works and deeds, but through relationship and intimacy. God is not calling us to embrace new cultural and religious forms; He is calling us to place less importance on them.

I have noticed that the religious spirit is not so much concerned with what type of form or structure a Christian relies on, as long as the Christian is relying on the structure as a substitute for God. Wild charismatics and trendy seeker-sensitive believers alike—they can all fall into systematic approaches to God, even though both groups are the most vocally opposed to such a thing. This is because we become what we judge. If we are always judging the "hopeless hypocrites," or those "stuck" in an old move of God, instead of looking for their potential as the beautiful Bride of Christ, then we are bound to reap what we have sown. We ourselves will imitate their hypocrisy in the end. It may have a different package, but it is the same religious spirit.

In Ecclesiastes 7:16-18, the Lord makes it clear that legalism and lawlessness are opposite extremes to be avoided. But the solution is to *fear the Lord*, because it keeps us humble and pliable.

Every effort of the religious spirit aims to *require* something before we approach God. This is the biggest demonic influence we have in the church today. We cannot work hard enough to earn entrance to God's courts. This is the epitome of human pride. It is only by the blood of Jesus that we have access to God's presence—not by our own works. And that access is complete and always available. To ever harbor guilt, insecurities, or rejection in the presence of God, is to call His blood insufficient. In the same way, we cannot wait until our motives are pure before we begin to chase after God, serve Him, or even enjoy Him.

Our motives will never be perfect. Our entire life on earth is a process of having our hearts purged. We must simply get used to being in *process* with Him. True humility is not a matter of simply acknowledging our own faults. Humility is to turn our eyes away from our problems and focus on God in all His vastness, looking to His perfection. By looking at Him, we naturally recognize our own need for improvement, but we also recognize our inability to improve without Him. Humility is to acknowledge that only God can purify me, and to approach Him in my weakness. Our spirits always have access to the inmost Holy of Holies, no matter our present condition. It should not take an hour of prayer and repentance for us to enter into God's presence. It is as simple as gently turning to Him at any given moment of the day. We can fully enjoy God and be enjoyed by God while we are still in the process of growing. The religious spirit not only repels unbelievers from wanting anything to do with the church or God—it also uses guilt and shame to block believers from walking in their spiritual inheritance. It makes us feel insecure in approaching God, although the blood of Jesus calls us to approach Him boldly—not of our own merit, but because of His righteousness imputed to us.

Of course, we understand this right of access in our head, but God wants us to *feel* accepted. He wants us to *experience* His divine communication at all times. Many of us can accept forgiveness and get past the condemning thoughts that hinder us from communion—but then what often hinders us, is the realization of our own religiosity! We have difficulty acknowledging our own hypocrisy, because that can dishearten us the most. However, God is not surprised at our hypocrisy. He was aware of it all the time, and He was loving us anyway. I think that the first step to having consistent encounters with God is to acknowledge our own spiritual bankruptcy every day, in order to buy gold refined in the fire (see Rev. 3).

"It is hard for many of us to grasp the fact that God loves us and enjoys us—even in our immaturity. We are lovers of God even in immaturity. When we stumble, we often see ourselves as hopeless hypocrites, and we lose the confession within our souls that we are lovers of God. We listen to an accusing spirit instead of holding fast to the truth about who God says we are in Christ Jesus," writes Mike Bickle in *The Pleasures of Loving God.*[6]

I believe that intimacy with God will strip away the hang-ups of guilt, shame, and religion—not in that these issues will cease to exist, but that we will be more adept to overcome them in our own hearts. Intimacy will also pave the way for cultural relevance, because we will naturally be prone to become all things to all men in order to share the love of God with our neighbors.

ENDNOTES

1. St. Francis Xavier sources:

    i. John S.J. Hardon, Fr., "The Miracles of St. Francis Xavier" from American Ecclesiastical Review Vol. 127 (Oct. 1952), 248-263. Accessed 10 Oct. 1998 <www.therealpresence.org/archives/ Miracles/Miracles_005.htm>.

    ii. John Laux, Fr. M.A., Church History: A Complete History of the Catholic Church to the Present Day (Rockford: Tan Books and Publishers, Inc., 1989 ed.), 465-467.

    iii. Kate O'Brien, "St. Francis Xavier." (Catholic Information Network, 2000). Accessed 10 Oct. 2004 <http://www.cin.org/franxav.html>.

2. Peter C. Wagner, The Third Wave of the Holy Spirit (Ann Arbor: Vine Books, Servant Publications, 1988), 87.

3. Che Ahn, Into the Fire. (Renew, 1998), 89.

4. Ibid., p. 92.

5. Samuel Zwemer, "The Glory of the Impossible" from The Unoccupied Mission Fields of Africa and Asia (1911).

CHAPTER 7

Bizarre Miracles

T HE tales of medieval miracles sound quite farfetched to the modern reader, and even the most Spirit-filled Christians are more apt to dismiss them as mythology than as legitimate history. But is God's power not boundless? In an era when society was completely open to manifestations of God's power, it is likely that miracles would have been much more common than today. In that age of poetry and spirituality that preceeded the age of rationalism, man was more positioned for encounters with the divine.

If there is a problem with believability, it should only be because of poor record keeping—but never should we question God's ability or desire to perform the phenomenal. God has always worked frequently and dramatically among men.

Thaumaturgy, or the working of miracles, was most documented by medieval writer Jacopo de Voragine in *The Golden Legend*. It was the most popular book in its day, and it was full of bizarre accounts of miracles in the lives of the saints. He did not always quote from firsthand documents, and his work is prone to embellishment, although most consider Voragine to have been a sincere man. By the Renaissance and the Age of Reason, this work had become the laughingstock of society. This is why we now use the word "legend" or "legendary" to describe something that is untrue or of fairy tale value.

It is clear that miraculous tales became stretched in the Middle Ages, and wherever there is hype surrounding God's power, criticism will follow. But skepticism was the undercurrent of the Age of Reason, and so every legitimate miracle from the past was thought to be just as phony as the contrived ones. It's as if society jumped from one extreme of believing just about anything, to the other extreme of believing nothing. No doubt most of us would scoff to read that Nicholas of Tolentino (that is St. Nicholas, i.e., Santa Claus) brought the partridges on his dinner plate back to life. But the medieval mind gave no thought to such a possibility when discussing the God of the universe. There is something remarkable about that.

Unfortunately, we have to be content with many questions regarding the actual lives of the saints. In some cases, we have to consider their stories purely as *apocryphal*, that is, we simply do not know one way or the other whether they occurred. But this is simply because of historical lapses before their stories were written down. Others were recorded quite well, and there is sufficient evidence to back up many miraculous claims. As we read about more recent revivalists, the recorded miracles are breathtaking. Nevertheless, with saints of old, we must be more prone to acknowledge that with God, all things are possible. When our first reaction is skepticism, we have erred the more. We should be more prone to presumption than we are to doubt about such things.

It is important to acknowledge the miracles of the Middle Ages, simply because many of them were completely off the charts. We will not have a framework for the supernatural activity that will be displayed through this last day church, so it is good to know at least that God has worked in uncanny ways throughout history. In that sense, there is precedent.

As in days of old, the coming revival will be marked by unusual miracles. Just as "God worked unusual miracles by the hands of Paul" (Acts 19:11), so will bizarre feats come through the hands of this people. Paul would touch handkerchiefs, and the presence of God would transfer over to them as they were used to heal people.

Supernatural translation from one place to another will be common in the coming days, just as it happened to Philip in Acts 8. Angelic activity and visitation will be normal. The first century church was so accustomed to interaction with angels, that when Peter was supernaturally freed from prison, and he came knocking on the gate, the believers were more apt to believe that Peter's angel was knocking than it was Peter himself! Healings and prophecy will abound. The church will again become a place of wonder and amazement.

As much as I love the gifts of healing, the Lord wants to break us out of a mind-set that focuses strictly on one gift. At any given time, the world today can flip the channel to Christian television and see Benny Hinn healing the sick. But there is coming a level of wonder and amazement back to the church which will leave the world in awe. They will not be able change the channel. There are coming phenomenal acts of power that are on par with the greatest works of Scripture.

Consider Samson's supernatural strength. The fact that Joshua commanded the sun to stand still in the sky. Moses split bodies of water, and Elijah called down fire from Heaven. Elijah also had super-speed to outrun a chariot! And on the same day he performed these great feats, he prayed for rain and broke a three-year drought! Talk about power. We must remember that these are just old covenant examples. These men were blueprints of the amazing power an entire generation can walk in, now that we can freely partake of God's Spirit. It doesn't require our perfection to walk in these exploits, it takes God's presence. Remember, Elijah was a man just like us (James 5). One day, he was performing all these great miracles, even ordering the execution of the 450 prophets of baal. And the very next day, he was running from Jezebel, sucking his thumb. God knows we are all weak and imperfect vessels. This level of power is not dependent on us. It is God's power that is made perfect in our weakness.

The Lord is schooling us in this hour to believe Him for more. He wants to take us off the charts of even the great miracles that have been done before. If we can first just come to the point of believing the miracles performed in the Bible, then we can move on to similar expressions of power in our own lives. Jesus said that even if the dead were raised in their midst, many people would not believe in Him, because they already did not believe the writings of Moses and the prophets. How can we believe for great miracles, if the inner recesses of our hearts are still in unbelief regarding the Scriptures?

God wants to blow the imagination of comic book writers out of the water. Super strength, super speed, invincibility—even bullet-proof warriors—it's all been done before. There's no creativity in that. Samson killed 1,000 men in one standing with a bone. We can step into any miracle that has been done before, if we can come to fully believe that any particular one actually occurred.

Miracles of healing are the most common type throughout history. The last day church will usher in a mighty healing revival prophesied by many great men of God throughout the ages, including John G. Lake, Kathryn Kuhlman, and others. We must recognize that just about every major stream throughout church history was marked by phenomenal healings. Why? Because physical healing is the clearest outward sign of what the Lord intends to do with our spirit man through salvation. And salvation itself, *sozo* in the Greek, is a word that speaks of salvation, healing, and deliverance all wrapped up into one package. This word is interchanged for "salvation" and "healing" numerous times throughout the New Testament. The Lord is interested in healing us completely, spirit, soul, and body.

Healing will be so broad-sweeping that Isaiah 33:24 will apply to this coming era: "And the inhabitant of the land shall not say I am sick." Even as the Israelites were brought up from Egypt without physical problems, so will this coming generation be.

He also brought them out with silver and gold, and there was none feeble among His tribes. Not one feeble or weak (Psalm 105:37).

Consider that these people had been under hard labor and bondage for 400 years, but millions of them came out of that place without being weak or feeble. Could this happen again? This may seem too good to be true, and we may think such predictions are fanciful. Yet Jesus Himself healed *every* sickness and disease. He healed *all*. As in the Book of Acts, we will again see healings even in the streets, as revival continues to break outside of the church walls.

> *They brought the sick out into the streets, and they were all healed* (Acts 5:14-16).

St. Bernard of Clairvaux

Why settle for a healing here and there if we can take hold of something this massive? I want more than a little healing here and there. I want to move in a *radius of healing* around my body like Peter, where even my shadow heals the sick. As with Jesus, may the hem of my garments heal the sick! That's demonstrating the power and glory of God.

St. Bernard of Clairvaux (1091-1153) was one of the greatest healers in history. Born to a noble Burgundian family, Bernard had an early appetite for prayer and study, as well as a hot temper. Joining a Cistercian order, Bernard was soon appointed abbot over a new monastery.

Modern historian Fr. John Laux, M.A., notes that, "Since the days of the early church there has been no greater miracle worker than St. Bernard. From far and near the sick were brought to Clairvaux to be healed by his touch and his prayers."[1]

Bernard's fame spread, and he was eventually drawn into spheres of power, against his will. Bernard became a great peacemaker. He quelled rivalries not only between bishops, but even between warring cities. God used this single man to prevent entire wars. But eventually, the pope called Bernard to preach and rally the Second Crusade. In what we would now call misguided loyalty, Bernard fulfilled the task. His great gift of influence was perverted to promote what he had always prevented. But despite the fact that he was summoning Christians to war, the gift of miracles continued to flourish with Bernard's preaching. During a single journey at that time, Bernard's companions documented 172 blind people healed, as well as nearly 200 crippled persons healed. At times, he would be swarmed with crowds, sometimes shuffling in the sick through windows.

Misguided though he was in the call to war, Bernard did not exhibit the anti-Semitism common to his day. When he heard of a fellow Cistercian advocating the destruction of the Jews, Bernard said, "The Jews are the living figures and letters, which remind us of the mysteries of our religion. Besides, they dwell peacefully in our midst. In warring against the unbelievers, we repel force by force, but it ill befits a Christian warrior to strike an unarmed foe."

The Second Crusade was a complete failure for the armies of the pope, leaving Bernard perplexed and confused. He found comfort only in the fact that he had been obedient to the pope in the matter. In Bernard, we see a common theme in all great men: Our greatest strengths are often the same areas of our greatest weakness. Bernard the peacemaker was trumpeting a religious war.

We are all prone to weakness, confusion and our best attempts can become misguided. But instead of focusing on our limitations, let us focus on God's potential to work through us. In the coming days, we will not have the luxury of not walking in the supernatural, so let us become accustomed to depending on God for miracles, despite our weakness.

WONDERWORKING

If we do not have the power of God—real prophecy, real healings, real miracles—we will be most prone to receiving the counterfeits. Millions of Christians call psychic hotlines, read horoscopes, and participate in other forms of "innocent" divination, simply because the prophetic word of the Lord has been rare in the church. Many Christians are also turning to alternative forms of healing—not that taking herbs is a bad thing, but many alternative practitioners use spiritist methods and mind control. These things are *acceptable* in our society and even in many churches. But as evil increases, demonic powers will execute more blatant signs and wonders to deceive the masses.

Some months ago, I had the opportunity to pray over a Tibetan Buddhist who was dying of jaundice in a Mexican hospital. As the presence of the Holy Spirit descended upon him, tears came to his eyes and he began to shake. Just feeling God's presence is enough to reach many people. Tangible power encounters are the only thing that will break intense demonic strongholds. For instance, Tibetan Buddhism is one of the most powerful forces of evil on the earth today. Its strength comes from the heavy emphasis on meditation and opening oneself to the spirit realm. Without the cross, though, any openness to the spirit realm is divination and an open door for the demonic.

I was told of a Christian convert whose father was a Tibetan Buddhist lama. One day, she was looking for him in the temple where he worshiped. He was so distraught that she had converted to Christianity, that when she found him, he thrust a sword right through his own stomach and it came out his back. The man was so possessed, that he pulled the sword back out again and he was demonically healed on the spot. This understandably caused the girl to backslide for about five years. Yes, there are demonically influenced signs and wonders. We should not ignore them. We must prepare to humiliate them by going deeper with the Lord. If the demonic realm is walking in a form of power, how much more is available to the Christian? The only way to cope with the evil that is coming, is to be equipped with reality.

Some of today's leading prophets have regularly encountered the spirit of the Dalai Lama himself as they were being drawn by God through the second heavens, into a third heaven encounter. He was there, trying to block them from ascending. The second heavens, of course, are made up of that spiritual realm where the angelic and demonic wage war. Much of our low-level prophetic knowledge is from God, but it comes filtered from the second heaven. But it is third heaven revelation—where sits the very throne of God—to which no demon of hell has access or can contend with. Despite their limited arsenal, demonic supernatural powers are only cheap counterfeits for what is available to the Christian believer.

Hitler rallied millions behind him and turned the world on end. He killed millions of Jews. And guess what? He did not perform a single sign or wonder. Understand that there is an antichrist coming who will hold tremendous demonic power. And the world will understandably fall to his feet. Why? Because the church is not walking in its inheritance. Where is the church demonstrating the power it rightfully possesses?

Miracles are not always God's seal of approval on a ministry. Remember that supernatural gifts do not always come in the same package as godly character and sound doctrine. Miracles are powerful testimonies of the gospel. But we trust in Jesus, not signs and wonders. That is why our faith should not waver when even powerfully gifted church leaders fall into sin, or when the enemy displays false signs and wonders to lead people astray. Miracles are tools for conversion, and can be used by God or the devil. But whenever there is a showdown, God always has the final word. Even Pharaoh's magicians could turn their staffs into serpents, but Moses' snake gobbled them up.

Todd Bentley's father, David Bentley, told me of a mission trip to Africa where a witch doctor would walk out from a river every morning and curse the crusade, then walk back into the river—completely submerged under water that was over his head—and stay there until the next morning. In another case, not long after David was saved, he was casting out a demon from a possessed woman, when suddenly she levitated about a foot off the ground , and said in stern but perfect English "What do you think you're doing, David Bentley!" Of course, he had never met her, and she should not have known his name.

I do not tell such stories to glorify demonic powers. I only hope to show that if witch doctors can perform such feats, how much more should Christians—who possess far greater power—demonstrate the true power of God. A good thing to understand is this: If the devil has it, we can take it back. This is understandably true with natural and cultural things like musical styles and the arts. Salvation Army founder William Booth used popular bar room melodies of his day and converted them to worship songs. He said, "Why should the devil have all the good tunes?" We should have an eye to redeem everything for the Kingdom of God. But this is especially true of the ability to move in supernatural power. Why should magician David Blaine be showcasing demonic levitation powers on the streets of New York City for television cameras? It makes a dry, religious church seem impotent and gives the appearance of rendering the living God powerless. But God is releasing Davids to challenge these Goliaths of our day. There are those fiery ones God is releasing who will stand up and say "who is this uncircumcised Philistine to defy the armies of the Most High God?"

We must understand that every demonic miracle is a weak, twisted shadow of what a Spirit-filled Christian can do through Christ. A Spirit-filled Christian has more power in his pinky than all the hordes of hell combined. Mediums, shamans, witch doctors, and a number of extreme Hindus and Buddhists have experienced well-documented levitations. They have been photographed well into the 19th and 20th centuries. I have even read of some levitating outside of third story windows. It is also a common occurrence in poltergeists and demonic hauntings. Many Christians tend to get intimidated by such stories, or allow such things to challenge their faith. But there is a history of many Christian saints who levitated and flew when they entered deep prayer. Didn't Jesus do this Himself when He ascended to the Father? The last time His disciples saw Him, He was levitating! Jesus even walked through walls after His resurrection. There is no limit to what we can do through resurrection power. Jesus said that greater things than these, we would do. And all things are possible for him who believes.

St. Luke the Younger (c. a.d. 946) was also known as the *Wonderworker*. A Greek, who eventually settled in Thessaly, Luke was given toward charity from an early age—often forfeiting meals to feed the poor, stripping himself of clothes to give to beggars, and sometimes sowing half his seed onto the fields of the poor—although his was only a peasant farming family. He is one of the first saints to have been seen levitating off the ground in prayer. After his death, Luke's hermitage cell near Corinth was known as *Soterion*, or the Place of Healing.

One might believe stories like this are mere medieval mythology, but in actuality, they abound. Joseph of Cupertino was recorded doing this stuff in the 17th century, well into the colonial era.

St. Joseph of Cupertino (1603-1663) is one of the best documented flyers in church history. Known as the *Gaper*—a derogatory term for his walking aimlessly about with an open mouth, absent minded, and forgetful—Joseph was later known as the Flying Friar. He was always in another zone, just walking in the Spirit, unshaken by his natural surroundings. Born in Cupertino in a shed, in dire poverty—his parents had lost their home to creditors—Joseph was abused by his family and eventually sought acceptance into a Franciscan order. But they would not have him. He was later kicked out of yet another order, because his spiritual ecstasies made him unfit for work. He was always focused on God—too much for their liking.

Joseph was sent from one monastery to another. Finally, his great virtue and devotion could not be denied and it brought him priestly orders by age 25, despite his near inability to read or write.

For five years, Joseph ate neither bread nor wine, and his fasts during Lent were very rigorous. He devoted

St. Joseph of Cupertino

much of his time to manual labor, usually routine household chores, which were all he seemed to be capable of performing. Nevertheless, he possessed great discernment and was often sought to answer complex questions. Joseph's life was primarily marked by extensive visions and supernatural trances, which could be triggered by things as simple as music, the mention of the name of God, church bells, thoughts of Christ's life, or the thought of Heavenly glory. He often supernaturally heard Heavenly music. Fearful and unfamiliar with such activity, others tried to pull him back from these ecstasies by means of yelling, beating, burning, and even piercing him with needles, but to no avail. However, when his spiritual superiors spoke to him, he was submissively able to return. Joseph would simply hear the sweet name, "Jesus," and begin to float off the ground.

There are more than 70 recorded instances of Joseph levitating, along with numerous miraculous healings that were "not paralleled in the reasonably authenticated life of any other saint," according to *Butler's Lives of the Saints.*[2] The most extreme instance of flight was when a group of monks were trying to place a large cross on the top of a church building. The cross was 36 feet high, taking the efforts of 10 men to lift, when suddenly, Joseph flew 70 yards, picked it up "as if it were straw" and put it in place. Such phenomena kept Joseph's leaders from allowing him to celebrate mass in public for 35 years. They usually confined him to his room with a private chapel. Joseph was also brought before the Inquisition, but he always remained joyful even during these persecutions.

As the church begins to understand and activate the spiritual realm through deeper prayer and contemplation, I believe there will be entire congregations that softly float off of their seats in the presence of the Lord. This will not be a spooky thing. The Lord once gave me a dream in which everyone in a church service reached such a level of stillness, soaking, and saturating in the sweet presence of the Lord that one by one, people started to float out of their pews. I do not think this was an allegorical dream. We will literally see this type of thing happen, and it will be a powerful witness to the reality of our God. We should remember that Jesus also suspended the laws of gravity when he walked on water, not just during His ascension. Christian saints Francis Xavier, John of the Cross, and even Gemma Galgani in the early 20th century were all reportedly lifted from the ground during prayer.

St. Teresa of Avila (1515-1582) was another widely known saint with a history of levitation. Eye witnesses said she would hover about a foot and a half off the ground during states of spiritual rapture for periods up to half an hour. She is reported to have said "it was much more violent than other spiritual visitations, and I was there-fore as one ground to pieces."

During her life, Teresa founded the order of Discalced (Barefoot) Carmelite nuns. She was frequently met with visions and prophetic encounters. Now recognized as a prominent mystic of her day, her con-

St. Teresa of Avila

temporaries were quick to condemn her experiences back then. After seeking guidance from a number of clergy who frowned upon such activity, Teresa was one day taken into an encounter where she heard the words, "I will not have you hold conversation with men, but with angels." Her revelatory happenings were extremely intense, including a number of clear, open visions and audible con-versations. She also received the *transverberatio*, or a supernatural piercing of her heart.

Teresa is well regarded for a number of deep, mystical writings, not the least of which is *Interior Castle*. In it, she describes various rooms of the soul, and the soul's purification or sanctification process. Her writings parallel the famed Christian mystic St. John of the Cross, who was also her contemporary and eventually cared for a number of spiritual foundations which Teresa established for men.

Teresa was probably quite reserved, and she preferred not to mention these levitations. She said that the experience frightened her at times. Whenever there were angelic encounters and other powerful miracles or visitations in Scripture, people were often afraid. I believe one of the things that prevents us from moving into more bizarre miracles and Heavenly experiences is our fear of the unknown. We must trust the Spirit of God to lead us.

We need to be prepared to press into the strange and unusual. Don't you think flaming tongues of fire were a little bit unusual and unorthodox on Pentecost? Where was the scriptural precedent when that happened?

We are often too afraid of demonic influence to try new things with God. Those who move in supernatural power are always accused of being demoniacs. Jesus Himself was accused of using demonic power. He was our prototype. If they said that about Him, they will say it about us. We must have discernment, but discernment is not just a cowardly feeling of warning and self-protection. It is also discerning the voice of Jesus when He is calling you to step out of the boat and walk on the water. Jesus is nudging us out of the boat right now. He is asking us "Are you so blind that you do not recognize the Spirit in which I speak?"

Just a quick glance at the ecstatic biblical prophets should tell us not to judge a book by its cover.

St. Christina the Astonishing (1150-1224) was strange by most standards. Born in Brusthem and left an orphan at age 15, she suffered a seizure at age 22 and was carried to church in an open coffin. During her own funeral, Christina sat up and soared to the beams of the roof. Everyone bolted from the building,

St. Christina the Astonishing

except for her sister. The priest made her come down, and Christina said she had gone up there because she could not stand the smell of sinful human bodies. Christina had visions of Heaven and hell during her death experience, and following the episode, she was the subject of numerous bizarre experiences. She often resorted to hidden places, climbing trees, towers, and hiding in ovens to escape the smell of humans. Fire would not burn her, and she would often jump into icy waters in the dead of winter. She would also pray while balanced on a hurdle or curled up into a ball. Many thought she was possessed and tried to confine her.

She behaved in a "terrifying manner," rushing wildly through the streets and living a life of begging and poverty with a wild appearance. However, she joined a convent and was sought for spiritual counsel by clergy and secular officials later in life. She was also submissive to spiritual leaders. There are a number of firsthand accounts and documentation about her life, offered by her contemporaries Thomas de Cantimpre, a theology professor, and Cardinal Jacques de Vitny.

The stories of wonderworking saints are far too many to include in a single volume. There are those who levitated, walked on waters, stayed alive without eating or drinking, whose bodies emitted fragrance or light, and those who were incombustible to flame like Daniel's friends in the fiery furnace. Many have multiplied food, read men's thoughts, been translated from one place to another and exercised dominion over animals and nature. Many have moved objects by thought—something of which telekinesis is only a counterfeit—and very many have raised the dead.

If these kinds of events were not still happening in our day, we may have room to doubt their veracity. Translations alone have been a common occurrence in recent decades. Many people are carried out of their bodies *spiritually* to minister in other places, or to see events before they happen. But even their physical bodies are carried off at times. Christian missionary H.B. Garlock was walking toward a flooded river in Africa, without any way to cross. He was suddenly on the other side of the river, with his own sweat being the only dampness in his clothes.[3] Another minister, David J. DuPlessis was also transported while ministering in Africa. He was needed very urgently for ministry while he was walking toward his destination. DuPlessis was walking with some friends, but was suddenly jolted to the place he was headed. It was 20 minutes before his friends ever arrived and caught up with him.[4]

Mel Tari

Mel Tari (1946-present) offers some of the most fantastic modern-day accounts of God's miracle working power, which he witnessed firsthand in the Indonesian revival on the island of Timor in the 1960s and '70s. Tari says a dead man was raised to life after decaying for two days in the tropical heat. He came to life in front of 1,000 people, and Tari credits this single miracle for causing many thousands more to come to Christ.

Tari rocked America with his book *Like a Mighty Wind* in the 1970s, which sat on the best seller list for 13 weeks and gave documented accounts of the revival. In the mid-'60s, Tari was sitting in his Presbyterian church as people were praying, when suddenly the Holy Spirit hit the place. Everyone began to audibly hear the sound of a mighty rushing wind filling the room. The village fire bell began ringing, and local firefighters rushed to the building. The church was covered in flames, but it was not burning. Many were saved that day. What began with a few dozen people would go on to impact the world.

Miracles of biblical proportions began happening. Water turned into wine for communion. People ate poison unwittingly and it did not harm them. Food was multiplied. Others were supernaturally protected from animals. Some once walked across a river that was 30 feet deep, in order to reach a village that needed the gospel. The revival spread throughout the islands, over into Malaysia and other nearby places. Young people were crying out for revival, praying all night long and going out in evangelistic teams to unreached villages—even very young children did this.

One group of young people was traveling through a dense jungle when a bright light appeared in front of them and guided them through to their destination. On another occasion, when traveling to a remote village through a jungle at night, the young people felt led to gather branches. Obeying this urging of the Holy Spirit, the branches became light as they broke off in their hands. They thought the tribe would be amazed to see this, once they reached the village. But when they arrived the light went away. They had to rely only on the power of the word of God and His presence—but that was enough!

Angelic visitations became very common. One group of children disobeyed the instruction of an angel that was leading them, and they went for a swim at an inopportune time. They later discovered that their clothes had landed in the top of a tree! They repented for their disobedience, and the angel instructed one of the children to climb the tree and get them. As he began to climb, he found that his feet literally stuck to the tree like a gecko, so that he would not fall.

Unfortunately, missionaries eventually quenched the revival, saying the move was not of God. Nevertheless, churches exploded during that time. The Indonesian Bible Society was completely unable to keep track of the statistics. Churches in Java jumped from 30,000 members to 100,000 members in less than a decade. Many mainline churches were revived.

A.J.B. Thomas, a local Methodist pastor in Bandung, said, "These people are very primitive. They always have lived in a spirit world, and they readily understand the conflict between good and evil spirits. With their childlike faith, miracles are no problem for them."[5]

On the island of Alor, Jesus revealed Himself supernaturally to a school teacher—not through a minister, but through a personal revelation. The man began evangelizing the locals, and they began repenting of various sins and living lives of purity. This enflamed the nearby Christian church, which was intimidated by the heartfelt repentance. They brought this fledgling group before the local magistrates and accused them of witchcraft. But later, they were vindicated. They had gathered together for prayer, when suddenly a whole host of angels appeared above the coconut trees around them. This was not just an internal vision—nor was it limited to their eyes only. The whole town saw this happen!

Tari tells of another peculiar happening at a Catholic church. A native missionary team told the priest that the Lord was displeased with idols. The priest said that he had no idols, but the team pointed out the iconic images hanging throughout the church. Arguments were getting them nowhere, so they decided to have an Elijah challenge. They asked the priest to gather the images in a pile and they would pray. If the Lord burned the images with fire from Heaven, then He was displeased with them. After they prayed, there was a short silence, and then a sharp bolt of crashing fire, like lightning, hit the images and burned them to ashes. Nothing else in the room was harmed. The priest was filled with excitement, rubbing his hands together, and eagerly gathered the rest of images from the back of the building, which he also burned. Many people repented of religious idolatry and turned to the Lord that day.[6]

THE COMING ECSTATICS

Marking the advent of the new mystics and ushering in the return of Jesus, is the final fulfillment of Malachi 4:5-6:

> *See, I will send you the prophet Elijah before that great and dreadful day of the Lord comes. He will turn the hearts of the fathers to their children, and the hearts of the children to their fathers; or else I will come and strike the land with a curse.*

This sonship dynamic and release of the prophetic Elijah spirit are closely intertwined. The release of this has already begun and will continue to escalate to its fullness. Many in charismatic circles today recognize the prophetic nature of the Elijah spirit, to hear and speak forth the word of the Lord. And the prophetic movement of the last few decades is a direct result of this scriptural decree. But we forget that the prophetic gift and office was only a part of Elijah's life and calling—it was also marked by radical *signs and wonders*. Extreme miracles and power encounters must accompany the prophetic word. In this sense, Elijah was more than a prophet. He was a *"sent one,"* a forerunner of the New Testament "apostle."

As for his prophetic call, Elijah was given much more authority than just to *speak* God's words. He was called as a mouthpiece of the Lord to exact the *judgments* of God, and the Elijah spirit is shadowed in the two witnesses of Zechariah 4 and Revelation 11—representing Elijah and Moses—who have the authority to speak God's judgments in the earth. While these two witnesses probably represent two literal people as well, they foremost depict the spirit of the sons of golden oil that will rest on the corporate church in the last days. The level of our prophetic authority has, for the most part, not yet matured to speak such words of judgment, but we are on the brink. God will not give authority to release His judgments until we have first been filled with His heart of compassion. It requires having His heart for restoration. Otherwise, we will be loose canons.

The two witnesses, like Elijah of old, will be given the power to shut up the heavens so that it does not rain. As did Elijah, they will literally be able to call down fire from Heaven. And the consummation of Elijah's life—his translation into glory, being carried away in a chariot without dying, as we saw typified in Enoch earlier—all speaks of the mantle of the end-time church, which will be changed and translated at the grand finale, though not in the way we have imagined or has been typified in rapture pop novels and Christian B movies.

A very real aspect of the spirit of Elijah is *unpredictability*. Despite the reams of teaching hitting the bookshelves today seeking to bring "balance" and guard against so-called "extremes" of the prophetic movement, Elijah prophets will always have some measure of eccentricity and wildness. John the Baptist, who walked in this spirit, is not the kind of guy you would leave your kids with in Sunday School. Radical. Unpredictable. Fiery.

As much as we should promote mutual submission in the church, and prepare the body to receive the prophetic office, ecstatic prophets will always be catalysts for change. There is no way to legislate a means for the church to accept them. We should advocate their freedom to operate as God leads, but when God leads us in a way we find distasteful, things can get ugly. Religious people have always historically sought to quiet, hamper, and bring such men into a sort of impotent submission to man.

Elijah typifies what we tend to call the *ecstatic* prophets. He did not simply sit around and write or compose psalms. His movements defied all human anticipation (see 1 Kings 18:12). His actions defied human comprehension, and he was quite an unorthodox fellow. God sends such men to be an intentional irritant to the old order, which, like a grain of sand in an oyster, eventually forms a pearl. I do not say that any manner of poor character, lack of healthy submission, inappropriate rebukes or the like should be tolerated in today's church under the guise of being a "prophet." That type of behavior is simply the mark of a spirit of rejection, or at best, an immature prophet. But even young, floundering prophets must have room to grow into their calling and gifting. Baby eagles are gawky, awkward looking things when they first begin to fly. Ah! But the glory when they learn to catch the wind!

There is no system that can be implemented in the church so that we will always receive and never reject ecstatic Elijah prophets. God purposely sends them to remind us of His own unpredictability. Since they are sent by God, and not by the church, they will always break our religious boxes, offend our traditions, and challenge us. But it is their same unpredictability that draws them into radical contests of power, even as Elijah challenged the prophets of baal and Moses confronted Pharaoh. Radical power encounters such as these are already hitting the streets today.

New Testament prophets are called to demonstrate mutual submission, as well as encourage and edify the body. Our prophetic standard is actually much higher than in the Old Testament, especially in the realm of personal character. We cannot simply justify ourselves with a "God says such and such…" There is a personal responsibility and ownership we must take for the things that come out of our mouths. We cannot blame God for poor prophecy. But this does not mean New Testament prophets must be predictable and fit the molds of institutional religion. It simply means they must demonstrate love and good character. Our lives are to be a sign and a wonder to the world in every way possible. The world should be drawn and mesmerized by our every action. As John Wesley said, when we set ourselves on fire, the world will come and watch us burn.

Of course, one could write an entire book on the Elijah anointing, and many have been written. But here we are only looking at a few significant elements, to begin to grasp how vast this transition and restoration will come about for the church and the earth itself. Our goal is to catch a glimpse of the new mystics who will walk in a corporate Elijah power anointing before the Lord's return. Jesus confirmed that "indeed Elijah is coming first and will restore all things" (Matt. 17:11). As we noted, John the Baptist walked in this Elijah spirit, and in John, we see the ultimate purpose of this mantle, which is to turn hearts to God. Love. John's simple message of "repent" was a basic call to restoration: Turn back to God. Let mankind's relationship with God be restored.

And so, the power, miracles, judgment, and prophecy are all given to capture hearts, and turn them back to the Father. In the coming days, we will see the Father's heart impacting nations. The Elijah anointing turns a nation back to God in a day, like it did on Mt. Carmel (see 1 Kings 18).

"Can a country be born in a day or a nation brought forth in a moment?" (Isa. 66:8). This is about to happen. Even Joel prophesied that the Lord is releasing an army that will take nations in a day.

Ask of Me, and I will give you the nations for your inheritance, and the ends of the earth for your possession (Psalm 2:8).

HEARTS OF THE SONS AND THE FATHERS

It does not take a rocket scientist to figure out that most of the church is not walking in the spirit of Elijah or performing Mosaic signs and wonders. But where is the first place we begin to bridge the gap from where we are now, and the destiny God is releasing to us? Again, let us look at Malachi 4:5-6:

> *See, I will send you the prophet Elijah before that great and dreadful day of the Lord comes. He will turn the hearts of the fathers to their children, and the hearts of the children to their fathers; or else I will come and strike the land with a curse.*

The primary purpose for the release of the Elijah spirit in this hour, is to turn the hearts of the fathers and the sons toward one another. The key to catching what the fathers had, is to walk in their footsteps, as Elisha did. To catch a double portion of what the fathers had will cost us everything. The anointing is an expensive thing. It costs your entire life. We must follow the Lord as Elisha followed Elijah—keep our eyes on Him and leave ourselves behind. But this following, this abiding, is all about relationship. While the Lord wants to restore all things, His main goal is to restore *relationships*. Relationship first with Him, then with others. Love is the absolute key to walking in power. This is one reason that the "love chapter" of the Bible, 1 Corinthians 13, is nestled right between two chapters that discuss spiritual gifts.

Love is the greatest miracle. A healed heart is the greatest demonstration of power around. One lost heart turned back to God—a single soul saved—turns Heaven on its heels in wonder. In this fallen world, love is actually the most bizarre miracle of all. In the garden, satan lured Adam and Eve to break relationship with God, amid the most perfect, pristine environment. But God will show His greatest wonder in these last days, as He turns the heart of His church *back* to Himself, amid the darkest, evil hour of this fallen world.

Elijah the *restorer* will not just restore relationships between blood-related fathers and sons. He will restore the anointing of every great ministry that ever moved in power, and impart it to this generation. To enter into last day's power, it is crucial that we remove every hindrance to relationship by rooting out the power of generational curses and sin. The element of sin that makes it most destructive, is the fact that it breaks relationship. This is also why the primary purpose of all repentance is to restore relationship.

Fathers and the sons represent many dynamics, not just parents and children. For instance, our generation must reconnect with former eras. Spiritual generations must reconnect just as family generations reconnect. This mandate is true for natural parents with children, spiritual fathers with their disciples, as well as God with humanity. Fathers and sons can also represent larger church movements that have birthed one another. For instance, God wants to turn the hearts of the Catholics and the Protestants toward one another: the Catholics representing the fathers, and the Protestants representing the sons. He wants to restore the hearts of the Jews the Gentiles to one another. Europeans could be considered spiritual fathers to a number of nations, to which they first brought the gospel. Whenever relationship is restored, ancient pathways of truth are rebuilt and ancient wells of blessing are reopened.

While we will be exploring a recovery of past blessings, do not think that we should live in the past. All of the forerunners in church history represent the floor at which we begin, but the ceiling is ours to build. Presently, we are walking under a number of generational blessings that are a direct result of our natural and spiritual forefathers. But we are also currently experiencing the effects of a number of generational curses that have been passed down from both natural and spiritual parents. Most curses and strongholds that we now deal with are signposts pointing to past breaks in the chain of relationship. If we can identify those breaches, we can overcome them with the blood of the Lamb and the word of our testimony. We can be a people who will "rebuild the ancient ruins and will raise up the age-old foundations; you will be called Repairer of Broken Walls, Restorer of Streets with Dwellings" (Isa. 58:12).

Jacob's generation is one that does not despise its inheritance—its birth right. And to feast on the inheritance of the saints—the blessings bestowed by the Lord Himself and our forefathers—we must learn to rest and receive from Him and from them. We cannot have relationship without restored trust.

Individually, the thing that is going to hinder your walk with God more than just about anything else is unforgiveness toward your parents. We are not called to criticize our parents, we are called to honor and bless them. The sins of the fathers—no matter how grievous—will always affect the sons, until we are able to surrender them to the Lord.

We are not called to judge our parents, but we are called to correct the errors they introduced. This is true for both natural and spiritual forefathers. This is one way we *make perfect* the things they began and were unable to finish. Space does not permit us to delve deeply into the subject of generational curses and inner healing here. However, we will never tap into old wells of blessing, if we cannot apply the cross to our old hurts and wounds and release forgiveness.

> ***Honor your father and your mother***, *as the Lord your God has commanded you, so that you may live long and that it **may go well with you** in the land the Lord your God is giving you* (Exodus 20:12).

We are called to honor our parents so that all will go well with us. In the same sense, any area in which we did not honor our parents, all will not be going well with us. If my father was an alcoholic, and I dishonored him for it, there is a very good chance I will have problems with alcohol or some other addiction in my own life. The same is true with financial matters, health, time management, and a host of other issues in life. To the degree we dishonored our natural parents in any particular area (whether they "deserved it" or not), so will we reap problems in that same precise area. Forgiveness releases great power. In our quest for exotic demonstrations of God's power, we must not neglect the cultivation of a healed heart. We must remove the bitter roots that hinder us personally in life, because the Lord wants to develop deep-seated character alongside our spiritual gifts.

The Lord is revealing to us, that one of the chief means of waging spiritual warfare is by *honor*. Honoring others disarms the enemy. It renders the enemy impotent. If someone sins against me, even a spiritual leader, I must see it as an opportunity to do damage to the enemy's camp by honoring and forgiving that person. Honor, like grace, is not an "earned" thing. If you are waiting for someone to earn your respect before you give it to them, you miss the point. It helps us to honor others, when we are able to properly identify our enemy. My brother is not the enemy, and I should contend for his deliverance by loving him.

> *For our wrestling is not against flesh and blood, but against the principalities, against the powers, against the world's rulers of the darkness of this age, and against the spiritual forces of wickedness in the heavenly places* (Ephesians 6:12).

We have forgotten our command to bless those who curse us. If judgment and criticism brings generational curses down on my head, then honor likewise opens up generational blessings. Generational curses pass to the third and fourth generation, but blessings are extended to a thousand generations (Deut. 7:9). We must honor not just the men we sit under for impartation today, but what God did through men of the past. If I honor the anointing of God that was on the ministry of Smith Wigglesworth, the same blessings of his ministry can come down into my life! If I honor what God did in Charles Finney, his anointing can come onto my life. This is turning the hearts of the sons back to the fathers. God is turning the heart of this generation to the former generations.

"Our own spiritual longevity will be determined by the humility with which we honor those who went before us, who made our way straighter and who spiritually gave birth to us. The pride of new spiritual generations—thinking they are better than those who preceded them—is a stumbling block that has tripped up every generation to date," writes Rick Joyner in *Shadows of Things to Come.*[7] This is such a profound principle. We are constantly trying to reinvent spiritual wheels, while ignoring a vast heritage that went on before us. The Book of Proverbs constantly reminds us to pay great heed to the fathers' instructions. History repeats itself.

After catching a glimpse of this principle, I can see how medieval Christians became sidetracked into reverencing the saints of old. It is OK to love dead saints. But foremost, we should honor the anointing on their lives. Love foremost that perspective of God that was reflected through them. When we make them our heroes, we are prone to read their writings, examine their lives, and open ourselves to be used in the way they were used by God. There are so many forerunners that the church has simply written off for various reasons. Perhaps because they were Catholic. Perhaps because they were Protestant. Perhaps because they lived hundreds of years ago, and seem to bear no relevance today. Jesus lived thousands of years ago; should we not listen to Him? In the same way, our spiritual predecessors left messages not just for their own generations, but for ages to come.

We should not elevate men anymore than we should ever elevate supernatural experiences above God Himself. God alone is worthy of worship. And even the greatest saints were mere men, prone to sin like you and I. You will find, throughout these chapters, that I have included their shortcomings as well. One way we can best honor our natural or spiritual parents is by looking objectively at their sins, so that we can correct the problems they introduced. Their shortcomings, when viewed in the right perspective, can actually teach us more than their successes at times. They took a lot of hard knocks that we can avoid.

It is Jesus who ministered to us through our forefather saints. Did you know that we are called to also minister to them? The way we do this is by bringing to completion the things that they began.

"God had planned something better for us so that only together with us would they be made perfect" (Heb. 11:40). We do this not by hiding from the mistakes of the past, but by going beyond where they stumbled. If we see higher and further than they did, it is only because we are standing on the shoulders of giants.

"(God is) going to take what's been lost in past revivals, the destinies that men and women didn't fulfill. God is going to take those mantles and put them on people," writes Todd Bentley in *Journey Into the Miraculous.*[8] "As the Father pours out His Spirit in power again, He will restore those mantles to the church all at once. It won't be 40 years between moves of God." We must honor and catch the anointing that was on their lives. In the past, the church idolized and put miracle workers on platforms. But instead of idolizing them, there is coming a generation that will *imitate* them. The church's stumbling into saint worship and the reverence of icons in the past was only a counterfeit for imitating the supernatural lifestyle mantles of those self-same spiritual heroes.

Part of the honoring process is to rightly identify the failures of the past. We don't expose and broadcast our fathers' nakedness like Canaan. But we rightly identify it, so that we can cover it. It is important that we likewise identify with the church's present problems, so that we can rightly correct those problems—past, present, and future. Those problems do not belong to others, they belong to you and I. We may not have created them, but it is our responsibility to correct them. That is one of the primary reasons we are here on earth—to serve as God's change agents. Instead of remaining ignorant of the past—of the historic sins of the church—it is important that we identify with them and repent on the church's behalf. The prophets of old modeled intercession for us, not by saying "God forgive *those* sinful people," but by saying, "God forgive *us*, for *we* are a sinful people." We must personally identify with sinful humanity. God doesn't need a holy roller or a critic. Jesus identified with us to the point that He became sin for us.

One of the very reasons God allows the effects of sins to be passed down from one generation to the next, is so that someone will be forced to deal with those sins. Once sin is set in motion, it continues like a pinball in the earth until someone puts it into contact with the cross. Sin corrupts more than just the individual who commits it. Sin affects the whole camp. It is corporate. And it does not just correct itself over time. Therefore, God is looking for a band of holy house cleaners who are willing to mend the mistakes of the past through repentance and application of the cross, and so become a people who will "restore the places long devastated; they will renew the ruined cities that have been devastated for generations." (Isa. 61:4).

Let us stop criticizing the church and recognize that we are the Church. Better yet, let us remember that Jesus loves His Church—His Bride—and He sees her for her potential, spotless, clean, and white. Jesus does not want His Bride criticized any more than I want my own wife criticized. We must find that place of acknowledging and repenting for sins, without crossing the line into judgment and condemnation. Biblical figures are given a very open and honest account of their lives, including their greatest victories and their worst failings.

Consider David. As king, he could have instructed scribes to brush over his affair with Bathsheba and his subsequent murder of her former husband. But instead, his openness about his own faults has set an example and a warning for every generation that followed. Transparency is vital.

"We must not hide our battle scars from our successors. Our testimony of moving through difficulty might provide just the strength they require to arrive at the destiny God has mapped out for them," writes Nigerian bishop Mike Okonkwo regarding the way we sustain a move of God.[9]

The truth does not cover up wrongs, but confesses them, so that by example, future generations can veer away from similar pitfalls. We know that all have sinned and fallen short of the glory of God. But when we choose to religiously mask over the failures of our fathers, we doom ourselves to repeat those errors. This is why we must look objectively at history.

"We have a strange illusion that mere time cancels sin. But mere time does nothing either to the fact or to the guilt of a sin," writes C.S. Lewis.[10] "Every uncorrected error and unrepented sin is, in its own right, a fountain of fresh error and fresh sin flowing on to the end of time."

There is a place to intercede for past wrongs, where we see the generational effects of sin still present in our churches today. But our task is not all about batting cleanup. Repentance and intercession is only part of the Christian life. Just as the cross is the doorway to resurrection, so intercession and repentance are the doorways to restoration.

We do not need to go through a church history book and say "forgive us" on every page. The best way to surpass the forerunners and heal history is to simply learn from old mistakes and draw near to the Lord. He is the ultimate Father, whose heart has drawn near to His sons. The spirit of Elijah will release fanatical miracles like the earth has never seen. But it is all ordained for a single purpose and destiny—one ultimate goal, from which the Lord will not relent: to restore intimacy between God and man.

ENDNOTES

1. Mike Bickle, *The Pleasures of Loving God* (Lake Mary: Charisma House, 2000), 15.

2. John Laux, Fr. M.A., *Church History: A Complete History of the Catholic Church to the Present Day* (Rockford: Tan Books and Publishers, Inc., 1989 ed.), 322.

3. Alban Butler, *Butler's Lives of the Saints*, ed. Michael Walsh (San Francisco: Harper Collins, 1991 ed.), 294-295.

4. H.B. Garlock and Ruthanne Garlock, *Before We Kill And Eat You* (Dallas: Christ for the Nations, 1974), 44-46.

5. David J. Du Plessis and Bob Slosser, A Man Called Mr. Pentecost (Plainfield: Logos, 1977), 84-86.

6. Mel Tari and Cliff Dudley, *Like a Mighty Wind* (Carol Stream: Creation House, 1971).

7. Ibid.

8. Rick Joyner, *Shadows of Things to Come* (Nashville: Thomas Nelson, 2001), 14.

9. Todd Bentley with Jackie Macgirvin, Journey Into the Miraculous Todd Bentley: An Ordinary Man Touched by a Supernatural God (Victoria, B.C.: Fresh Fire Ministries, 2003), 14.

10. Mike Okonkwo, "Sustaining the Move of God." Out of Africa, ed. Peter C. Wagner and Joseph Thompson (Regal Books, 2003), 67.

CHAPTER 8

Reformation

WE cannot look at the church age without briefly discussing the Reformation. Many books have been written about the Protestant reformers, and we are indebted to them as some of the greatest heroes and pioneers of the faith. But an even greater reformation is coming to the church. It is not a reformation of doctrine or theology. It is a reformation of love and power—an apostolic reformation that restores the element of the supernatural in the daily lives of believers.

Rick Joyner points out that the institutional church, up through the 12th century, claimed to be built upon the authority given to Peter. Then the rediscovery of Paul's epistles in the Reformation, seemed to represent Paul rising up to rebuke Peter, as he did in Antioch in the Book of Acts.

"Even so, Paul is not the foundation of the church; Jesus is. Since the Reformation we have tended to use Paul to interpret Jesus, rather than the other way around," says Joyner.[1] While Paul was focused on building the church, establishing doctrinal issues and dealing with practical affairs of the body, Joyner rightly points out that the church itself is only one small part of the Kingdom of God. Jesus' teachings were largely focused on the Kingdom, but He only made a few references to the church. We are entering a Kingdom age, and it is time to take Christianity to a whole new level.

Most of us are living in the healthy changes brought about by the Reformation, so there is no need to reiterate them all here. But what I hope to do is to move beyond celebrating past victories and go beyond where the Reformation left off. We are living in a post-Protestant society, and most Protestants are no longer protesting their Catholic brothers and sisters. Now that we are living in a post-Protestant, postmodern era, we can safely look back to the days prior to 1500, to recover things that were actually *lost* in the Reformation. I do not suggest we all become Catholics again. Instead, I think we are about to become something altogether new.

Many Protestants believe that God fell asleep after the Book of Acts, briefly rolled over and snored during the Reformation, and that's the extent of church history. In the process of having our heritage truncated by the enemy in this way, we lost the tradition of the mystics, the Desert Fathers, and countless other revivalists throughout the years.

Is it possible that there are ancient streams of truth that the Lord specifically wants to restore, which were lost in the reformers' zeal? For one, we should understand that the reformers were fallen men, just like us. Martin Luther created horrendous doctrines against the Jews that were still held right up through the German Holocaust. John Calvin, another great reformer, melted down pipe organs throughout Europe, because of his distaste for Catholic tradition and the spiritual neglect he had received. In his zeal against dead religiosity, he unwittingly reintroduced a number of gnostic tendencies toward instrumental worship. This undermined Luther's restoration mind-set in the area of instrumental worship. Examples of this kind are endless. We can look at them honestly, without detracting from their great accomplishments. We should always be thankful for the reformers' boldness, and I believe they did far more good than evil. But it is time we acknowledge that they opened some gates that need to be closed, and closed some gates that need to be reopened.

Primarily, we need to deal with the root of division. During the Reformation, we see the beginnings of a problem that continues today—the pattern of formulating our theology based on *woundedness*. First of all, the reformers did not always "confront in love." The Reformation opened a huge door to the spirit of rebellion. This was largely because they were wounded from centuries of religious error. I believe this is the reason why priests in the Old Testament were not allowed to have scabs when they ministered before the Lord. God does not want us to minister out of our unhealed hurts. Otherwise, we are bound to twist the truth.

Luther took a monumental and much-needed prophetic stand. He will forever be rightly remembered as one of the greatest men of the faith, whose impact on the Kingdom was unrivaled since the first century. He heralded the very rediscovery of salvation by grace. His bold challenge against indulgences, idolatry and superstition in the church was incredible. He put the Scriptures back into the language and hands of ordinary people. Nevertheless, like all great men of God, he also possessed a sinful nature and made some poor decisions that have affected the church ever since. Since our focus here is re-digging ancient wells, I think it is important to be candid. Rather than giving Luther more repetitive applause, the Protestant church has grown up enough to look frankly at some of Luther's pitfalls that linger on today.

For instance, Luther's temper was such that he had Anabaptists put to death. I think this one sin has limited our experience of the very sacrament of water baptism in a phenomenal way. We have learned to view it as just a symbolic, religious act, rather than a heaven-rending revelatory experience. When Jesus was baptized in the Jordan, the heavens split open and He had a visitation along with an audible voice from the Father. I believe that if the Anabaptists had not been so rejected, we would understand the sacrament of baptism in a completely different light today.

As for sacraments, the reformers lost a wealth of truth from the communion table by rejecting doctrines of transubstantiation to the extreme. Catholics believed that the bread and wine literally turn to Jesus' flesh and blood when you eat them. Many are still strongly opinionated about it. Clearly, the Lord's Table was a place of great superstition at the time. However, the reformers clearly went over-board in trying to strip the elements of their mystery. The Lord's Table is a spiritual contact point in the life of the believer that unlocks tremendous power. This sacrament eventually became a symbolic, religious ritual, devoid of meaning or passion over time.

Luther also resorted to using political power to accomplish his purposes. Much like Constantine many centuries before, Luther eventually represented a church/state hybrid, which had suc-cumbed to a political spirit. This same spirit of control by carnal means is still preaching from many Protestant pulpits today. It is an ancient tap root of many of our power plays, jostling and maneuver-ing for position in the present-day church. This spirit was at work in the church long before Luther, but he had ample opportunity to avoid going there. It was not until his influence had broadened, that this once lowly monk took one of the most fatal steps a spiritual leader can make: To trade his spiritual authority for political author-ity. This was a huge step downward, though in natural appearance it may have seemed advantageous. This was a temptation faced by Jesus Himself, when the devil offered to trade Him temporal author-ity over the kingdoms of the world, in exchange for the spiritual authority He would receive by abdicated His own identity and wor-shiping satan. Today, we still have hundreds of churches that are run by power brokers and businessmen who sit in the pews—good ol' boys and small town politicians who keep their pastors on puppet strings.

But again, the worst of the Reformation's excesses was the rebellious nature in which it took place. This has spilled into the genetics of the church by building a tendency to split and schism over minor doctrinal issues. I honestly believe that America's high divorce rate is an indirect result of the Reformation. After the reformers violently broke away from the church, there were count-less other movements that followed precedent and broke away from the reformers. America was founded by such schismatics, who have built into their mind-set "when the going gets tough, run." Any little church problem or feud turns into a split these days. And what is modeled in the church spills over into the home—hence divorces at the drop of a hat. As goes the church, so goes the world. How many thousands of denominations do we have today? Of course, I think there is some good in denominations. Without them, the church is still too immature to foster true diversity. I think the Lord allows denominational separations to preserve some differences in worship style and calling. But I am sure the Lord would prefer that we did not need them.

Yes, I think the Reformation really did need to break away from the Roman Catholic church. Were the doctrinal issues which Luther faced minor? Not by any stretch of the imagination. Did he have a chance of working them out internally? Not a snowball's chance in hell. Luther was like a bottle of Clorox to cleanse a filthy church. But Clorox needs to be used sparingly. To this day, most Protestant churches sit constantly on the brink of a potential church split because parishioners prefer to escape problems rather than deal with them. We split over the color of carpet in the sanctuary. We split because Deacon A was promoted to an eldership over Deacon B. We have split over water sprinkling, tongue talking, building projects, song preferences, women preachers, hair length, service times, racial prejudice—you name it. We split until there are four people left in the church and we can no longer afford to pay the electric bill. We split because we are bored. We split because we are escapists. We split because we are rebellious.

> *How good and pleasant it is when brothers live together in unity! It is like precious oil poured on the head, running down the beard, running down on Aaron's beard, down upon the collar of his robes* (Psalm 133:1-2).

Luther did try to first work out his problems with the Catholic church from the inside. Despite our opinions on his tactics, or those of the Roman Catholic church, we know the battle became ugly and bloody. And let's cut Luther a break—the times were a lot bigger than him. Never in the history of the church has her division been so brutal. Never has Christ's body been so torn and fragmented, but on Calvary itself. Much of it was unavoidable, but I think time now gives us the needed distance to look more objectively at the Reformation. Luther may have been right on a million points besides the 95 theses he nailed on the Wittenberg door. But if we do not champion our cause in the *nature* of Jesus, we just lost half the battle. Religiosity had so suppressed the church for ages that the natural reaction was to rebel against authority. Mob mentality ruled for a time and was passed down to us ever since. But those days are over.

For too long, the Protestant church has felt license to defame the Body and Bride of Christ by calling her Catholic brothers and sisters the "whore" church of Revelation. Every time we say such a thing, we are pounding another nail into Jesus' hands. He died for Catholics and Protestants both. And Catholics can no longer afford to categorize Protestants as mere schismatics, heretics, or *lesser* Christians. For too long, some Protestants have cursed Catholics, rather than embraced them as brothers—and vice versa. Of course, we are all starting to realize our error. We all need the humility to embrace Christ within one another, though we may never agree on any other doctrinal issue.

It is all too childish to paint one another in black and white stereotypes. We all can learn from one another, and we are all riddled with error. In his imaginary games, my 3-year-old son loves to pretend there are "good guys" and "bad guys." But real life is not that simple. We have all played the harlot. It is time that we grow up.

The reason nearly every move of God tends to stagnate, is because it judges the last move of God. We become what we judge. If we judge religious people and hypocrites, we eventually become religious hypocrites. Never criticize the old wineskin, just let it be. The wine itself will burst the old jug. And it will eventually burst yours. There is no quicker way into bondage than falling into spiritual pride and thinking we are on the cutting edge of what God is doing. That we have somehow ascended beyond where the old order got stuck. First of all, we don't know all that the old order had to put up with, and what spiritual ground they broke through on our behalf.

It is important not to adopt a rebellious spirit, and to remember that our battle is not against flesh and blood. Yes, religion is a foul thing. But *religious* people are often just wounded Christians seeking identity and comfort in the wrong places. To criticize the old guard is often a sign that we are still operating out of rejection, and somehow needing their affirmation rather than the Lord's. Truly mature Christians, who have overcome insecurity, will see people beyond the veil of their religious bondage and empathize with the hurts that landed them there.

Is Christ enough? Is it enough that He wants a Bride whose body parts are not strewn about—a Bride who cares about nothing except Him and Him alone? We are told to first love God, then to love others as ourselves. Unity does not mean compromise on the basics. And we want to take doctrinal errors seriously. But we need to give one another a lot of latitude and grace to grow. Some of the greatest divides in the church are being healed at this time. I was encouraged several years ago to learn that Roman Catholic and Lutheran theologians published a joint document, with both agreeing that justification comes by faith, and that the faith/works debate is now a moot point. That is absolutely huge, considering the church's greatest point of division *ever*—the catalyst of innumerable wars and Inquisitions—is now a *moot point.*

"This document is historic in that it begins the healing of the initial breach that started the splintering of Christianity through the debate over faith and works, and scripture and tradition. But it is only an initial step," writes Catholic monk and popular music artist John Michael Talbot. "I think that this means that we all are now in an era where we do well to emphasize our growing communion with Jesus and the Church, rather than arguing with and condemning those who do not see Jesus and the Church as we do."[2]

This document alone, though relatively unnoticed, could signify the church's introduction into a new era.

REVOLUTION

A violent revolution is truly on the horizon for the church. But we will be rending our hearts and not our garments. We will be taking the Kingdom of Heaven by force—not bickering over the kingdoms of this world.

I believe that Christians should be salt of the earth and influence politics, economics, and society for the good. But we can never forget that we are the partakers of an eternal Kingdom. The perishable cannot inherit the imperishable. The kingdoms of this world will become the kingdoms of our God, but there is no such thing as a "Christian nation" this side of heaven. We can never confuse our spiritual mandate with earthly authority.

The Cevennes prophets (17th century) of France are an interesting case study in corporate Holy Spirit outpourings. God began an awakening in the Cevennes when in 1688, 16-year-old Isabeau Vincent began to have ecstasies, shaking and fainting, wherein she could quote Scriptures she had never known and prophesy. She would sometimes sing or preach sermons in her sleep. She impacted many, leading them to repentance. Dozens of people in her village were ignited with a prophetic gifting, and as news spread, visitors flocked to the area. Many in the Cevennes had angelic visions, and they were sometimes led to secret meetings

The young prophetess Isabeau Vincent is brought before authorities, as illustrated by Samuel Bastide.

by means of lights in the sky. Specific words of knowledge were common, and all were driven to a thirst for holiness.

People began to pray and fast, and their meetings were marked by unusual spontaneity, as well as exuberant and demonstrative worship. Physical manifestations of God's presence were also present on believers. At this time, France's Catholic king had placed hundreds of laws into effect restricting Protestant religious freedoms, even having many persecuted and killed. Protestant leaders were explicitly killed or banished, and many of their churches were destroyed. But the twisted dilemma of the church wielding a worldly sword did not end at the Catholics' hilt. Protestants also shed the blood of their brothers.

With their spiritual leaders deported, French families being killed, and their homes burned, those who had learned to walk in God's Spirit through this outpouring were led to extremes. They began to lean on far-fetched prophecies and strange predictions, and many thought God was inspiring them as to who they should kill and what they should destroy. Those who turned to such military resistance were known as Camisards, and they were eventually wiped out by the king's forces. But much of the fruit of the original outpouring did remain through the centuries.[3]

Let us learn from the Camisards that sinful men can twist even a mighty move of God to their own carnal benefit. Where can we trace back this initial confusion between the Kingdom of Heaven and the kingdoms of the earth? It's been the case since Adam's fall. But to look at the specific confusion between spiritual warfare and political force in the church, let's jump back in time to the era of Constantine. It was then that the weapons of love and self-sacrifice were first exchanged for the sword. In fact, the Reformation and the Constantinian era have together made the greatest impact on how Christianity is *practiced* than any other periods of history.

Emperor Constantine (a.d. 274-337) was the pagan ruler of the Roman Empire who, in a.d. 312 when marching into Italy for war with 25,000 troops claims to have seen a cross of light in the heavens, around which were woven the words: *In hoc signo vince*s, "In this sign you shall conquer." The historicity of this is questionable, but Constantine supposedly began leading his armies to war under the symbol of a type of cross, the *chi roh*. In a.d. 313 he issued the Edict of Milan, which officially tolerated the church and ended Christian persecution in the Roman Empire.

Suddenly, church leaders from local bishops to popes were given governmental power. It sure seemed like a good idea back then. But as church leadership gradually moved into power trips and politics, church office became associated with money and control.

Constantine began a massive program of church building projects in a.d. 323. As any experienced pastor knows, a good way to kill revival can be to get involved with new building projects! Prior to that, the church had never even considered buildings—the church was a living network of people that met in homes, and really had nothing to do with physical structures. Church buildings became more elaborate with high vaulted ceilings. On one hand, they spoke of the vast beauty and glory of God, but on the other hand, the mesmerizing architecture made God seem distant and out of reach.

Previously, Christians had always gathered for love feasts, but now, with crowds swelling in these massive new church buildings, the community focus dissipated. Mere crowd control merited that only one or two people could speak or share, out of the hundreds in attendance. Christianity became a spectator sport. The layman lost his voice. Where once you may have been a participant, suddenly all eyes were focused on a centralized pulpit. Services became ordered. Professional speakers replaced the spontaneous sermons given by average believers.

Understand that these must have been exciting times for believers. You could be a Christian for free, without it costing your head! But the celebratory love feasts were soon banned. The priesthood of every believer was handed over to a select few, who approached God for you. The Roman system of hierarchical government was transposed into the church leadership model with bishops, archbishops, etc. Scriptures would eventually leave the hands of ordinary believers, and theological baggage would be piled on top of them for centuries until the Reformation.

During the time of Constantine, Christians jumped from about 4 percent of the population up to 80 percent, but it is doubtful that most of these were real conversions. Pagans flooded into the church. *Clergy—a* term that originally described pagan priests—suddenly began wearing costumes that set them apart from average believers. Church buildings were named after saints, like the pagan temples were named after their gods. Pulpits and choirs originated in pagan practice. Sunday, the "day of the sun," or *dies solis*, was the state instituted holiday that gave preference to Sun worship—"Christian" Constantine even built a number of pagan temples as well, just to cover all his bases with other religions. He even did this in Constantinople—the great city he built in dedication to Christianity.

I believe the Lord longs to redeem practices and cultural trends we see in the world around us, but it is clear that in Constantine's day, the church jumped to a quick, false maturity based on institutional religion and half-converted pagan practices. Why do you dress up on Sunday? It is because your forefathers tried to look good to impress Constantine's friends. Why has the operation of the fivefold office gifts been lost from the church? It is because Constantine's hierarchy established a one-man, priest-like hierarchy.

Pagan rhetoric practices would soon bring polished, snappy oratory into the church. Professional sermonizing would replace prophetic utterance and the "simple speech" used by the apostles. Eventually, every practice of the faith would become established and taken out of the hands of average believers. By the time of Pope Gregory, around a.d. 500, even singing was relegated to the clergy! And even then, they were only allowed to chant in one specific scale.

But it was the twisted unity between civil government and church authority that still gives us the most problems today. Constantine promoted church leaders that agreed with him and quietly dismissed those who spoke up against state interference in the church. At that time, no one knew how to handle a government that was friendly toward the church. It was not easy to resist the tempting siren of the state, after the church had been persecuted for so long by it.

Constantine called the famous Council of Nicea, largely as a means to hold together the empire, which was beginning to fall apart by that time. His primary interest was unity within the empire.

Here, Constantine weighed in on doctrinal matters and, in effect, became the virtual leader of the church. Church leaders who would not sign the Nicene Creed were persecuted—for the first time, Christians were persecuting their brothers. State permits were needed to become a leader or teacher in the church. Conversions were made by political influence or outright force, not by the Lord's leading.

As noted earlier, Augustine's writings would soon be used to justify war, not just in the name of Christ, but also against fellow Christians. Religious wars would begin to sweep the nations from that day forward until now.

We may never know whether Constantine was a legitimate believer. He was clearly full of superstition. For instance, he refused to be baptized until just before he died, because he thought it somehow cleared you from sin. He wanted to do it at a time when he would be least likely to commit more sins afterward. Of course, the cross alone can absolve sin. I believe Constantine was a legitimate believer, but a very confused, immature believer at best. He may have been sincere in his efforts to further Christianity, but without much depth of understanding, he did much more harm than good. The church cannot be built by human means.

There must be a distinct separation between church and state. No civil authority or human force can change a man's heart or force a conversion. The Lord does not work this way, and ever since the garden, He has given mankind a choice whether or not to follow Him. The worst problems the world has ever seen have come from this unholy blending of church and state. The two can co-exist amicably, but one should not control the other.

Obviously, this separation between church and state is now being interpreted in America as a means of ridding church influence from society and politics. Of course, this violates the words and intent of the Bill of Rights and the U.S. Constitution. We can never allow government restrictions or man's opinion to silence us in matters of faith. As Christians, we must always seek to obey and honor civil authorities, but never in violation of God's commandments. The revolutionary army prophesied by Joel will not be one to wield a human sword, but neither will it be afraid of the human sword.

Many American Christians are timidly sitting by as our blood-bought rights of free speech and freedom of religion are turned against us and used as excuses to restrict Christian speech and thought in public places. When the authorities commanded the apostles to stop speaking and teaching in the name of Jesus, Peter and John answered, *"Whether it is right in the sight of God to give heed to you rather than to God, you be the judge; for we cannot stop speaking what we have seen and heard"* (Acts 4:19-20).

The church is waking up into the boldness of her calling. No longer will we keep silent. The sweet temptations of human and political acceptance will no longer muzzle us or emasculate us with religious idolatry.

RECKLESS ABANDON

There will be a holy boldness coming upon the church in this hour that has not been seen for centuries. Power baptism brings boldness. In Acts 4, we see the church walking in a level of signs, wonders, and miracles that were far greater even than were recorded at Pentecost in Acts 2. It was then that the apostles asked the Lord to "stretch out Your hand to heal and perform miraculous signs and wonders through the name of Your holy servant Jesus," and the place of their meeting was shaken like an earthquake. Immediately they were filled with the Spirit "and spoke the word of God boldly."

Miraculous power brings a release of reckless courage. Today's church, however, has confused humility with timidity. Jesus was meek, but he was not a coward. Meekness is defined as strength under control. But Jesus was bold, and used His strength and fearlessness in an appropriate manner. For instance, He stripped the temple of God bare with a whip, overturning the tables of the merchants and money changers. He was bold enough to separate corrupt men from their cash. And He was never afraid to tell the truth.

Pride is the *opposite* of humility, but cowardice is the *counterfeit* of humility. Many Christians who have the appearance of being humble are really just chickens—bound by fear. We need to pray for a release of holy boldness in this hour. Nothing will make you as bold as spending an hour in the prayer closet in the electric presence of God. Boldness will come through a display of God's power, but even more so, it comes through a revelation of Christ in us.

In many ways, we have known Jesus from a natural understanding. This is not entirely bad, but we must move on to know Him as the Lord of Glory—the Lord of hosts, King of the armies of heaven. The disciples were shocked when sleeping, natural Jesus stood up in their boat in the middle of a storm and commanded even the wind and waves to obey Him. They were awed at this man whom they thought to have known so well now ruling over the very forces of nature. Or when He was on the Mount of Transfiguration with Peter, James, and John, we see that they had no context of how to approach Him in the glory.

I believe that this level of glory, where Jesus' face and clothing became bright as a flash of lightning, is about the extent to which the believer can physically manifest the glory of God on earth. This will be happening on a more regular basis in these latter days. Moses' face also shone with the glory under the old covenant, and Scripture is clear that we are under a better covenant. While Moses' glory was fading, we are called to walk from one level of glory to another. But on the Mount, Peter was still trying to cater to Jesus, Moses, and Elijah in a natural manner, after the flesh, offering to build them a little tent for the night. This incident shows that the natural mind and human means cannot contain the glory of God. Even Jesus had to lay aside the fullness of His glory just to fit inside the natural realm. We have thoroughly discussed how the natural realm is not evil—but it is perishable and limited. Flesh and blood cannot inherit the Kingdom of God. This is why we must be born again.

John was called the disciple whom Jesus loved, and John was so intimate with the Lord that he even laid his head upon Jesus' breast.

But when John saw Jesus later in life in the Book of Revelation on the Lord's day, in a much greater glory, John fell to the ground as though he was dead (see Rev. 1:17). He was encountering God in a much more intense, exhilarating way than he had ever known Him in the natural realm.

Or let us consider Peter again. When Jesus was resurrected, just after Peter had denied Him, Jesus approached him and asked "Do you truly love Me more than these?" Peter answered Him, saying "Yes Lord, You know that I love You." But Jesus asked him this question two more times. "Do you love me?" "Do you love me?" In that culture, this must have been humiliating for Peter. The first two times, Peter answered, "Yes Lord, You know that I love You." But Jesus was using the word *phileo*, or "brotherly love." And He was speaking to Peter's *old man*, or human nature, calling him "Simon, son of John."

Finally, after being asked the third time, "do you love me," Peter answered more truthfully, knowing that Jesus saw into the depths of his heart. Peter had run from the cross. He had known Jesus in a natural sense, but had never ascended to the highest, sacrificial type of love, *agape*, also known as "Godly love."

"Lord, You know all things; You know that I *phileo* You," said Peter. Peter realized that he had only loved Jesus in a natural, *phileo* way, but he had not fully learned to love the Lord after the Spirit. The All Consuming Fire. The Lord of Glory. Peter had known that Jesus was Messiah. He probably had a *saving* knowledge in that sense. But like many Christians, he did not fully comprehend that Messiah was building more than a natural kingdom—He was restoring mankind's spiritual relationship with God. If Peter had received a revelation of the full measure of Christ, he certainly would have had the boldness not to deny Him. We must know Him as the Lord of Glory. Peter had to honestly come to grips with his own spiritual bankruptcy.

It was in the boat, after the storm, where Jesus remarked at the disciples' lack of faith. If they had really known who was in the boat with them, they never would have had to wake Him up. In the same way, when we recognize what it really means to have Christ in us, the hope of glory, anything becomes possible. It does not matter how much you try to imagine or exaggerate, the sky is the absolute limit to the power that flows from that revelation—that we have access to every spiritual blessing in Christ.

Miracles are a sign of Christ in us, but it is that same revelation of His indwelling which is the true source of boldness. As this revelation increases, the miracles will abound, further releasing an unprecedented aggression in the preaching of the Kingdom. God is releasing a holy, revolutionary army that will know Him after the Spirit. And the violent are going to take the Kingdom by force.

George Fox (1624-1691) is a great example of apostolic boldness. Fox is known as the founder of the Quaker movement. We generally tend to think of Quakers as quiet, timid believers, known for their pacifism and nonviolence. But their founder was absolutely fearless and volatile. Quakerism, like many movements, was founded on the dauntless sacrifice of those who braved persecution.

George Fox at Houlker Hall in 1662.

Born in Leicestershire, England, Fox always had a burning desire for true faith, free of religious hypocrisy. Fox detested anything that remotely smelled of institutionalized religion: church buildings, paid clergy, and the observance of Sunday services. In his early 20s, Fox had a miraculous encounter, wherein he saw a vision of God's glory and gained a heart of evangelism for the lost. Suddenly, he was driven to dynamic feats of boldness.

Fox would walk into church services, and as soon as the vicar finished a sermon, he would step right up front and begin to preach the gospel. This caused him more than a few problems. He would get physically thrown out of churches, locked up, beaten, and even stoned—by "Christians!" Sometimes he was supernaturally healed, and other times, he would just wipe up the blood and walk away. Fox was thrown into prison three times, and the term "Quaker" was stamped on his followers as a derogatory remark given by a judge at one of his trials, when Fox admonished the court to "tremble at the word of God."

Where did Fox get his boldness? Fox left behind a *Book of Miracles* in which he documented at least 150 healings and other supernatural miracles in his life and ministry. As the power of God was released in Fox's life, it brought with it a daring resolve. Eventually, Fox's following amassed greatly, and revival swept the common people to whom he preached. Many Quakers died for their faith. Their Christianity was the kind bought with blood. They were even given a death sentence in the American colonies.[4]

It is not coincidence that *naturally* passive Quakers were some of the most spiritually violent men on earth. The revelation that we belong to a Heavenly Kingdom, outside of this world, gives us a radical boldness to lay down our natural swords and sacrifice all. This is how Jesus sacrificed all. He said:

> *My Kingdom is not of this world. If it were, My servants would fight to prevent My arrest by the Jews. But now My Kingdom is from another place* (John 18:36).

Jesus said His Kingdom is now from another place, but one day, it will include this earth as well. Our job is to be channels for God to bring as much of that dominion into this world as we possibly can. But we do it His way. This may seem an odd point to hammer, since Christians don't take up guns to defend their faith. But when persecution starts to notch up, you better believe that it will be a temptation.

Boldness is a sure sign that you really believe in the unseen realm. The first people who are called unfit for the Kingdom of Heaven are the *cowardly and unbelieving* (see Rev. 21:8). God is calling a people who will step out in risk and faith, even risking spiritual error at times. Movement and spiritual progress means that errors will sometimes happen. Many are so afraid of wildfire that they have no fire at all. But any mistakes made will be well worth the benefits. Those who overreact to error are the ones most prone to ditch faith. As Bill Johnson says, the church is focused on committing sins of presumption, but the Lord is more concerned about our sins of unbelief. Walking by faith means having the courage to step into new territory and risk the unknown.

Christians should not be looking for ways to avoid defeat. We should be looking for ways to win. If we're going to avoid something, let it first of all be a lukewarm heart. There's no such thing as a stationary Christian. You are either moving forward or you are slipping backward.

THE NEW APOSTLES

The church has been hearing a lot about the coming apostolic reformation over the past several decades. The restoration of the apostolic office will surely mark a release of corporate power, because they will carry gifts of impartation for the body. They will be releasers and reproducers. And with this power will come boldness in the body.

The apostolic movement could have as dramatically positive an impact on the church as the Constantinian era was negative. The true apostolic movement will come in a completely opposite spirit than the hierarchical priesthood of old Rome. Apostles are under girders. Theirs is a type of servant leadership—not from the top down, but from the bottom up. Paul calls the apostles *scum of the earth*, put on procession at the end of the age. They are humble and not self-appointed. They are also entrusted with secrets from God, and are therefore called to a higher measure of faithfulness (see 1 Cor. 4).

We noted earlier that "apostle" literally means *sent one*, and a similar word was used to describe Elijah in the Old Testament. He was a forerunner of the type of apostolic ministry the Lord seeks to bring to His New Testament church. Clearly, like Elijah, apostles will move in power as well as revelation. They will be able to operate in all of the other fivefold ministry gifts: pastoring, teaching, evangelism, and prophecy. They will also plant churches and often be extra-local in nature; that is, they will not be tied down to a single local church, but will truly be "sent ones." The first century apostles traveled the globe. In the same way, many of those we have called "missionaries" throughout the centuries were really just apostles. Or, one could at least say they were engaged in apostolic endeavors.

Apostles, like pastors, teachers, and other fivefold ministries, have always been among us. But they have usually not been recognized, and were therefore limited in their giftings. Apostles will not be untouchable superheroes. They will be normal men like us. We have long made the mistake of not recognizing prophetic people for their gifting, because we were expecting a "prophet" to be some kind of God-incarnate super-human. The same is true for apostles. When we understood that *all may prophesy*, the charismatic church's understanding began changing toward prophets. There are still only a few people in the earth today who I would call fully *mature* prophets, but there are very many others who are legitimately maturing in a prophetic gifting. The same will be true for the apostolic office. When we realize that the apostles are not given to us to idolize, we will be able to recognize them more easily.

I think that, at this point in the game, there are lots of people starting to move in apostolic power. And there are many among us who have latent apostolic callings. But by biblical standards, we have yet to see the full release of apostles back into the body. At least not mature ones. We are guilty of calling a lot of things "apostolic" which do not meet the level of New Testament apostolic ministry. Many, in their zeal, who have rushed ahead to call themselves apostles, have not always done so out of selfish ambition or pride. It has largely been from misunderstanding concerning this office. Truths regarding the apostolic arena are just now being broken open by forerunner saints and ministries.

It is difficult to discuss the new mystics without addressing their role in this apostolic reformation. Apostles will lay strong foundations. They will plant. They will break open new territory. And they will work in relationship with teams—never as a one-man show.

We learned the hard way, after a lot of disappointment, that prophets are not perfect. We must be willing to accept as apostles those who are still "human," and who still make mistakes. While the stakes of holiness and devotion must be kept high for the apostolic office, we must be patient in the meanwhile as the parameters of this ministry are still being defined for us by the Lord.

The Lord Himself is the one who supernaturally places His apostles into their offices. They were not established or ordained into that position by any man. The apostle Paul seems to define himself as an apostle because he has *seen the Lord*. This seems to be a prerequisite. In the age of modernity, governments, corporations, and even churches have been controlled from the top down, with systems of rules and regulations, with the guiding *virtues* of strife and selfish ambition. The postmodern era, however, seems most ripe for apostolic leadership, which leads by relationship in a servanthood position. True apostles will not be interested in maintaining control. Instead, they will seek to reproduce themselves. Their goal will be to raise up others capable of taking the reigns—"establishing elders"—then moving on to break open more ground for the Kingdom. They will be spiritual fathers who want to raise up children who surpass themselves.

As silly as it seems, many churches have pursued a fivefold system of leadership in recent years and quickly fallen into the trap of filling five slots in a type of pecking order—who is the prophet? Who is the evangelist? The coming generation wants something real, not something artificial or contrived. They will not just want a man-appointed institutional leadership, but a charismatic, God-appointed leadership. When the sent ones, the *smeared* ones, come forth in the anointing of Heaven, this will be a generation that can recognize them. And we will marvel at what the Lord has done.

In summary, however, I would like to point out that the coming reformation is not so much a reformation of church government, structure and politics, as much as it is a shift of vision, focus, and a revolution of the heart. It is not that the original vision of the church will change, but that we will actually get back to the true vision.

The church, for the most part, still acts like the slave son of Hagar, serving God under the task master of the law with no true understanding of its sonship or inheritance as the seed of promise. The revolutionary change that is coming to church government is that we will possess that Spirit by which we call out "Abba, Father!" The church will not be an institution of leaders and laypeople, as much as it will be a family of sons and fathers, daughters and mothers. Regulation will be washed away by heartfelt relationship. Law-focus will be replaced by faith-focus, and Jacob's striving will be replaced by Israel's ruling and reigning.

ENDNOTES

1. C.S. Lewis, *The Problem of Pain* (Touchstone Books, 1996 ed.).

2. Rick Joyner, *Shadows of Things to Come* (Nashville: Thomas Nelson, 2001), 25.

3. John Michael Talbot, "Luther." (Little Portion Hermitage, 2003).

4. "Toronto in the Cevennes." (Jesus Fellowship Church). Accessed 13 Oct. 2004 <www.jesus.org.uk/ja/mag_revivalfires_cevennes.shtml>. Article sources: Henri Bosc, La Guerre des Cevennes (1985-1993 reprint); Hillel Schwartz, *The French Prophets* (1980); anon, *The Protestant Prophets with the Accounts of Various Marvels* (1707).

CHAPTER 9

Ancient Pathways

I N this chapter, we will be looking at "Christian mystics" in the traditional sense of the title—those who flourished between the 14th and 17th centuries whose lives were marked by deep, contemplative prayer. In fact, the truest definition of a Christian *mystic* is one who lived a life of deep, extensive prayer. They were not all known for miracles and healings as much as intense prophetic experiences and, primarily, for intimacy with God. Throughout the course of this book, however, I have defined "mystic" very loosely, including miracle workers and all who pursue a supernatural journey of divine experience based on intimate communion with the Lord.

I first began my studies of the Christian mystics—the *contemplatives—in* a search for spiritual insight that was not available in most mainstream books and churches. I wanted a language for the spiritual experiences I was having, that modern prepackaged theology was too lifeless to offer. Why did I want to run away and sit in the presence of God all day without talking? Is that normal? How do we pursue the deeper, inner life? I wanted to explore new frontiers mapped out by forerunners—and I wanted to break new ground myself. Every insight or answer I gained only opened the door for 20 more new questions, and I learned to live in the suspense of unknowing.

Whenever I read the mystics, I am humbled. After Job's friends spend 37 chapters giving pat answers and reasons for his calamity, God finally speaks and says, "Who is this that darkens My counsel with words without knowledge?" These words are spoken to me, whenever I read the mystics. I see that I know nothing.

Trappist monk and 20th century mystic Thomas Merton often found himself like the prophet Jonas, "caught up in the belly of paradox." He said, "the very contradictions in my life are in some ways signs of God's mercy to me." The cross itself, and the entire Christian life is full of paradox. We die to live. We lose to gain. God is utterly complex, yet remarkably simple. He is tangible, yet untouchable. He is unseen, yet fully revealed. We can know Him who is unknown. We can search out the One who is unsearchable.

The mystics lived in the midst of this spiritual tension of paradox. The mystics did not settle for one form of theology over another at the expense of missing out on God. They were often excommunicated, martyred, or forced to undergo extreme church "discipline" because of their deep pursuit of personal interaction with God. They were often labeled as heretics, just because they expressed themselves in a clumsy way. Theirs was an intimate language of love—of the bedchamber. Their words naturally tended toward exaggeration. The deeper one goes into the presence of the Lord, the more difficult it can be to describe. Often, the mystical journey so tends to strip one of superfluous words, that he is reduced to a simple confession of God's love. All becomes silent in awe of an all-consuming, holy God.

Along the journey, the fire of God's love that begins to burn within causes us to surrender the things of the world that we lean on for fulfillment. We willingly submit to His inner, cleansing flame. In doing so, we find that prayer becomes an exercise in resting in Him. The mystics are known widely for their practice of the presence of God.

Brother Lawrence (1605-1691) held as his lifelong endeavor the practice of the presence of God. People traveled from miles around just to come watch this humble monk wash dishes because he was so saturated with the substance of God. His was the most simple, yet profound type of walk a person can have. I believe there is no greater purpose a man can set out to attain. Lawrence composed the best rule ever written for holy life, and it is simply this:

"I wouldn't even lift a straw from the ground against His order or for any other motive than love for Him. Pure love of Him is all that keeps me going," he said.[1] He gave up all his other forms of prayer besides intercession, in order to focus all his attention on the presence of God. This experience of God's unceasing presence filled him with such uncontrollable joy, that it compelled him to sometimes do childish things to try and contain it. "My prayers consist of a simple continuation of this exercise (of practicing God's presence). ...If I am deceiving myself, the Lord will have to remedy it. I want Him to do whatever He pleases with me; all I want is to be completely His," he said.

Lawrence said it is key to recognize that God is always intimately present with us. He renounced everything that did not lead Him closer to God. But Lawrence said we are not so much to *change* our activities, as we are to begin doing them for God instead of ourselves. To Lawrence, life became a prayer. He says it is wrong to think of our prayer time as different from any other. All the actions of our daily activities should unite us with God's presence as much as our prayer time does. This set him aside from many others, in that his natural life of service was directly linked with his inner life.

This practice is to become a pleasurable habit we do without thinking. He said that we should not become discouraged when we fail at this initially. Our attitude should be so focused on faith, hope, and love that we are not concerned with our own shortcomings. "Although the habit is difficult to form, it is a source of divine pleasure once it is learned," he said.

Lawrence embodied perhaps the purest form of Christian mysticism, but there were many forms of contemplation. During the spiritual renewal of the past decade, we have used the broad term "soaking prayer" to describe various modes of contemplation. Simply speaking, contemplation is that form of prayer in which the mind and soul become stilled, in order for the Holy Spirit to come upon us and bring us into new levels of transcendent intimacy and holiness.

IMMERSING INTO ELECTRIC SOLITUDE

"Soaking prayer" has been a buzzword in Christian renewal over the past decade. However, it is more than the latest religious trend. Throughout the ages, those who walked closest to God were those who basked in His electric radiance. Those who best knew Him were those who allowed their thoughts and interior turbulence to be silenced and drank deeply from the living streams of life.

> ...*Drink, yes, drink deeply, O beloved ones!* (Song of Solomon 5:1)

It is clear that we are tasked to drink constantly from the river of life, and all too often, we take a sip—drink of His sweetness for a season—then return to our patterns of strife. We know that walking in the Spirit must become a lifestyle. But without waiting and lingering in His midst, we forfeit intense Kingdom revelation and power. Most of all, we miss God Himself and His destiny for our lives. If we literally miss a day without pulling aside to drink of His new wine—to miss out on His "rivers of pleasure," His never ending delight—we should count the day a waste. I work much better under the inebriating peace of His nearness, and the best work is often done when I'm too sloshed in it to get off the floor.

Americans want results—productivity. God just wants to get us plastered in His love.

Soaking prayer, or contemplation, is simply the practice of the presence of God. It is a place of stillness and meditation, wherein we enter the "secret place of the Most High," merely for the sake of being near Him. It is a response and a culmination of intimacy, wherein we cease to perform for God, and instead choose simply to be with Him. It is a posture of rest and repose, wherein we literally baste in His power and closeness as He flows over us and through us. We encounter the supernatural.

Sadly, studies have shown that American pastors pray an average of 15 minutes a day. Fifteen minutes—no kidding. How can this be? God did not ordain His servants to be first of all administrators, second of all organizers, and thirdly good orators. He wants men who get before Him on their faces and pray. Yes, this may take a violent pressing in at times. Prayer is the front line of combat against the devil. God is not looking for a bunch of sissy Christians who won't sacrifice themselves in prayer. If you look at the greatest saints and revivalists of old, you will see one thing in common—they were all staunch men of prayer. How hungry are you to change the world for your King? It will show by the time you put into your prayer closet.

But prayer is not just about exhaustive, repetitive intercession, trying to twist God's arm to intervene in the affairs of men. Nor is it just about tongue-talking yourself into a delirium for three hours. All of that kind of prayer is good, but you will burn out if that is your only staple. The only way a man can maintain extended prayer before the Lord is learn the practice of His presence, and how to still himself before God in silence. It is there that prayer becomes interactive. Prayer is much more about listening and basking in God's presence, than it is about talking and asking.

"I still believe that all spiritual life consists of practicing God's presence, and that anyone who practices it correctly will soon attain spiritual fulfillment. To accomplish this, it is necessary for the heart to be emptied of everything that would offend God. He wants to possess your heart completely," writes Lawrence. I am convinced that it is all a matter of our *desire*—we can each have as much of God's manifest presence in our lives as our hearts truly want. Fourteenth century mystic Jan Van Ruysbroeck was once approached by two priests, who came to ask his opinion on their spiritual state, and he told them "You are as holy as you wish to be!"

We have to get hungry. No measure of prayer, reading, or spiritual discipline can replace the fire of passionate hunger which God desires from us. And how can we ever become hungry for Him unless we stop to taste and see that He is good? If we truly want more of God's presence in our lives, we will get it.

"The Lord says: 'These people come near to Me with their mouth and honor Me with their lips, but their hearts are far from me. Their worship of Me is made up only of rules taught by men" (Isa. 29:13). And yet, when the flame of divine love does begin to kindle in our souls, we know that "the eyes of the Lord range throughout the earth to strengthen those whose hearts are fully committed to Him" (2 Chron. 16:9).

There is no form. No methodology to the practice of His presence. It relies heavily on silence—on listening—but the only DNA which separates it from other systems, is that it is not a *system*...it is a relationship.

> *This is what the sovereign Lord, the Holy One of Israel,*
> *says: 'In returning and rest is your salvation, in quietness*
> *and trust is your strength ...'* (Isaiah 30:15).

In the place of His nearness, in hearing His still small voice, we are supercharged. We can do super-human feats and receive heavenly visitations. Taking the time to experience God kindles the fire of heaven until it is raging within us. It is my belief that, in today's postmodern era, the discontinuity of life, the discontentment with religious formulas and the evident limits of rationalist thinking are simply signposts to a cultural cry for true *spiritual* intimacy.

Who still believes in the supernatural? More tend to worship a dead god that lives in a building. But there is a generation of new mystics on the rise who will unlock the mysteries of God that have been sealed and hidden throughout the ages. This is because they do more than believe He is alive—they believe He is near, and they walk with Him like Enoch. They will walk in unprecedented revelatory power that will even put the first century apostles to shame. In fact, it is already beginning. Many are young people—the first fruits of the army foretold by the prophet Joel—who do not rest on the laurels of a seminary degree, but simply understand their access to the war room of heaven itself. There is a rapid maturation process when one dwells with God.

We are also on the brink of seeing a full restoration of the contemplative monastic tradition of divine listening in the vein of St. John of the Cross, St. Terese, and others, which has been largely lost in the modern era. And it will be amplified in these latter day rains of God's glory.

My inner man must first learn to *be still and know that He is God* (Ps. 46:10), before I can hear the thunder in the distance. My pride has so geared me to trust in human strength and my own stubborn efforts to succeed—even to succeed in spiritual matters—that I am unable to truly quiet myself and just be with Him. It feels unproductive. What will it take for us to just lie down and trust God?

> *The Lord will fight for you; you need only to be still* (Exodus 14:14).

> *Therefore, since the promise of entering His rest still stands, let us be careful that none of you be found to have fallen short of it. … There remains, then, a Sabbath-rest for the people of God; for anyone who enters God's rest also rests from his own work, just as God did from His. Let us, therefore, make every effort to enter that rest…* (Hebrews 4:1, 9-11).

Even as we long to rest in God, so the Son of Man is still seeking a place to rest His head. We are His resting place. The emerging church is shaking off dead works, turning her eyes back to the fiery passion of her Savior. There are a people arising who hunger for the deeper under-currents, no longer content with the mental gyrations of churchy legalisms. The coming generation longs for true intimacy with God alone, out of which will flow true power. And the reality of the spiritual realm, with signs, wonders, and miracles—which are needed to reach a world in critical darkness—will only come forth through the cultivation of soaking in God's presence. The inner chamber of His glory, opened by the blood of Christ, is the secret source of all power.

"There is no sweeter manner of living in the world than continuous communion with God. Only those who have experienced it can understand. However, I don't advise you to practice it for the sole purpose of gaining consolation for your problems. Seek it, rather, because God wills it and out of love for Him," writes Lawrence. "If I were a preacher, I would preach nothing but practicing the presence of God."[2]

Yes, there is Kingdom work to be done. There is a world hungry for the true gospel of Jesus Christ. There are goals to be accomplished and battles to be won, with no room for complacency. But the work begins in the closet. It begins with knowing God, and not just knowing about Him. Being with Him, and not just doing for Him. Listening to Him, and not just talking at Him. This does not always sound like practical Christianity. Christianity was never practical.

When we first stop and tap into the vine—our fruitfulness multiplies. We can no longer afford to serve *for* intimacy. We must learn to serve from a posture of intimacy, receiving His love which is so freely given. Soaking in His love will naturally propel us forward into supernatural Christian service.

Jesus is really our model for prayer. He constantly pulled aside to spend time with the Father, often leaving everyone to stay the night alone in hidden prayer. He pulled aside to get wisdom for decisions. Often, the Father showed Him things in prayer that He would later carry out in ministry. We know that Jesus did only what He saw the Father doing (John 5:19). It is in this place of prayer that Jesus gained strength for trials, such as in the Garden of Gethsemane.

Jesus would pull aside *long before daylight* to pray, and when the disciples found Him, He would sometimes have direction to move on to other towns for ministry. He was given revelatory direction and purpose in that place of prayer (Mark 1:35-38). In the Book of Acts, we see that the apostles were first *empowered* in a place of prayer. Jesus was also empowered in prayer, but He did not just pray before He preached, in order to be filled with the Spirit. He would also draw away *after* performing some of His greatest miracles, which kept Him in a place of humility and rest in the Father. The place of prayer covers us from the temptations of the world. It is a place of protection, wherein we die to the cares and worldly desires that seek to pull us away from our destiny. Prayer is the number one place where the Christian is called to carry his cross.

Yes, greatest saints and miracle workers were all marked by vast amounts of time in prayer. But this is impossible to do without being led by the Holy Spirit. Otherwise, it is a boring exercise in sitting by yourself in the corner. It should never—ever—be an exercise in boredom. It is the lifeblood of the believer. The man who is bored in prayer has not yet learned how to pray. True prayer is a place of travel into the multi-dimensional heart of God. You should never know what to expect in that place of meditation. Soaking is an inner sojourn, where Christ within us is revealed and manifest in our outer man. It is a journey we all must endeavor to take.

> *Blessed is the man whose strength is in You, whose heart is set on pilgrimage* (Psalm 84:5).

There is no formula for getting into the presence of God. Practicing the presence is not a *movement*. It is a lifestyle. It is Christianity 101. Even many renewal churches that have undergone periods of corporate soaking and meditation have grown agitated after some time, and backed away from intimacy. The religious urge to *do something* often cuts short our seasons of deep worship. Todd Bentley says, "Even if renewal was over, I would still be a closet drinker!"[3]

We cannot depend on others to affect this journey for us. This is a solitary escape, where we must press in and learn to linger where the Lord is for us. It requires a lot of waiting and patience, but the reward is great. Our outward performance will be far greater in due season, because it will be supercharged. Yet just being with the Lord is an end in itself. The goal is to be with Jesus, not to do for Jesus.

Surely I have calmed and quieted my soul, like a weaned child with his mother. Like a weaned child is my soul within me (Psalm 131:2).

Meditate within your heart on your bed, and be still (Psalm 4:4).

Come to me, all you who labor and are heavy laden, and I will give you rest. Take My yoke upon you and learn from me, for I am gentle and lowly in heart, and you will find rest for your souls for My yoke is easy and My burden is light (Matthew 11:28-30).

He gives power to the weak, and to those who have no might He increases strength. Even the youths shall faint and be weary, and the young men shall utterly fall, but those who wait on the Lord shall renew their strength. They shall mount up with wings like eagles: they shall run and not be weary, they shall walk and not faint (Isaiah 40:29-31).

Wait on the Lord; be of good courage, and He shall strengthen your heart (Psalm 27:14).

Todd Bentley (1976-present), a modern-day miracle worker, spent three months of intense soaking, plastered in the presence of God up to 12 hours a day, until finally the Lord launched him into an international healing evangelism ministry in his early 20s. He has now seen hundreds of thousands saved, and many thousands healed in his few short years of service as a healing evangelist. When Bentley travels into the nations, he will literally clear out entire schools of deaf children. He seems to have a particular anointing for healing the deaf. But I have seen the Lord affect even more bizarre miracles in his meetings. Traveling with him to Mexico, for instance, I saw a child with Down syndrome who was

Todd Bentley prays for a man at a foreign crusade

healed of the affliction. I have been an eye-witness in his meetings as metal plates disappeared, knees were recreated and blind eyes were opened.

Bentley had a background of drug abuse and prison from an early age. He had overdosed three times, and was converted after hearing the audible voice of God in his drug dealer's trailer. After his deep season of contemplative prayer, Bentley now regularly receives prophetic encounters, divine visitations, and spiritual translation into the third heaven. It was all birthed out of the practicing the presence of God.

I have seen Todd pop open the ears of rows of deaf people and work all manner of healings under the power of the Lord both on the mission field and in conferences in the United States and Canada. He also carries a powerful prophetic mantle. The words of knowledge he receives are very detailed, calling out complete strangers' names and illnesses in a church service, calling them forward to be healed. Yet this is all the fruit of lingering and drinking in the presence of God until He empowers us to do the work. The gospel has reached multitudes because of Bentley's passion for God's presence.

The lie we've been told is the same that has been used against monks and intercessors for centuries: We've got eternity to soak in the presence, but right now our job is to be *productive* and save souls. Productivity increases exponentially when we first pull aside and wait on God. It is there we are most significantly equipped. Not that we go to God strictly for productivity. We go there to give Him our hearts, and to receive His. Western churches have forgotten how to wait and listen to God. Five minutes of silence is considered a waste of time in most modern, mainline church services. People get fidgety, until finally someone feels they have to say something. Not that silence is the only mark of practicing God's presence, but we have forgotten how to wait—how to watch and listen. Jesus said to *watch* and pray.

Obviously, when we talk about stilling the thoughts, modern fundamentalism is severely opposed to such practice. But it is important that we distinguish clearly between biblical contemplative prayer and pagan counterfeits. Contemplation is about "being still and knowing that He is God" (Ps. 46:10); it is about intimacy and soaking in the River of God's presence. It is there that we meditate or reflect on the Lord, taking the focus off our own selves and our own issues. Although, in doing so, we often discover our *true selves*—our identity in Christ, our purpose and destiny. Contemplation is not about abandoning the mind, but about embracing the Lord with our full heart. The mind is a fortress to guard us against evil, but it can also become a stronghold to keep out the presence of God.

The broad term "mysticism" itself has been used to describe everything from occult practices, pantheism and outright divination, to all other sorts of false spirituality. But it is time that the church rediscovers our rich heritage of Christian mystics and takes back some spiritual ground they pioneered for us. New age mysticism is only a counterfeit for true, Godly mystical experience, and it will never compare in depth, intimacy, and the power that is found in Christocentric, cross-based spirituality. Christ alone is the door, and anyone who tries to enter the realms of the spirit without entering through the doorway is a thief and a robber.

The wells of mystical Christianity must be rediscovered in our day, otherwise the present prophetic movement is in danger of becoming another trend—the latest move of God that dissipates into formulas and techniques. God does not want a movement; He wants a prophetic people. When we fail to recognize the inexhaustible dimensions of unseen divine love and all its mysteries, we are rendered powerless by religion. The contemplative understands that he has found every answer in Christ, but in a paradoxical way—because in humility, his gaze at God causes him to realize he knows nothing. Therefore, his spiritual journey never ends, although he has already arrived at his destination. I believe we settle too quickly for an *understandable* God of religion, because we are intimidated by the unknown. We need the mystics to shake us up now and then to show us God is not so black and white.

"Heaven will solve our problems, but not, I think, by showing us subtle reconciliations between all our apparently contradictory notions," said C.S. Lewis.[4]

In this day, the writings of the mystics are beginning to resurface. Even now, the Lord is restoring the hearts of the children back to the fathers. Many of their words were intended for our day—for this generation. As far fetched as that may sound, there are many, many passages in the Bible itself that have also been waiting for our day for their fulfillment. One such mystical writer who has gained recent popularity is Madame Jeanne Guyon.

Madame Jeanne Guyon

Madame Jeanne Guyon (1648-1717) lived during one of the richest eras of Christian mysticism. She was admired for her teachings that, at one time, impacted those in the king's court, but she also served time in prison for her beliefs.

She lived 12 years with a harassing husband who refused to let her pray, and so she would steal away in the middle of the night in secret. Relatives would be sent to spy on her. It was several years after her husband's death that Guyon truly was blasted with an infilling of the Holy Spirit's peace.

"All I had enjoyed before was only a peace, a gift of God, but now I received and possessed the God of peace," she said. She had intense visions and encounters with the Lord, but the hallmark of her life was her intimate walk with Jesus. Her works *Intimacy with Christ and Experiencing the Depths of Jesus Christ* are saturated with such a thick anointing, it rivals only Brother Lawrence, who was her contemporary. In fact, Lawrence and Guyon lived in a generation that saw a number of spiritual giants, including Archbishop Francois Fenelon—a friend of Guyon—and Michael Molinos, credited for starting the Quietist movement. Guyon spent seven years in prison for her controversial writings, four of which were in the Bastille. Molinos died in a Roman dungeon.

Each of these mystics heard from heaven. As Guyon put it, "When Jesus Christ, the eternal wisdom, is formed in the soul, after the death of the first Adam, it finds in Him all good things communicated to it."

Our study here is neither a theological work, nor a scholarly historical work—though it is smattered with theology and history. I say this, because we are not looking intently at "mystical theology." The mystics have been analyzed and interpreted for centuries. The goal here is not to interpret the mystics, so much as to *imitate* the mystics. The language of the Christian mystics has often been a topic of confusion for scholars, theologians, and just about anyone who is not a mystic himself. They use erotic terminology—love language— for their relationship with the Lord. Theirs was a Christianity of relationship and intimacy at times when the corporate church was gripped with formalism, structure, and control.

"My words," said Jan Van Ruysbroeck, "are strange, but those who love will understand." Ruysbroeck, like others of his vein, were *experiencing* the ultimate Reality, which others had only dreamed or taught about. They were trying to describe interaction with God in human words and were often misunderstood.

The apostle Paul notes that he did not come with wise and persuasive words of human wisdom, but of "God's secret wisdom, a wisdom that has been hidden and that God destined for our glory before time began" (1 Cor. 2:7).

This is what we speak, not in words taught us by human wisdom but in words taught by the Spirit, expressing spiritual truths in spiritual words. The man without the Spirit does not accept the things that come from the

Spirit of God, for they are foolishness to him, and he cannot understand them, because they are spiritually discerned (1 Corinthians 2:13-14).

The mystics depart from theologians because they are not teachers per se, in the sense of a mathematician breaking down spiritual truth into logical, rational fragments. Their words are the experiential outbursts of love and divine exhilaration.

Jan van Ruysbroeck

Jan van Ruysbroeck (1293-1381) spent vast amounts of time alone with God—launching out to give more than 38 years of his life to contemplative prayer in the Flemish forest at age 50—yet he balanced his inner journey with outward acts of service. Unlike many strict contemplatives, Ruysbroeck made use of a well-trained intellect, and his writings are many. They are considered some of the most important mystical writings of the 14th century. However, he never let the mind encroach upon divine intuition, and he would never teach or speak unless he felt led by God to do so. Ruysbroeck said, "God is an ocean that ebbs and flows." His brothers would sometimes come looking for him after he had been gone for many hours in prayer, to find him lost in a state of ecstasy and surrounded by a visible, divine light.

Ruysbroeck taught that Christ should be experienced in the active (outward) life of the believer; in the interior (mind/soul) life; and in the deepest, supernatural place of spiritual contemplation. Ruysbroeck sought to keep sound theology in his mysticism and remain submitted to church discipline.

There are many other great contemplatives than mentioned here—Meister Eckhart, Bonaventura, Julian of Norwich, Walter Hilton, and the anonymous author of *The Cloud of Unknowing* to name a few. Some were hermits. Others combined their contemplation with acts of service. The mystics used imagery, romance, and poetic expression. They were often rendered silent by an inability to express the inexpressible. They produced numerous revelatory writings, and they always considered divine downloads of supreme importance over theological speculation.

"Mystical knowledge proceeds not from wit (the mind), but from experience; it is not invented, but proved; not read, but received; and is therefore most secure and efficacious, of great help and plentiful in fruit; it enters not into the soul by ears, nor by the continual reading of books, but by the free infusion of the Holy Ghost, whose grace with most delightful intimacy, is communicated to the simple and lowly," writes Michael Molinos, in The Spiritual Guide. "There are some learned men, who have never read these matters, and some spiritual men that hitherto have hardly relished them and therefore both condemn them, the one out of ignorance, and the other for want of experience."

Molinos mentions "mystical knowledge," which today we would probably call revelatory or prophetic insight. In fact, when we discuss the "Christian mystics," we are really just talking about prophets, in an age where the prophetic office was not recognized in the church. Molinos points out that many condemn the revelatory things of heaven out of ignorance. Others reject revelation out of their own envy and selfish desires. "If this is of God, why wouldn't He speak to me first?" We can all fall into the latter trap. Pride and covetousness can cause us to quickly miss out on the Lord's work and not recognize the prophets He sends us.

ROAD OF CONTEMPLATION

The road of contemplative prayer is an ancient pathway that is not highly traveled. There are no rules or methodology for entering contemplative prayer, and there are many contemplative and silent prayer traditions within Christianity. There is listening prayer, meditation, lectio divina (meditation over Scripture), centering prayer, the prayer of quiet, the prayer of union, the prayer of silence. I will not attempt to define each of these, because many of the great mystics seemed to have their own definitions anyway. However, we will look at three basic phases of contemplative prayer that generally match up with most common practices. Understand that many of the mystics sought to map out various forms of prayer and inner experience as a way to describe interaction with the Holy Spirit at the deeper levels of the spiritual life. Prophetic out-of-body experiences and visions were commonplace for many of them.

It may help to first understand that contemplation/meditation is not an intellectual exercise aimed at considering theological ideas. In fact, in contemplation we are not thinking of God the Father, Jesus, or the Holy Spirit. In contemplation, we are attempting a far greater feat: We are seeking to *be* with God the Father, Jesus, and the Holy Spirit. Contemplation is *firsthand* prayer.

Also, it is good to note that true mysticism is not a means of self-deification. Nor is it a "path to God," except that it is taking hold of Christ, The Path, and applying Him to our lives. The mystics saw spiritual growth as an ever-deepening relationship with God. The mystics undertook an intense process of inner sanctification, by which they were purged in order to decrease, that Christ might increase within them. The chief aim was the practice of the presence of God. Each was aware that his own human efforts were powerless to accomplish the deep union they sought with God, yet they positioned themselves in the place of quiet to receive their Lover.

Now, let us look at the three general phases along the way:

The first of these steps is sometimes called *recollection*, in which the Holy Spirit ministers healing and cleansing to the soul. It is here where we release the hurts, guilt, and wounds of the past. Let go of the sins and anxieties of the day. We release our burdens to the presence of God. We are also cleansed from the expectations, fears, or longings for the future. In this state of recollection, we begin to see God in the present, without the weight of old baggage or future anxieties that would otherwise hinder us. This first stage is a place of purification. It is where we lay our cares at the cross.

As our hearts become cleansed along the way, we will find that we can actually use our imagination in a healthy way in prayer. It is not bad to picture the Lord in our mind. This is not the same as the new age practice of visualization. Most visions do usually come to us internally, in the realm of the imagination. We usually learn which ones are from God and how to discern His voice, by first recognizing those that are confirmed in Scripture and in the natural realm. For example, on more than one occasion, I have prayed for musicians, and without knowing what instrument they play, I may see a violin, or drumsticks, etc. in a vision. When I ask them about it, I find out that this person is a violinist, or that person is a drummer. The vision on the backdrop of my "imagination" is confirmed in natural reality.

The imagination is a God-given mode of thought that modernism has written off as useless—and the church has largely taught us that the imagination is evil. However, we need to become child-like again. The Lord longs to give us the desires of our heart. He wants us to dream and envision great things with Him. He wants us to lift our vision higher, and God created the imagination for a very real purpose. Before He blesses us with a thing, He wants us to be able to envision it in our heart. But it is not until our desires become purified, that He can grant them.

"Delight yourself in the Lord and He will give you the desires of your heart" (Ps. 37:4). Notice that the prerequisite here to gaining your desires is to *delight yourself in the Lord*. When we are seeking first the Lord's heart, our imagination and desires become purified, because we long to do and accomplish only the things that please Him. We want Kingdom things. We want souls saved. We dream about ways to please Him in our imagination. Often we are trying to quiet our imagination in prayer, while in actuality, the Lord is trying to speak to us through it. Yes, the imagination can become a distraction, but we must learn to sense when the presence of God is drawing us into visions. The key is to follow the Lord's lead. If the imaginations become a distraction from His presence, we do not try to wrestle them away. Instead, we learn to gently release them to

Him. Contemplation is not a striving prayer, it is a soaking prayer. A place of rest and release.

Just to clarify something here: few people are aware that the imagination is very closely linked to one's *spiritual eyes*, or the *eyes of the heart*. As we become filled with truth, the imagination becomes less a place of unholy fabrication, and more of a place of creative prophetic vision.

The next step of contemplative prayer is often called the *prayer of quiet*. It is a place where the thoughts and cares are softly released to the Lord in a place of stillness. Teresa of Avila describes this place of quiet. It is a place where we recognize our inability to calm our own thoughts with our own strength. We become utterly dependent on God to lead us in prayer. "If I'm distracted, He calls me back in tones that are supernaturally beautiful," writes Brother Lawrence.[5] It is a place of pure listening and quietness. Divine love pours over us and our spiritual senses are awakened. We can have no agenda in this state of stillness.

Many contemplatives feel that to try and hold onto any vision or spiritual delight in this state of prayer will only lead to distraction. I agree to some extent, but it is pointless to listen to God, then reject what He is saying to you. When I am entering into deep prayer, I have found that it is best to let God do the talking; listen to the vision; and then not hold on too tightly to what I've heard in a way that prevents me from going deeper. We can idolize the revelations we receive in the lower states of prayer. Sometimes, we have to sacrifice second heaven revelation, in order to arrive in the third heavens.

The third phase of the contemplative journey is sometimes called spiritual *ecstasy*. It is scripturally known as a *trance*, or pure contemplation, and it is a place in which one is caught up in the Spirit into heavenly realms of interaction with God. This is not a practice that you can initiate, but something that God does to you. It is not a common occurrence, and many mystics referred to it as the "gift of contemplation" because of its rarity. It is often a fleeting experience, but those who grew to enter it regularly, would sometimes be caught up into heaven for hours or days at a time. Those who entered deeply into divine ecstasy could often not be shaken back into natural consciousness very easily by other people. Those who have experienced it speak of the utter delight, joy, and pleasure of God that is inexpressible in human terms.

Believers are not called to seek out ecstasies, experiences, and manifestations. But as we pursue intimacy with God, these are welcome gifts and byproducts. Like 14th century mystic Walter Hilton, I do not claim to have the grace of contemplation "in feeling and in working, as I have it in talking." But from what experience I have, I can say that when one is soaking in God's presence, he is rarely concerned with whether he has entered into this or that state of prayer. We are just there to enjoy the goodness of God. Our aim is simply to be with Him. He is the delight of our soul. It is His love that is both the goal and the pathway of prayer.

EMERGING

Churches are seeking to explore how the Christian faith will reconfigure in the postmodern matrix. There becomes a discontinuity in our religious forms, which, though providing stability in good times, are unable to offer adequate explanations when life is not going well. Those who learn to "let go" will eventually become disembedded, moving into a transition area which the Lord intends. This state of spiritual limbo is rarely comfortable. Many mistake this God-inspired disconnect from the insupportable religious system to be a personal abandonment of their faith. They can't seem to see God, or feel God anymore.

During this transition, we want to deconstruct and reconstruct our spiritual walk, based upon our experience and knowledge. We may flounder and give up hope. However, the deeper vein of the Spirit is to allow God to deconstruct our systems, and then to allow God to reconstruct our walk.

Unless the Lord builds the house, its builders labor in vain (Psalm 127:1).

This is why the waiting and patience of contemplative prayer are so critical. It all sounds easy and polished, but in the shadowy throes of the dark night, it is rarely clear who is at work—God or myself—or whether any particular work (internal or external) is for the good or for the bad. We get confused. Shouting at the dark. Sometimes we find ourselves rebuking a voice, just to find out it was really God. But an active and living faith will always be marked by paradigm shifts, in which our existing framework of faith is constantly challenged. No true progress can be attained without opposition—we have to swim against streams. Only *living* fish swim against the current.

Our faith is best stretched and grown, when we are challenged to step into areas that are seemingly contradictory to that faith. Think of when the Lord challenged Ezekiel and Peter to eat those things which they deemed "unclean." There are always going to be gray areas of conscience, in which we are uncertain whether we are stepping into the waters of apostasy and compromise, or the river of God. But this is the walk of the one who follows the Lord—we are often called to walk a fine line between light and darkness.

On the surface, a higher level of faith will very often appear heretical. And what looks holy can often be deceiving. Hence Christ's constant challenges with the religious men of His day:

> *Woe to you, teachers of the law and Pharisees, you hypocrites! You clean the outside of the cup and dish, but inside they are full of greed and self indulgence. Blind Pharisee! First clean the inside of the cup and dish, and then the outside also will be clean* (Matthew 23:25-26).

There is a thin line between advancement into deeper levels of the Kingdom of God, and utterly falling away. It is commonly said that the believer is either moving forward or falling backward, but never standing still. We are constantly in spiritual warfare and flux. At the point of military engagement, there are really only two options—to be victorious, or to be defeated. There is no in-between;

there are no treaties with hell. We see in the cross that victory some-times looks like defeat. But in the end, death loses its sting.

Christian music pioneer Keith Green said he always liked it when his picture of God was turned upside down. That is the only way our vision can grow. Unless the idol of our tiny perspective of Jesus is laid on the altar, there is never room for the real Jesus to enter the room. If the real Jesus had to die to give us life, how much more should our limited perceptions of Jesus be put to death? Even the good things must find their death on the cross. The good must be put aside to make way for the best—which is God Himself. This is the path from glory to glory. This is the path from the outskirts of God's heart, to the very center of His true nature.

DARK NIGHT OF THE SOUL

One dark night,
fired with love's urgent longings
- ah, the sheer grace! -
I went out unseen,
my house being now all stilled.

In darkness, and secure,
by the secret ladder, disguised,
- ah, the sheer grace! -
in darkness and concealment,
my house being now all stilled.

— *St. John of the Cross*

There are only two books I can remember ever throwing across the room. One of them was *Dark Night of the Soul*, by St. John of the Cross.

I recall the day I bought his collected works at a monastery bookstore. Mostly, *Dark Night* sat on the floor of my bedroom. I can still remember the white, torn edge of an envelope that I had used as a book mark, and the way it would stay tucked into the same page of the book for weeks, until I was broken down enough with anguish to finally open it again. It was a time of purging for me, and I did not want to believe God was behind it—that God worked that way.

Among contemplative Christianity is a stream of *dark mysticism*. Understand that this is a holy darkness. It is a purgative, refining purification process which leads the soul to a deeper illumination and unity with God. A basic understanding of this is needed as a prerequisite for every aspiring contemplative or mystic. Anyone who has a prophetic call on his life will be crushed and broken. It requires great sacrifice, and we are often purged accordingly to our calling. As for this dark night, it varies in degrees of intensity. It may come all at once or in seasons. It could last for any given period of time. But it is a season of utter crushing in which a man is called to step out of himself, away from his carnal desires and appetites, and thereby embrace a closer communion with God.

We learn that God actually *woos* us into this place of darkness "fired with love's urgent longings."

There is often an outer trial or tribulation involved in the life of the one going through the dark night, but more often than not, it is the internal testing that is most difficult. It is a dry and arid place for us spiritually, from which many will turn back. We rarely see that it is actually the Lord who is tenderly calling us out of the window into a deeper place of intimacy with Him. In fact, we feel abandoned by God in this place. It is the place of utmost loneliness, and without God's grace, it would be a place of utter despair. We are usually unaware even of His grace in that hour. It is not until afterward that we often realize the great benefit of this night. During it, we abandon the natural supports of the soul that no longer satisfy the spiritual hunger that is kindled within us. Our house of our soul becomes stilled.

> On that glad night,
> in secret, for no one saw me,

nor did I look at anything,
with no other light or guide
than the one that burned in my heart.

This guided me
more surely than the light of noon
to where He was awaiting me
-Him I knew so well-
there in a place where no one appeared.

Anyone who is called to pursue a life of abandoned devotion to God must be prepared to have their understanding of Him totally wrecked. And there is a season of entombment, between losing our vision and having our vision resurrected. Such a person will first experience the feelings of utmost neglect by God. This isolation will often continue until the soul can see through it and enter an awareness of God at all times. Such a one must be willing to be completely raked over the coals of suffering and broken to pieces. I love the Jabez prayer—Lord bless me, bless me—but any theology that denies the reality of suffering is not a Christian theology. The cross is a bloody, painful, agonizing thing, and Christians are called to carry crosses.

"God prepares a cross for you that you must embrace without a thought of self-preservation. The cross is painful. Accept the cross and you will find peace even in the middle of turmoil. Let me warn you that if you push the cross away, your circumstances will become twice as hard to bear. In the long run, the pain of resisting the cross is harder to live with than the cross itself," writes 17th century mystic Francois Fenelon in *The Seeking Heart*. "See God's hand in the circumstances of your life. Do you want to experience true happiness? Submit yourself peacefully and simply to the will of God, and bear your sufferings without struggle. Nothing so shortens and soothes your pain as the spirit of non-resistance to your Lord."

For me, the dark night came in waves over a period of 10 years. And the Lord thankfully told me how long it would take beforehand.

For some it is less, for some it is more. For the apostle Paul, it was also 10 years. Fellow believers hauled him off to Tarsus after his conversion for a long season of preparation, and the Scriptures say the church "enjoyed a time of peace" (Acts 9:31). Paul caused tremendous havoc trying to minister before the Lord had time to work him over. The dark night, to some degree, is a necessary process for those who will be the Lord's ministers. But it should be approached as an invitation of honor, not as a dreaded thing. The Lord will still use you during this period—He did with Paul. He did with me. But your full fruitfulness comes after He has sent you through the wringer, emptied you out, and filled you with Himself.

Teresa of Avila, in her mystical writings, defines the soul's purging process as a seven-level progression. With each level, there are ups and downs as we lay aside our life and take up the life of Christ. There are intervals, in which the presence of God returns in ever amplified proportions, because the soul is more refined to experience Him. Then on the sixth level, she says, there are no more ups—it's all a downward spiral. It is as if we cannot see the light at the end of the tunnel. That is the dark night. All downward. Finally, at the seventh stage, the soul has acquired a peaceful submission and rest in the presence of God.

These are good concepts to understand, to know suffering is a part of our walk and that it reflects God's discipline of us as sons, not His rejection of us. However, I don't think there are any sure-fire, seven-step formulas for becoming sanctified. Throughout our lives, we are all in a continual process of growth until the day we die. And as we have mentioned, Christian mysticism is not a matter of the human soul trying to ascend to God (though one will find a little of that bent in any Christian tradition). This is impossible—the very reason for the cross is our inability to access heaven in our own strength and power. It is Jehovah M'Kaddesh, "The Lord Who Sanctifies," that is doing the purging work. We simply submit and agree with Him in the process.

In fact, this is the very reason for the dark night—to strip us of our own attempts and abilities to reach God on our own human strength.

While I understood the need to purge the appetites of the flesh, I did not fully grasp the depth to which the soul must be purged: mind, will, and emotions, not just of *bad* things, but also good things to which it becomes attached. And not only are we called to detach from good things. There is a very real dynamic where we have to detach from *God things*. Our perception and the way we experience God can become a thing of idolatry at times, and He has to break our shadowy concepts and inner experience of Him, in order to take us to a higher level. And let me say this: it is almost a guarantee that while we are being broken, we will not be able to see or comprehend the new level of glory to which we are being taken until we get there.

"The ordinary way to contemplation lies through a desert without trees and without beauty and without water. The spirit enters a wilderness and travels blindly in directions that seem to lead away from vision, away from God, away from all fulfillment and joy," writes Thomas Merton.[6] "It may become almost impossible to believe that this road goes anywhere at all except to a desolation full of dry bones—the ruin of all our hopes and good intentions."

O guiding night!
O night more lovely than the dawn!
O night that has united
the Lover with His beloved,
transforming the beloved in her Lover.

Upon my flowering breast
which I kept wholly for Him alone,
there He lay sleeping,
and I caressing Him
there in a breeze from the fanning cedars.

Within the dark night, we are making a place for the Lord in our hearts. We begin to realize that the refining fire of the Lord is actually a *good* thing, and as crazy as it sounds, we begin to desire death to self, because we are gradually learning to desire Jesus more. As those things we once relied upon give way beneath us, the only constant absolute we have left to cling onto is the refining fire itself. The soul begins to embrace the night. It embraces the cross. As the spirit man is called out to walk alone with God, apart from the senses, we find that the senses were never really capable of providing pleasure or fulfillment in the first place. Throughout this process, there is often a feeling of frustration, because our faculties seem no longer able even to pursue God.

The human pursuit of God will be burned out of us—and then we feel utterly helpless, afraid we are doing something wrong or that we are completely lost. The old way of doing things religiously for God doesn't work anymore. We see whole new levels of cleansing that are needed within us. It is then that the Lord begins to infuse us with His own divine hunger that supercedes our frail human ability to love God. Our own efforts to draw near to Him must be fully stripped away and replaced. But almost as soon as we depart from the futility of the senses, they are reawakened with a resurrected intensity and a heightened vision of holy love. Usually, the one being purged is not aware of the "stages" through which he is being led until he has actually arrived at that state of deeper union. He just knows, during the process, that he feels distant from God in a state of limbo and restlessness. It is this suspension of the senses that most defines the dark night.

For those willing to go into these realms "no matter how much they suffer perplexity and uneasiness in the wilderness where God begins to lead them, still feel drawn further and further on into the wasteland. They cannot think, they cannot meditate; their imagination tortures them with everything they do not want to see; their life of prayer is without light and without pleasure and without any feeling of devotion," writes Merton.[7] "On the other hand they sense, by a kind of instinct, that peace lies in the heart of this darkness.

Something prompts them to keep still, to trust in God, to be quiet and listen for His voice; to be patient and not to get excited."

When the breeze blew from the turret,
as I parted His hair,
it wounded my neck
with its gentle hand,
suspending all my senses.

I abandoned and forgot myself,
laying my face on my Beloved;
all things ceased; I went out from myself,
leaving my cares
forgotten among the lilies.

The ultimate end of the dark night is not when we have quenched our own sinful appetites. The end is when we are simply no longer aware of ourselves, and fully aware of God. The goal is intimacy. We have become so deprived of any earthly satisfaction, that the love of God alone is what "guides and moves her, and makes her soar to God in an unknown way along the road of solitude," says St. John. We see that *Beauty* has been with us all along. It is for intimacy that we climb out of the window of ourselves and enter the dark night. And it is for intimacy that the Lord pierces us and breaks us, to draw us into Himself.

The dark night is that place we enter, like the Beloved in Song of Solomon, who searches the streets and dark alleyways for her Lover. "All night long on my bed I looked for the one my heart loves; I looked for Him but did not find Him. I will get up now and go about the city, through its streets and squares; I will search for the one my heart loves, so I looked for Him but did not find Him" (Song of Sol. 3:1-2).

Yet, by the end of the Song, we discover that "love is stronger than death," and that even the darkness is as light to Him.

*A preserved drawing by
St. John of the Cross*

St. John of the Cross (1542-1591) whose stanzas you have been reading, was a Spanish Roman Catholic reformer and mystic, whose influence on Christian mysticism has perhaps been greater than any other since his day. He was the most renowned of the dark mystics. As a Carmelite monk and priest, he was influenced by St. Teresa of Avila, and began a reform within his own monastic order. There was resistance to this new move of God, and John was imprisoned for a year in Toledo, where he was brutally treated with weekly public lashings and kept in a very small, isolated room. It was during this time of suffering and imprisonment that he began writing and reflecting on his spiritual journey. After his escape, he continued to write and found monasteries until his death.

Let me say that most Christians are unwilling to go through the burning sands of these spiritual deserts which John and many other mystics describe. But the paradox is that the mystics are really chasing the intense, fiery presence of the Lord that drives them like a heroine junkie for a fix. One of the reasons prophetic people get stuck, is because they begin to idolize the revelatory level they have attained. Our human perception of God must be allowed to die like a seed, falling to the earth.

John Sandford poses the scenario quite clearly. When Jesus gave His life for us on the cross, what was this life that He gave? What was the single source of His living? The life of Jesus, notes Sandford, was His very relationship with the Father. It was on the cross that the words were echoed "Eloi, Eloi, lama sabachthani?"—which means, "My God, My God, why have You forsaken Me?" (Mark 15:34) Jesus obediently died to His very relationship with God the Father, so that it would, in turn, be made even better. This is a very hard concept to grasp—how Jesus became sin for us, so that we could be reconciled with God. Consequently, the Father had to turn His face from Him. In the same way, we are called to progressively lay down our own spirituality in a sense, to advance as Christians. Of course, we are never forsaken by God—and we cannot fully enter into that place of burden bearing that Jesus did. In speaking of this inner crucifixion of our spiritual life, we should guard ourselves so that the age old tide of pietism does not draw us to an unhealthy reverence over death.

INTO THE MORNING

Of course, we did not discuss gnosticism and extreme self-denial by chance in earlier chapters. Reading the mystics, especially the darker ones, must be balanced with a strong understanding of grace—which was not a heavy theological concept for many in their era. Many enter unhealthy ascetic lifestyles and reject normal, natural desires in a religious, Augustinian way. Despondency and outright depression needlessly will follow, and are sometimes glorified. But depression is only a counterfeit for true contemplation.

We should never *look* for suffering. That is downright masochistic. But we gladly embrace what comes our way if it draws us closer to the Lord. Remember that Jesus was led into the desert. It is not something we try to bring on or conjure up. We seek God, and sometimes deserts come. We need not panic. The Lord calls us, for the most part to prosper, not suffer. Even Job's sufferings were one tiny sliver of a very long life of prosperity, health, blessing, and anointing—one year of his life, and he lived 210 years. Our attitude should be like his, "Though You slay me, yet I will trust in You" (Job 13:15). Yes, the Lord refines us, but only in seasons. And out of it comes tremendous resurrection power. Like the children of Israel, the desert changes you from a slave into a warrior. Notice here that, as with any righteous lamentation, Job's prayer contains the word "though," as well as "yet." He does not deny the negative circumstance, but neither does he stay there. Though we accept the present state of reality, yet we contend for a greater reality.

We do not wallow into depression, nor do we attempt self-masochism to speed up the dark night process. We embrace the fire when He brings it, but we shouldn't try to kill ourselves. Jesus *endured* the cross. That is, He put up with it for a greater cause, but He did not self-inflict it. He calls us foremost to love and joy and prosperity—and such things are the very purpose for refinement, inasmuch as they are grace extensions/fruits of Himself. We should not overly focus on death, even death to self. We shouldn't try too hard. Many of the darker mystics opened themselves to demonic attack—even physical, outward assaults, and demonic beatings—which, in retrospect were probably avoidable with a stronger framework of grace and the Father's love. We live in an exciting time, in which we can recover the wells of pure mystical experience dug out by the Christian mystics, yet we also have 500 years of solid, post-Reformation teachings on grace so that we don't go overboard. For too long, we've let the devil beat us up because of our religious striving. Prophetic teacher Graham Cooke notes that, "The cross can be a source of joy and pleasure. It doesn't always have to be a place of suffering and pain." We must remember that Jesus endured the cross *for the joy set before Him*. The Lord once spoke to Cooke, saying, "Graham, please understand there are times I want you to die laughingly."

This improper perspective of self-denial is the main problem with the dark mystics, which we can learn to avoid. Nevertheless, even the dark mystics have their place in formulating a full theology. We would do well to revisit many of their principles today. One thing you've got to admit about these guys: They would do anything for more of Jesus in their lives. Some are afraid to press into the heroes of the faith in the Dark Ages because there are so many pitfalls, heresies, and weirdness to contend with. However, the Dark Ages and the church's darkest hours have only been the backdrop of nighttime sky, upon which the Lord is about to illuminate with the lightnings and the fireworks of heaven. The night season is a canvas which will be broken open with Renaissance and light. Unless a seed falls to the earth and dies, it bears no fruit. Much that was sown in the Dark Ages, though it was sometimes sown in ignorance, is about to blossom into a heavenly dawn in this hour. What we thought was church history's shadowy closet, will actually be opened to display hidden treasure.

BLOSSOMING THE WASTELANDS

We can always be assured that when we are led into a desert, it is in order to bring us to a place of abundance and resurrection life. We are drawn into deserts, in order to make them blossom. This is the very essence of restoration and is charted out in Isaiah 35:

> *The desert and the parched land will be glad; the wilderness will rejoice and blossom. Like the crocus, it will burst into bloom; it will rejoice greatly and shout for joy. The glory of Lebanon will be given to it, the splendor of Carmel and Sharon; they will see the glory of the Lord, the splendor of our God* (Isaiah 35:1-2).

The purpose of the dark night, of the refining fire, is to strip us down to sheer faith. We have no comfort or feeling to rely upon, only blind trust in the faithfulness of God. We learn to wait on Him. I learn to know that He is not only waiting for me on the other side, but He is in the furnace here with me. Even though I do not see Him, even though I do not know where I am or where I am going, even though I seem lost in the shadow of death, I learn to trust in God. I learn to lay aside fear.

> *Strengthen the feeble hands, steady the knees that give way; say to those with fearful hearts, "Be strong, do not fear; your God will come, He will come with vengeance; with divine retribution He will come to save you"* (Isaiah 35:3-4).

I learn to strengthen myself in this place. I get outside of myself by learning to strengthen others, even though I myself am in a desert. I become confident enough in God's care that I spend myself caring for others. When we have arrived at this state of trust, this state of faith, that no longer fears the outcome, then the desert no longer has power over us. Even as Jesus came forth from the desert in great power, so do we come forth from our dry places in great power when we have let the testing flames run their course.

Then will the eyes of the blind be opened and the ears of the deaf unstopped. Then will the lame leap like a deer, and the mute tongue shout for joy. Water will gush forth in the wilderness and streams in the desert. The burning sand will become a pool, the thirsty ground bubbling springs. In the haunts where jackals once lay, grass and reeds and papyrus will grow (Isaiah 35:5-7).

This is a place of revelation, healing, deliverance and renewal. It is also a place where joy is restored. Not just a little bit, but leaping, shouting joy. In whatever way I died to self, I have gained the authority to minister in that area and obtained the power to set others free. My level of spiritual authority is only as great as the extent to which God has increased and I have decreased. Wherever this has been accomplished, a stream has been opened that will water the dry places. Those places which were barren wilderness will become a well traveled highway for the redeemed.

And a highway will be there; it will be called the Way of Holiness. The unclean will not journey on it; it will be for those who walk in that Way; wicked fools will not go about on it. No lion will be there, nor will any ferocious beast get up on it; they will not be found there. But only the redeemed will walk there, and the ransomed of the Lord will return. They will enter Zion with singing; everlasting joy will crown their heads. Gladness and joy will overtake them, and sorrow and sighing will flee away (Isaiah 35:8-10).

The Lord brings us into the desert, so that we learn to lean on Him through it. "Who is this coming up from the desert leaning on her Lover?" (Song of Sol. 8:5). It is the Bride. The pure Bride. Stripped away of every hindrance to love. She has entered a state of supernatural rest and power. She has entered into intimate union.

This is the path of the pioneer. This is the walk of the forerunner.

ENDNOTES

1. "God's Trouble Maker." (Jesus Army/Jesus Fellowship Church). Accessed 13 Oct. 2004 <http://www.jesus.org.uk/ja/mag_revivalfires_fox.shtml>. Article source: Vipont, E. George Fox and the Valiant Sixty (London: Hamish Hamilton, 1975).

2. Brother Lawrence, *The Practice of the Presence of God* (New Kinsington: Whitaker House, 1982 ed.), 37.

3. Ibid., 29-30

4. Todd Bentley, "Secret Place 2," conference audio recording (January, 2004).

5. C.S. Lewis, *A Grief Observed* (San Francisco: Harper, 2001).

6. Lawrence, *The Practice of the Presence of God*, 38.

7. Thomas Merton, *Seeds of Contemplation* (New York: New Directions Publishing, 1986 ed.), 153.

8. Ibid., 155-156.

CHAPTER 10

Joel's Army

Out of the dry, desert sands the Lord is raising up an exceedingly great army. Some saw it coming before the days of Christ. Great men of faith predicted it through the centuries. And now, for more than 50 years, countless prophetic voices have been heralding a massive outpouring of God's Spirit that will impact an entire generation. What is coming has no precedent in human history. It will be a cataclysmic release from Heaven to earth. On Pentecost, Peter spoke of this end-time spiritual army as he recited the words of Joel:

> *In the last days, God says, I will pour out My Spirit on all people. Your sons and daughters will prophesy, your young men will see visions, your old men will dream dreams. Even on My servants, both men and women, I will pour out My Spirit in those days and they will prophesy* (Acts 2:17-18; Joel 2:28-29).

This is Joel's army, reserved for the end-time harvest. Earlier we noted Psalm 110:3, wherein we see that in the day of God's power, His troops will volunteer willingly. Christianity itself will be radically altered in a single generation.

"During this generation, the kinds of powerful displays of the miraculous released through Moses and those witnessed through the apostles will be combined and multiplied on a global dimension. The combination of miracles that affect the natural order in the earth and miracles that restore individual lives will affect the entire world," writes Mike Bickle in *The Pleasures of Loving God.* "I personally believe we are in the early days of this final generation."[1]

While it may not outwardly appear that we are on the threshold of a supernatural generation, Bickle points to the lull before the storm in the days of Moses.

"It looked like business as usual during Moses' fortieth year in the wilderness tending sheep. I'll bet Moses never dreamed that he was about to operate in the power of God in a way that would cripple an empire," says Bickle.[2]

We will see mass healings and salvation like no revival has ever before experienced. There will be unprecedented guidance and intimacy with the Lord. We will finally see the fulfillment of Jesus' words in John 14:12, "greater works than these, you shall do."

"There will be not only individuals, but an entire generation that will step into that anointing. Into that realm of authority on planet earth in the preaching and demonstration of power," says Bill Johnson.[3] "Jesus wants to end this thing on a high note, not a low note. I'm a little bit nauseated by the idea of getting rescued."

We hear of this end-time generation in Matthew 24, when Jesus says "this gospel of the Kingdom will be preached in the whole world as a testimony to all nations, and then the end will come." We know that the gospel of the Kingdom is more than just a salvation message. And it is followed by signs and wonders when it is preached—healing the sick, casting out devils, and raising the dead. This will be demonstrated throughout the earth before the end will come.

Several major prophetic voices have said that modern stadiums were actually built not for sporting events, but God intended them to ultimately hold crowds gathered for worship during this cataclysmic outpouring. Already this has happened for decades in major crusades throughout the world, but at the height of revival, these meetings will last day and night without ceasing.

"No prophet or apostle who ever lived equaled the power of these individuals in this great army of the Lord in these last days. No one ever had it, not even Elijah or Peter or Paul. No one else enjoyed the power that is going to rest on this army," said the prophet Bob Jones, who has been telling of this army since the 1970s.[4]

In a prophetic experience, nationally recognized speaker Bobby Conner told me he was shown many people checking their mail boxes to find a letter of induction into Joel's Army. Conner believes that the massive, intercessory youth assemblies that have begun to sweep the nation, such as *The Call* have been critical in activating this young army, which is now being called and commissioned.

Bob Jones has also seen reams of draft notices for this army in the Spirit. In a vision, other forerunners throughout biblical times and church history were looking for the keys to this revival in the sand. After those great men came up empty, Bob was told to put his own hands into the sand. Bob did not think he would find anything either, but he uncovered literally millions of draft notices for God's end-time army. "He is sending them out now!" the angel of the Lord told Bob, "God has saved the best of every blood line until now."

Along with Joel's message of young people prophesying and seeing visions, many believe this worldwide revival will largely be carried by youth. Many of the movers and shakers in this revival will be young children who hear the word of the Lord like Samuel, at 10 and 11 years old and younger. At an early age they will heal the sick, cast out evil spirits, and prophesy. My own daughter was prophesying, speaking in tongues, and seeing into Heaven at age 5; my 3-year-old son sees angels; and my 1-year-old daughter has already learned to lay her hands on people to pray in tongues, although she can barely speak any English yet. Children will have eyes to see the Kingdom, and in many ways they will lead us.

"What will Joel's Army accomplish? Mighty signs and wonders on a level not experienced in our life time. These will not be so called big shots; these will be ordinary everyday men and women, boys and girls with an awesome anointing of God's presence and power upon their life. Expect to see great and mighty displays and demonstrations of God's power," says Conner.[5]

SIGNS AND WONDERS

This move will be highlighted by the same specific signs and wonders demonstrated by Moses and Elijah. This will be a generation that literally can call down fire. Like Elijah, they will have power to order the sky to stop raining at their word. But their hearts will be established in intimacy and compassion before God will ever entrust them with the authority to speak forth His judgments. The spirit of the church in that age will be as the two witnesses in Zechariah 4 and Revelation 11, the sons of golden oil, walking in the spirit and power of Moses and Elijah, who represent the Word and the Spirit of God.

This may sound harsh, but when we realize that God's judgments are only given to eradicate every hindrance to love, we welcome them. Joel 2:17 shows us that this will be a weeping army, as the ministers of the Lord cry out in intercession for God to spare the people. Their primary job description will be this: Out of intimacy, destroy the works of the devil.

The Pentecost passage reveals the restoration of Mosaic signs by describing the same kinds of miracles displayed to bring the children of Israel out of Egypt.

> *I will show wonders in the heaven above and signs on the earth below, blood and fire and billows of smoke. The sun will be turned to darkness and the moon to blood before the coming of the great and glorious day of the Lord. And everyone who calls on the name of the Lord will be saved* (Acts 2:19-21; Joel 2:30-32).

Again, we are reaffirmed of God's intent to restore Mosaic signs and wonders in the last days through the writings of the prophet Micah:

> *As in the days when you came out of the land of*
> *Egypt, I will show them wonders; the nations shall see and*
> *be ashamed of their might; they shall put their hand over*
> *their mouth; their ears shall be deaf. They shall lick the*
> *dust like a serpent; they shall crawl from their holes like*
> *snakes of the earth. They shall be afraid of the Lord our*
> *God, and shall fear because of You* (Micah 7:15-17).

What will these people look like who actually do this stuff? Many of these guys will be absolute freaks. And I hope I am hanging out with them. By appearance, they may be no different than your next door neighbor.

But the ultimate focus of this last generation will resemble that of Moses far less than it does Joshua. While Moses' work was that of deliverance and of a pastoral administrator—guiding, organizing, and teaching the nation as it plodded slowly through the desert— the Joshua generation will be different. Its eyes will be set not on escaping Egypt, but on conquering the Promise Land. They will not be escapists; they will be spiritual conquerors. They will not be on the defense; they will be on the offense—and the gates of hell will not be able to hold up against them.

"As a prophet, except for the Lord Jesus Himself, Moses was without peer in giving the oracles of God to His people. ...In these things Joshua could not compare to Moses, but Joshua had a different purpose. His purpose was to help Israel possess its inheritance," writes Rick Joyner.[6] Joyner says that leaders throughout the church age, like Moses, have been effective in helping us to walk in the ways of God, in order to cross this "great, nearly two thousand year wilderness. However, there is a new leadership about to arise that is not here to lay those foundations again, but they are here to lead God's people into their inheritance. The church must have a fundamentally different kind of leader to take it into the promised land."

Joyner notes that this Joshua generation will not be composed of administrators, but instead will be a company of generals and warriors. He says that, as we near the end of the church age, we will stop trying to emulate the first century church, but will focus on preparing today's church for her purposes.

"We are coming to the time when we will see authentic apostles, prophets, evangelists, pastors and teachers, like they have not really been seen since the first century. Then they will go to even new heights of effectiveness. This is not necessarily because they are greater leaders than the first century apostles, but because this is not the church coming out of Egypt, but the one coming out of the wilderness ready to conquer its inheritance," writes Joyner.[7]

UPRISING

Now is not the time to hesitate. We must advance. Satan has sought to oppose this army even before its birth. Today, you can type "Joel's Army" into a search engine and a thousand heresy hunter Websites pop up, decrying the very mention of it. Religious spirits despise the fierce aggression with which this army will take ground, and the enemy would seek even now to keep us back from this destiny. But no weapon formed against us will prosper. The Kingdom will be clearly demonstrated with signs and wonders in the name of Jesus. We will not need to defend this move of God. We will simply need to move out of the way and join the Lord's ranks.

The Lord thunders at the head of His army; His forces are beyond number, and mighty are those who obey His command (Joel 2:11).

That which is coming borders on fantasy, so let us first cultivate our own hearts, that we do not disqualify ourselves from this army through unbelief. Understand that this army will be mighty, and in fact, will operate in the Spirit of Might (Isa. 11:2). This army is fearful and will strike dread in the nations. Joel compares them to locusts, devouring gardens and turning them into wastelands. A fire goes before them and behind them. The earth shakes and the sky trembles before them. But this is not a wicked army, as some have thought. We want to be among those radical, militant believers who will hate sin. The power of this army will not be in military or political strength—but it is a spiritual army whose weapons are love and righteousness, prayer and fasting, demonstrating God's power through miracles, signs, and wonders.

> *For the weapons of our warfare are not carnal, but mighty through God to the pulling down of strongholds. ... We are destroying speculations and every lofty thing raised up against the knowledge of God, and we are taking every thought captive to the obedience of Christ* (2 Corinthians 10:4-5).

"When this army comes, it is large and it's mighty. It's so mighty that there's never been anything like it before ... they won't be able to kill this army," says respected author and prophetic teacher Jack Deere. Not only does Joel say this army is invincible. The Lord Himself will take the lives of those who oppose them.

"Those in this army will have the kind of anointing...His kind of power...anyone who wants to harm them must die," said John Wimber, founder of the Vineyard movement. The Lord Himself will be our shield, and we never need to defend ourselves. Joel 3 says that God will gather all nations and wake up the *men of war*— destroying wickedness with a *roar from Zion*. Many have prophesied this great outpouring at the end of the age. Many have seen this emerging army in the Spirit. The Latter Rain revivalists of the '40s and '50s thought they were already walking in this last day army— and in fact, they were tasting its beginnings.

Lonnie Frisbee, the prophetic hippie evangelist we discussed earlier, also believed that the outpouring of the Holy Spirit of Joel's prophecy was a precursor to the Lord's return. He said that Joel's prophecy placed youth "on the vanguard of the spiritual revolution," and even thought the Jesus People were fulfilling much of this in the '60s and '70s.

"At Christ's second coming the church will be found with the same power that the apostles and the early church possessed. The power of Pentecost is manifest in us. The Christian religion must be demonstrated. The world wants to be shown. Then let God's power be manifest through us," said Pentecostal pioneer Charles Parham at the birth of that movement nearly a century ago.[8] Parham only reiterated what many others believed in his day, that the church would see true apostolic faith, signs, and wonders before the end of the age. Even a prophecy from 1679 predicted the coming of such a generation. It states:

> The most prophetical generation, will the Most High raise up who shall deliver His people by the force of spiritual arms; for which there must be raised up certain head powers to bear the first office, who are to be persons in favour with God whose dread and fear shall fall on all nations visible and invisible, because of the mighty acting power of the Holy Spirit which shall rest upon them. For Christ will appear in some chosen vessels to bring into the Promised Land the New Creation state.

The Lord has been preparing us for this outpouring in various stages. We could trace revivals and movements until we are blue in the face. But the recent move of God has been simple: out of a restoration of true, intimate worship in the church has come the prophetic movement. Intimacy brings hearing. And this restored ability to hear the Lord is now releasing a healing, signs, and wonders revival that will bring in the end-time harvest. Hearing brings miracles. Miracles bring in souls.

PURITY BRINGS VICTORY

We must carefully guard the vision for this great move of God. At the time of this writing, a very sobering development occurred, as one of the most gifted prophets of the nation was confronted on serious personal sin issues and for some time remained unrepentant. Because of the freshness of the development, I will not mention him by name. But it came as a shock and a wakeup call to the church. His prophetic gifting was proven and intense, beyond where most of us could ever dream to go. He has predicted earth-quakes and other major events. He operated in nearly 100 percent accuracy with words of knowledge, and received numerous visita-tions from angels and even Jesus Himself. This prophet also had impeccable character, humility, and purity in his life leading up to this point. For such a man to stumble into delusion should send the fear of God into all of us, to be careful lest we fall. No matter what our level of gifting or experience, sin is always at the door, and we are never above backsliding except by the grace of God. We must remain pliable.

I bring this up for several reasons. I had intended to list this great prophet's life in this chapter as one of the new mystics of our day, prior to hearing this tragic news. I am believing for his full restoration, and I look forward to the present situation becoming a testimony to God's grace in the end. But I want to point out that this man was one of the clearest visionaries to herald Joel's Army in the church today. While this will be a nameless, faceless army, there will still be leaders—and the enemy wants to pick them off in any way he can.

This is truly warfare. This battle is not a game. Satan hates God's army, and he has sought to destroy it from the onset. He has seen a new breed of deliverers and champions on the rise, and he has even tried to kill them from birth. In the days of Moses and Jesus, a satan-ic decree was released to kill all newly born children, because the enemy could see that the heavens were being aligned for a mighty move of God in their generation. When abortion was legalized in the 1970s, it was an overt attempt by the enemy to stop this Joel's Army generation. Everyone born after abortion's legalization can consider their birth a personal invitation to take part in this great army. The enemy has sought to rob us of that destiny. If satan cannot kill us outright, he will seek to bring temptation and compromise to strip us of power.

The aforementioned prophet had experienced open visions of Joel's Army more than 100 times over the past few decades and was being mightily used by the Lord to rally the troops. He regularly saw a vision of a TV anchorman saying, "There are no sporting events to report tonight because all the stadiums, ball parks, and arenas are being used for large revival meetings and are filled with people crying, 'Jesus is Lord, Jesus is Lord.'" This vision was repeated for years, until one day he finally saw the real, live anchorman on TV that he had always known from the vision. The time is surely drawing near. Those he saw ministering in the stadiums would heal the sick and preach for three days and nights without food, water, or change of clothes. The vision was always marked by a large billboard at a crossroads saying "Joel's army now in training."

This was not an immature prophet with shallow character. He not only moved in power and maturity, but was a spokesman for purity. He had deep roots, even operating as a major healing evangelist in the powerful Voice of Healing Revival at age 18 in 1947, working with the greats like William Branham and seeing thousands of healings, salvations, signs, and wonders. He was even obedient to the Lord at the height of his ministry, laying it down and going into seclusion at the Lord's command. In doing so, he watched from the sidelines as other revivalists were crippled by the sin and excesses of sex, money, and power that eventually squelched that revival and brought down many ministries of that era. But he, himself, was preserved from that corruption. We will read about that revival later in great detail and see how it was a prototype of the coming Joel's Army. I have even seen old newspaper ads from the healing revival era with the words "Joel's Army" emblazed across them. In all that we learn from that generation, let us not forget that our own purity and holiness must exceed even theirs. Jesus told us that our righteousness must exceed even that of the Pharisees—the legalistic religious order of His day. This can only happen through deep, inward passion for the Lord. Our level of victory is measured by our purity, and our purity will only come through intimacy with the Lord.

With all the talk about miracles, I want to be clear that the biggest miracle of all is to carry the anointing for repentance. There is clearly an *anointing* that brings repentance that no volume of empty arguments or loud preaching can conjure up. The prophet

Jonah took a whole city without mention of one miracle. John the Baptist had no miracles accorded to his work, yet he had a nation's ear. I do not believe that every believer will be walking on water, but we will all carry the flame of repentance.

The church of Acts was a church that walked in the fear of the Lord, and that was a source of great power. With Ananias and Sapphira dropping dead in their midst for lying to the Holy Spirit, it is no doubt that *"fear came upon every soul."* (Acts 2:43).

Charles Finney
(Photo c.1883)

Charles Finney (1792-1875) is one of the greatest examples of fiery holiness and purity we can learn from in our day. He, perhaps more than any other public figure in past 150 years, carried a terrifying mantle of the *Spirit of the fear of the Lord*, one of the sevenfold persons of the Spirit of God seen in Isaiah 11. The very presence of Charles Finney would cause complete strangers to weep and repent, before he spoke a single word. This is a tangible anointing that is coming back on the church in our day, where people will be gripped with conviction just by coming into contact with the air around you.

Smith Wigglesworth had some measure of this anointing. He was once walking into a train carriage when a man simply looked at him and said, "Sir, you convict me of sin." But if Wigglesworth tasted this anointing, Finney swam in it. Finney once walked into a cotton mill and just stood there silently. He carried the fear of the Lord so intensely on his physical body, that all of the mill workers became swept with it, and they began weeping, even though he never said a word. He carried the fear of the Lord as a tangible, transferable anointing that emanated like an atmospheric radius around him.

The account of his conversion follows:

Finney was born the year after John Wesley died, perhaps picking up his very mantle. Finney became a Presbyterian minister and one of the leading figures in the holiness movement. He went to church only to meet girls in his younger years, but as a law student, he began to study Scripture and seek after God. One day, he determined to press into God, no matter the sacrifice. He simply walked off into the woods one day, determined to meet God in a real way. At that time, he was suddenly consumed with an awareness of his own sin, and feared that he could instantly fall into hell. There in the forest, trembling, he surrendered his life to God.

When he returned to his office, Finney saw the Lord "as I would see any other man," and fell to his feet weeping. Here is the account:

> I received a mighty baptism of the Holy Spirit. Without any expectation of it, without ever having the thought in my mind that there was any such thing for me, without any memory of ever hearing the thing mentioned by any person in the world, the Holy Spirit descended upon me in a manner that seemed to go through me, body and soul. I could feel the impression, like a wave of electricity, going through and through me. Indeed it seemed to come in waves of liquid love, for I could not express it in any other way. It seemed like the very breath of God. I can remember distinctly that it seemed to fan me, like immense wings. No words can express the wonderful love that was spread abroad in my heart. I wept aloud with joy and love. I literally bellowed out the unspeakable overflow of my heart. These waves came over me, and over me, and over me, one after another, until I remember crying out, "I shall die if these waves continue to pass over me." I said, "Lord, I cannot bear any more," yet I had no fear of death.[9]

Just sitting in Finney's presence after this incident caused his boss to also flee to the woods in surrender to Christ. Finney would go on to set the nations ablaze with revival and evangelism. The very next day, he entered a church prayer meeting, and as he walked in, the power of God caused people to fall on the ground confessing their sins.

Finney also faced resistance. A man carried a pistol into one meeting, intending to kill him, before he was gripped with conviction and repented. A pastor tried to keep Finney out of one town by threatening to stop him with cannons. Another pastor who publicly denounced Finney in his church died immediately after speaking against him. In one city where Finney traveled, he met initial resistance, but when he began to preach, fear began to grip everyone and they fell to the ground in repentance. "If I had had a sword on each hand, I could not have cut them down as fast as they fell," he said. Many of them had to be carried out of the meeting, which lasted all night long. In another city, an entire tenth of the population was converted.

After a life of itinerant evangelism, Finney taught theology at Oberlin College. Overall, he is credited for winning more than half a million souls to God. He also renounced slavery and allowed women to speak in church in a day when such views were unpopular.

The Spirit of the fear of the Lord was the main element of God's nature that He most revealed through the holiness revival stream. This same mantle rested on the Pensacola revival in the 1990s, as hundreds of people would literally bolt out of their seats and run forward during the altar calls every night in holy fear. I visited Pensacola at the height of the revival, when a line of people stretched around the parking lot just to get in the doors every night. It was impossible for anyone to sit through one of those services without being consumed with conviction.

Robert Murray McCheyne, a minister in Dundee, Scotland, in the 1830s and '40s carried a similar anointing. He would just walk into the pulpit and before he said a word, people would begin weeping with conviction of sin. This is because he stayed in the presence of God, and it emanated from him. But over the next century, the church was quick to forget Isaiah 11:3, which says "he will *delight* in the fear of the Lord." There is a certain ecstasy that mankind was created to enjoy that only comes through a raw terror of God. Fear of the Lord is only the beginning of wisdom, but the love of God is the fulfillment of wisdom. We need both to walk in purity. Without the revelation of the pleasure and delight of God, we cannot properly embrace this holy reverence of Him. As God restores this man-

tle of the fear of the Lord on our lives, we will see the complete fulfillment of John 16:8—"When (the Holy Spirit) is come He will convict the world of sin." In addition, as we are again pursuing a gospel
of power, instead of a gospel of mere talk, we must remember to
engage the anointing for conviction. "Because our gospel came to
you not simply with words, but also with power, with the Holy Spirit
and with deep conviction" (1 Thess. 1:5).

HOLY ROLLERS

Lying between the 18th century Methodist revival to the 20th
century Pentecostal movement was the American Holiness Revival—
a broad sweeping, multi-denominational move of God. Like every
move of God before and after it, the Holiness Revival was also accompanied by healings, miracles, and physical manifestations.

Besides Finney, others received what they called a "second conversion" though not all identified the experience as a "baptism of
the Holy Ghost," as did Finney. The holiness preachers, like Phoebe
Palmer and others, were all birthed out of the earlier work of the
Wesleys. D.L. Moody and William Boardmann—even Oswald
Chambers—all experienced a "second blessing" after salvation
which some referred to as the "higher Christian life," "perfection" or
"entire sanctification." American Quakers Hannah Whitall Smith and
Robert Pearsall Smith were also among these revivalists.

Most received this Spirit baptism through a period of waiting,
or "tarrying" on the Lord. It was a time of extended prayer and
pressing into God. Let me say this—if you want to experience God,
there is nothing holding you back. Wait on Him. Pursue Him. You
will find Him. This lingering in the Lord's presence was a carryover
practice from several precursors. Congregationalist Thomas Upham
studied Catholic mystic Madame Guyon and Lutheran mystic
Johann Arndt during the holiness movement. We see that the flame
of the mystics—the very presence of God—has been the common
thread passed down in every revival since Jesus first breathed on
His disciples.

These men knew how to persevere in prayer and linger in the presence of God. There were no four-minute conversions and comfortable Christianity in those circles. They spent long hours on their knees. And only one thing can drive you to stay in that position: the manifest glory of God.

The 19th century revivalists all restored the truth of holiness and purity to the church—the importance of sinless living. Were there abuses? Every time God moves in the church, He always calls His people to a higher state of holiness. But without fail, we always botch it and jump over into legalism and control. We turn to the letter that kills. But true holiness is love, joy, peace—it is bearing the fruits of the Spirit. "True holiness is love hanging on a cross," says John Sandford. It is measured by our willingness to love and sacrifice for one another. God is calling us to a tremendous level of holiness, but it is measured by the level to which we abandon selfishness and self-focus, and reach out to meet the needs of others. The level to which we learn to love God and love other people.

As for positional holiness with God, we ultimately rely on the blood of Jesus, and there is nothing we can add to His work. But God is calling His church to a holy lifestyle as well—appropriating the benefits of the blood here on earth. The Holiness Revival eventually put too much emphasis on the work of the believer to attain this holiness. Many believed it was possible to live a sinless life. Theoretically this is true through the blood of Christ, and should always be our goal. But when we claim to have no sin, we are most in error. There were fringe movements, like that of John Humphrey Noyes, who claimed to be free from sin and founded a utopian community where he instituted group marriage and practiced eugenics. The apostle John warns us that when we think we are without sin, we are deceived. This was the deception of the Pharisees—but Jesus said that our holiness must exceed that of the Pharisees. That type of holiness is the kind that lays its life down for a friend.

Overall, I think we are missing the whole point of the holiness revival. In its prime, it was not about legalism or human effort—though it devolved into that. There was a principle that many of these men and women were tapping into, which seems to have gradually been lost in the church today—although I doubt they understood it entirely themselves. They were actually reaching into a tangible impartation, an *anointing* for holiness, that we can also tap into, which is beyond our own effort to attain and is a gift of grace. There is a dynamic of the presence of God—the *spirit of burning*, the refining fire—wherein holiness is imparted not just as a result of years of trial, testing, and maturity. It can be a sudden download. It is a first fruit of the infilling of God's Spirit.

Yes, free will and choice will always be required on our part. I don't just wallow in sin until God supernaturally anoints me to be pure. Repentance is very much a lifestyle and a choice not to sin (keep in mind that sanctification is a lifelong process, too). But there is a place in the anointing where—and I do not mean this presumptuously—sin is no longer an issue. By no means do I mean to downplay the severity of sin, nor should we ever let down our guard against it. But there is a grace from the Lord that can enable us no longer to be defeated and bound by sinful practices. This holiness anointing enables us to focus outwardly and get Kingdom work done, because we are no longer wrestling internally with personal sin problems.

This anointing enables us to see the beauty of repentance and gives us a deep inward passion for purity. It is closely tied with the spirit of deliverance, where our senses grow to hate sin and despise the things we once craved that were evil. Holiness is not a matter of abstaining from the object of our addiction. It is a matter of redirecting our addiction. We are born to be God addicts. We were made for worship.

The new mystics will be marked by radical holiness. The kind only God can produce. The only way Jesus will have a spotless Bride is by His own, supernatural intervention. Purity brings victory. In whatever area a Christian achieves purity in his life, he is given authority to conquer and move in power.

"The greatest revelation I have received is that holiness has everything to do with love," says Che Ahn. "What many people do not realize is that in this (recent move of God), more true repentance has been taking place inside most people than at any other time in their walk with Jesus. …Nothing changes us like the love of God."[10]

Often we think that we have to move God to kindness by our holiness. But it is God's loving kindness that actually draws us to holiness. "We've been told that repentance brings revival, but the opposite is true. Revival brings repentance," says Bill Johnson.[11]

The thick glory God is releasing on His last day army will be a consistent, keeping flame. This will be an army that conquers because the Lord Himself has birthed purity deep within.

THEY WILL NOT BREAK RANKS

This army will be a "nameless, faceless" generation that is not interested in position or personal recognition. These end-time warriors, Joel tells us, will not break ranks—they will not jostle for position. They will know their place and walk in it. They will scale walls and make nations tremble. In fact, some entire nations will literally be taken in a day for the Kingdom of God. Major prophets have said that stadiums will fill up around them, with news reporters trying to get in to interview these miracle workers. But there will be no point man, except Jesus. As soon as one performs a sign, he will move out of the spotlight and another will step onto the platform and raise the dead.

This army will be pure and free from selfish ambition and lust for personal glory. The Lord is raising up a priesthood of spiritual eunuchs. These will be those shepherds who have no desire to draw the King's Bride to themselves. Thus, the King can entrust them to watch over Her—His Church. This army will be separated to the Lord, giving no room to the devil or the desires of the flesh. This purity will come from intimacy with the Lord. And out of purity will come unity. Out of unity will come revival. Jesus' prayer to the Father in John 17 is that we would all be united with one another and with Him, "so that the world may believe." This has not yet been fulfilled, but Jesus does not pray hit-or-miss prayers. We *will* see church unity like never before, and combined with deeper unity with Christ in the individual believer, the world cannot help but believe.

If we are not walking in unity with the body, then we are not walking in full unity with Christ. There is tremendous power in unity, *"for there the Lord commands His blessing, even life forever more"* (Ps. 133:3). Note that He *commands* the blessing. And when the church is in unity, life forever more—salvation—is released to the nations. That is revival. But there is yet another layer to this. When we are in unity, the Lord commands that we be able to access our eternal blessings here and now. That is, He releases Heaven on earth. It was when all the believers were together in one accord that the fire first fell on Pentecost.

The Lord is not just looking to bring unity between churches. He is also looking to bring unity between the church of the ages. As we move closer to the end, hindsight will bring into clarity God's plan for the entire church age.

Unity does not mean slowing down for others to catch up. Many forerunner ministries think they have to back away from the "edgi-er" things God is doing, in order to preserve unity. This is not true. If we set a higher standard, others will follow. God wants us all to run full throttle into the calling He has released into our lives.

However, unity does not criticize those who do not run as fast as I do, or those who do not meet my standards. Unity respects every believer where he or she is, and trusts God to lead them without judgment. Unity also is receptive to the gifting and ministry of others who are different from us. Unity does not require conformity of style or function. It requires perspective change, in which we value a brother with the eternal worth of Christ that has been placed upon him. Unity is achieved only through love for one another. Unity itself is not really the ultimate goal. Love is the goal. Unity is just the fruit of love. We may completely despise one another's calling, function, and ministry tactics, but if we have love for each another anyway, we can still achieve unity. We must learn to prefer

one another, despite our differences. Consider how Abraham preferred Lot. There was no competition or selfish ambition in
Abraham. He let Lot choose the choicest, fattest portion of the land
without the slightest argument. And God blessed him with an eternal covenant, giving him spiritual land and blessing that far out-
weighed Lot's acreage.

Most divisions come through envy over one another's gifts,
blessings, and callings. And this is rooted in a slavery mentality. It is
a form of spiritual poverty, in which we do not feel worthy to
approach the Father's table for ourselves. We then become jealous
when He favors someone else. Like the elder brother when the
prodigal son returns, we become envious, not knowing that the
Father would have thrown us a party anytime we wanted. We feel
we must fend for our own—even in ministry. But God is big enough
to bless everybody, each and every one.

We need to be creative and blaze new trails. Envy and jostling
for position only breeds copycats, look-alikes, and drones. True unity
is found in diversity. We will never be able to work together if we
are just copying one another's style or ministry, because it will only
lead to competition. Once we come to a place of believing the Lord
has individual provision, inheritance, and destiny for our own lives,
we can begin to search those things out without the pressure of
personal ambition.

We will be amazed at the colorful diversity of this army. God is
creative and He is not looking for us to conform to any mold except
for His Son. Jesus is the most creative element in the universe.
Through Him, the Father created everything that has been made. In
the same way, the Father wants to create through us. Only by operating in our true individual callings and identities, can we ever fit
together as living stones and arrive at perfect cohesion. Otherwise,
we may have a perfectly united "shell" of a ministry, but no real unity
in our hearts—because outside of our unique, individual destinies,
we will never find satisfaction or purpose. Every leaf, every
snowflake, every fingerprint is uniquely different. The tribes of
Israel were different, but still, they each worked together to help

one another take their inheritance. The "unity of the faith" is not uniformity, but it does pack exponential power that no one man or ministry could accomplish alone.

So many pastors and churches have realized the benefit of unity in recent decades that joint meetings and citywide ministerial associations between denominations have become popular. There was a time when coming together in unity was a fragile thing, like a newborn baby, that had to be cared for and nurtured so that everyone didn't splinter again. But these little "unity parties" must mature. The baby is growing up. It is time we stop just celebrating our unity and slapping one another on the back, and actually learn to *do things together*. Unity is great, but it must go to the next step. Our relationships do have intrinsic value—unity is an end in itself. But it is also for a *purpose*. It must begin to bear fruit in other areas. We can no longer afford to be like the child who threatens to walk away if everyone doesn't play his way. We need to discover how we can all play together in the way we were designed, and begin doing the work of the ministry as a unit.

In our home church in Alaska, if we do not feel someone will be receptive to our ministry style, we simply recommend another congregation that would better suit their needs. There is no need for competition. Once you know your niche in the Kingdom, the pressure to compete subsides. Find your calling and stick to it. The Lord is not looking for a bunch of carbon copy grunts. He is enlisting an army of highly trained specialists.

DRUNK AND DESPERATE

Many in the Lord's Army will be complete ecstatics. The fact that such a diverse and peculiar people could march in spiritual formation will be due simply to the order of the Holy Spirit working within them—not man's order. Whenever God moves, it is always marked by strange manifestations. Church services always look like glorified chaos during revival. That's historical fact. Consider the demonstrative expressions of worship and the emotive outbursts that have always accompanied a new move of God. When humanity is slapped with the electric power of God, we flop, wiggle, laugh, cry, and express it in a number of ways. And the more desperate a people become for God, the more He is apt to show up in such a manner. As we learn to cultivate the presence of God, and He literally possesses us to a deeper degree, we see that these emotive power encounters were all the time teaching us how to respond to the slightest nudgings of the Spirit. There is no better tutor than the presence of God. No better school room than the place of worship.

It is interesting that many Christians will accept that a donkey talked to a prophet and that God called Hosea to marry a prostitute, but they cannot accept that God would cause people to laugh or shake during a church service. There are a surprising number of Christians who would classify themselves as *cessationists*, that is, they believe God no longer operates through spiritual gifts or moves on people in a way they can tangibly experience. That, too, is gnostic. They believe God sort of sits in a spiritual vacuum somewhere. But most of these Christians are not very familiar with their roots. Nearly every popular revival in the past three centuries had a measure of healings, prophetic experiences, or wild manifestations of the Holy Spirit's power in its midst. Some would be surprised to discover that the Pentecostal denomination does not have a corner on Holy Spirit manifestations, and He has always moved radically whenever He moved.

Physical, corporate manifestations of God's power have been one highly criticized aspect of the Toronto Blessing renewal over the past decade. From people falling over, flopping on the floor, shaking, rolling and feeling drunk to laughing, and roaring under the weight of God's presence—none of it is entirely a new phenomena. In fact, the Shakers and the Quakers are both denominational trends that got their very names from such physical manifestations—shaking and quaking. Each of the Great Awakenings and every major revival was marked by similar activity. Of course, this spiritual drunkenness that always accompanies intense supernatural power is most clearly highlighted in Acts 2 during Pentecost as the Holy

Spirit fell, when Peter points out to the crowds that, "These men (the disciples) are not drunk as you suppose." Notice, Peter never said the disciples were not drunk. They were extremely intoxicated, but "not as you suppose." They were drinking the new wine of the Holy Spirit, and their bodies were buzzed. They were being impacted by the glory presence of God. The more they saturated themselves in that heavy glory, the more they were empowered to work miracles and preach the gospel with boldness.

It is this inebriation that allows the prophets to be such nutcases. Most prophets are highly intelligent, but they do ridiculous things because they are buzzed in God. We are called to walk in the Spirit. Paul tells us not to be drunk with wine, but instead to be filled with the Spirit (Eph. 5:18).

Even in the natural world, drinking wine makes you bold. So it is with the Holy Spirit. When we sit in His presence to the point of intoxication, we become bold in that place of power. The Holy Spirit is the "Helper." The generation of young warriors on the rise will be heavy drinkers. The early apostles had to get loaded before the miracles exploded. Without the drinking, you do too much thinking. It is God's presence that prepares you for the miraculous.

Joel says that in the time of the Lord's army, *"the mountains will drip new wine"* (Joel 3:18). Joel speaks of the wine of God more than any other writer. This will be a generation that stays intoxicated on the presence of the Lord. The best wine has been saved for last, and the Lord will pour it out without measure. When we think of military soldiers on furlough, we often think of party animals. Warriors like to drink. There will be a true *party spirit* among these warriors of exuberant joy and reveling in the love of God. Drinking the wine of Heaven will bring supernatural boldness and recklessness that will be necessary to overcome spiritual intimidation and fear in these last days.

Doesn't the natural order clearly spell out that man was made for this type of thing? Why is that Bacchus, bar room, Mardis Gras experience such a stronghold in the heart of man? Because it is the counterfeit experience of being filled with the Holy Spirit's joy and exuberance—what we were created for. The lusts of the flesh, in this regard, are simply shallow substitutes for this deep spiritual truth. In fact, the sin of drunkenness is the only core issue that Joel really preaches against in his book of prophecies. Either we will be drunk with the spirit of the world, or we will be drunk with the presence of God.

When this overflows, the emotions and the body get involved. Obviously, outward manifestations have drawn criticism as being demonic, or at best, sensational. Fearful of criticism over physical manifestations, many powerfully anointed ministries have backed away from revival, or at least pushed the manifestations off into a corner—thus missing out on a greater glory. Often, this is because of fear of deception. But it can moreover be rooted in a desire to build a ministry for oneself, which is laced with the fear of men's opinions. Many simply are unfamiliar with such activity and they fear disruption and uncharted territory. However, nearly every revival has been preceded by the physical prayer of trevail—an intercessory birthing that not only serves as an outward prophetic sign of what God is doing, but also incorporates the believer's entire body, soul and spirit in some of the most intense, enjoyable, and beneficial kind of prayer. Remember, God sends ecstatics specifically to offend our pride and religious boxes. But He is not just looking to offend. God simply wants to play with His children, and He is prone to mix things up when we least expect it.

Why would God design prayer to be so fun? Isn't it nice to not know what you're going to get whenever you enter the prayer closet? I am not saying that we should seek physical manifestations—much less build a ministry around them—but we should always be seeking to have fun with God. That's a big part of our job description.

Manifestation is primarily a gasoline explosion in the soul realm, but it is sparked by something at the spirit level. Unless we allow spiritual things to filter out into the outward life, our faith will always be an esoteric type of gnostic detachment. We do not invert our priorities and place manifestation above the higher call to intimacy, character building, etc. But neither do we discount it, simply because it is bizarre and unorthodox.

Dramatic emotive responses, as well as miracles and manifestations, have been a part of just about every major move of God in the past several centuries. Overall, we see that man has long tanked up on God. It is psychedelic Jesus who still offers the best trips. Let's look at His power in several popular revivals:

The Moravians of Herrnhut, Saxony, were a group of about 300 refugees living on the estate of Count Nicholaus von Zinzendorf, when in 1727 a great outpouring of the Holy Spirit fell. "We saw the hand of God and His wonders, and we were all under the cloud of our fathers baptized with their Spirit. The Holy Ghost came upon us and in those days great signs and wonders took place in our midst. From that time scarcely a day passed but what we beheld His almighty workings amongst us."[12]

Count Nicholaus von Zinzendorf

The Moravians were some of the greatest missionaries the world had ever seen. They sent out more than 1,000 missionaries throughout the world, and held non-stop intercession, 24 hours a day for 100 years. The Moravians were responsible for converting Methodist founders John and Charles Wesley and even ignited the Baptists to amp up their missionary efforts.[13]

The apostles' drunken behavior on Pentecost only signaled the unpredictable course their lives were about to take, as they would be strewn wildly across the globe spreading the fires of revival under the dancing hand of God. Every great revival or season of harvest is marked by similar orchestrations of demonstrative glory.

The Methodists, believe it or not, were known for being absolutely loud and obnoxious. Their services, during the

Wesleyan revival, were marked by excessive emotional demonstrations of worship. They were so loud, in fact, that they were called the "shouting Methodists."

John Wesley walks peacefully and miraculously through a bloodthirsty mob in 1743. Such mobs were purposely incited by church leaders.

They would interrupt their preachers with their shouts. As one convert wrote by 1807, "I thought they were distracted, such fools I'd never seen. They'd stamp and clap and tremble, and wail and cry and scream."

Many of the movements' earliest hymns give reference to shouting, and many saw it as a very viable weapon in spiritual warfare. They saw it as an act of worship that "displaced satan from the camp." A report by Devereux Jarratt, a former Methodist, described a gathering in 1776 wherein "the assembly appeared to be all in confusion, and must seem to one at a little distance more like a drunken rabble than the worshippers of God."[14] John Wesley also believed in divine healing.

The revivalists of old were simply experiencing into the age old principle of Jesus' first miracle—turning the water of the word into wine. God enjoys order, and He despises confusion. But on the same token, He is a God of wildness. He is not afraid of chaos. In fact, His Spirit can hover over the swirling waters of chaos, as it did at the very formation of the earth, whenever He is about to create a new thing.

Hugh Bourne joined the Methodists in England in 1799, and became a fiery evangelist. He would convert coal miners and drunks on the streets, and thousands were saved under his ministry. His meetings were so loud, some said you could hear them a mile away. Hugh's meetings were the roots of the Methodist "camp meetings," as people would camp overnight to hear him preach the next day.

Hugh Bourne

Once, when speaking to thousands of people in a single meeting on God's judgment, "many ran away, while others fell upon each other in heaps." And one of his meetings in 1807 was so large, there were four separate preachers speaking simultaneously to the crowds, and it lasted for four days straight. Bourne was eventually booted from the mainline denomination and formed the Primitive Methodists.[15]

George Whitefield (1714-1770) was associated with the Wesley brothers at Oxford University in the 1730s, then in America on an evangelistic mission to Georgia. His meetings would later spark the Wesleys' itinerant meetings. Whitefield was a major player in the Great Awakening started by Jonathan Edwards. Many were saved in his missions, and it is estimated that he preached to six million without the use of radio or television.

George Whitefield preaches to a crowd at Leeds in 1749.

Whitefield's meetings were criticized for their emotional expressions of worship. John Wesley describes a prayer meeting with Whitefield, in which the Spirit of God moved on them in 1739. "About three in the morning, as we were continuing instant in prayer, the power of God came mightily upon us, insomuch that many cried out for exceeding joy, and many fell to the ground. As soon as we were recovered a little from that awe and amazement at the presence of His majesty, we broke out with one voice, 'We praise Thee, O God, we acknowledge Thee to be the Lord.'"[16]

Understand that we are not referring to hype or a striving, emotional attempt to garnish experience from God. This is about the sudden, undeniable surprises of His sovereignty.

Jonathan Edwards

Jonathan Edwards (1703-1758) converted thousands during the Great Awakening. He learned Greek and Hebrew by the time he was 13, and soon after graduating he was born again. Edwards evangelized Native Americans for seven years before becoming president of Princeton University. There were many emotive expressions and manifestations of the Spirit in Edwards' ministry, and he exhorted believers to be patient and judge the long-term fruit of the revival. "Miracles accompanied the revival as well. Many people were healed of sickness and disease, and other mighty acts of God were evident. Some would lose the strength in their legs and fall to the floor in divine ecstasy. Critics said this was due purely to emotionalism, but the manifestations continued."[17]

Many may find it interesting that the 19th century revivalist D.L. Moody, namesake of the renowned Moody Bible Institute and hero to many cessationist evangelicals, himself claimed to have had a deep encounter with God in New York in 1871.

"I was crying all the time God would fill me with His Spirit. Well, one day in the city of New York—oh, what a day! I cannot describe it. I seldom refer to it; it is almost too sacred an experience to name.

Paul had an experience of which he never spoke for fourteen years. I can only say that God revealed Himself to me, and I had such an experience of His love that I had to ask Him to stay His hand. I went to preaching again. The sermons were not different; I did not present any new truths; and yet hundreds were converted. I would not be placed back where I was before that blessed experience for all the world—it would be as the small dust of the balance," wrote Moody.[18] Moody's secret was not keen Bible knowledge. It was the anointing. Keep in mind that those who most revere Moody are from denominations that despise the very mention of the baptism of the Holy Spirit for the believer today. In fact, many probably think the Trinity consists of the Father, the Son, and the Holy Bible.

Lester Sumrall met a man in England who even heard Moody speaking in tongues. The man told him, "I was in this city with Dwight L. Moody. As I knelt in prayer with him, he did the same thing you are doing. He spoke in some words that I could not understand."[19]

We have only mentioned a few examples of historical moves of God, but understand that God has moved miraculously and prophetically on a consistent basis throughout church history. The Adventists and Churches of the Brethren were also marked with healings in the early days of America. And even the most liturgical churches, at least in theory, acknowledge that miracles still happen today. Maybe the reason we aren't seeing more of them is because we need to relinquish control. We can no longer afford to expect God to move in the way that we have predetermined. He wants to bring us beyond our expectancies. What does that mean? For one, it means you haven't visualized it yet. You may have seen it in part, but it is above and beyond your wildest imaginings.

An army follows orders. It obeys the will of its commanders. It marches in formation. And the way this happens, for the Christian, is to come into line with the inner working presence of God. For us, marching in formation may look like a wild rabble at times, but God's order is different from our own. Sometimes standing firm in the word of God means you can't get up off the floor.

ENDNOTES

1. Mike Bickle, *The Pleasures of Loving God* (Lake Mary: Charisma House, 2000), 154.

2. Ibid., 154.

3. Bill Johnson, "Strategic Keys," conference audio recording (April, 2004).

4. Transcribed by Todd Bentley with Jackie Macgirvin, *Journey Into the Miraculous Todd Bentley: An Ordinary Man Touched by a Supernatural God* (Victoria, B.C.: Fresh Fire Ministries, 2003), 3.

5. Bobby Connor, "The Commissioning of Joel's Army." (November, 2003).

6. Rick Joyner, "The New Leadership." www.eaglestar.org, Word of the Week. 16 Aug. 2004.

7. Ibid.

8. Roberts Liardon, *God's Generals* (Whitaker House, 1996), 109. From Mrs. Charles Parham, The Life of Charles F. Parham, (Birmingham: Commercial Printing Co., 1930), 59, 74.

9. H. Wessel, ed., *The Autobiography of Charles Finney* (Minneapolis: Bethany, 177 ed.), 20-22.

10. Che Ahn, *Into the Fire*. (Renew, 1998), 122-123.

11. For more information on Bill Johnson resources, visit www.ibethel.org.

12. Geoff Waugh, "Fire Fell: Revival Visitations," and "Spirit Impacts in Revivals." Renewal Journal No. 1 (Brisbane: Renewal). Accessed 13 Oct. 2004 <http://www.pastornet.net.au/renewal>. Article source: Greenfield, John. "Power from on High." (London: Christian Literature Crusade, 1950 ed.), 14.

13. Ibid.

14. "Shouting Methodists." (Jesus Army/Jesus Fellowship Church). Accessed 13 Oct. 2004 <http://www.jesus.org.uk/ja/mag_revivalfires_methodi sts.shtml>. Article source: Winthrop Hudson, Encounter (Winter, 1968, Vol. 29).

15. "Hugh 'stoked' up the old fire." (Jesus Army/Jesus Fellowship Church). Accessed 13 Oct. 2004 <http://www.jesus.org.uk/ja/mag_revivalfires_primi-tive.shtml>. Article source: Joseph Ritson, The Romance of Primitive Methodism (publ. E. Dolton).

16. Geoff Waugh, "Spirit Impacts in Revivals." Article source: C. Idle, ed., The Journal of John Wesley (Tring: Lion, 1986 ed.), 55.

17. Mark Trigsted, ed., *Jonathan Edwards His Greatest Sermons* (Bridge-Logos Publishers, 2003), 3.

18. W.R. Moody, *The Life of D. L. Moody* (New York: Revell, 1900), 149.

19. Lester Sumrall, *Pioneers of Faith* (Ben Publishing, 1995), 185.

CHAPTER 11

Enter the Healer

THROUGH the next few chapters, we will focus heavily on the miracle workers of the past two centuries. Our goal here is not to elevate Pentecostal or charismatic history above its neighboring streams in the Body of Christ. But our study is not one of theological development, as much as a look at supernatural power players. In a hagiography of mystics and miracle workers, it only makes sense to study the well-recorded lives of modern day healers, most of whom filtered through charismatic streams.

Of course, there has always been a steady stream of miracle workers and healers in the church, from Bernard to Xavier, from the early apostles to Francis. Divine healing conferences have been traced back to London from 1885, decades prior to the Azusa Street revival that launched Pentecostalism. And many healing ministries were operating in the 1800s, which came directly out of John Alexander Dowie's Zion City. Raymond T. Richey and Gordon Lindsay, who were major figures in the Voice of Healing Revival of the 1940s and '50s, were actually living in Zion as children. As we walk through history, we can follow the passage of this supernatural influence as it is handed down from one miracle worker to the next.

Maria Woodworth-Etter (1844-1924) not only walked in a powerful miracle and healing anointing prior to the turn of the 20th century, her ministry was also marked with radical prophetic experiences as well as physical manifestations of God's presence. All of this brought considerable attention from the press. Etter was well known on the itinerant circuit, and was a contemporary to John Dowie, although he openly denounced her methods. Perhaps had he learned to rest in the presence of God as Etter did, many of the control issues could have been avoided which later brought down his own ministry. Etter was quick to stop and soak in the presence of God, even in the middle of her preaching. In this sense, she identified more with the contemplative mystics who preceded her centuries before.

Maria Woodworth-Etter

The manifestations of the Spirit in her ministry largely included trances and people being "slain in the Spirit" when Etter preached. Of course, the phenomenon was not a new one, but was largely popularized through her ministry as never before in mainstream Christendom. In fact, the term "slain in the Spirit" likely originated from Etter's meetings. Upon first entering ministry, she was given a vision of the harvest, with angels coming into her room, telling her that people would fall as "grain fell from wheat."

Etter was called to preach at age 13. Early on, she was intimidated to preach because she was a woman, and by the time she had a large family, it was all but impossible. But after losing five of her six children to disease, Etter finally responded to the call at age 35. In some of her first meetings, people fell to the floor weeping in repentance. As this continued to happen, people would subsequently have visions and trances on the floor. Sometimes, Etter would have trances herself, standing frozen for hours during the middle of her own services, with her hand raised up in mid-air.

Etter described some of the first encounters with people falling down under God's presence, by saying, "Men and women fell and lay like dead. I had never seen anything like this. I felt it was the work of God, but did not know how to explain it, or what to say. I was a little frightened, as I did not know what the people would think of me, as I was the leader of the meeting. While the fear of God was on the people, and I was looking on, not knowing what to do, the Lord revealed wonderful things to me in a few moments.

"'This is My slaying power. I told you I would be with you and fight your battles. It is not the wisdom of men, but the power and the wisdom of God that is needed to bring sinners from darkness to light.'

"Those who were lying all over the chapel as if dead, after lying about two hours, all, one after another, sprang to their feet as quick as a flash, with shining faces, and shouted all over the chapel. I never saw such strong conversions, nor heard such shouting. They seemed light as a feather."[1]

This continued until Etter was preaching to thousands who were all experiencing the same thing, "when the Holy has fallen on them, and swept over, wave after wave, till the multitude would sway back and forth like the trees in a forest or grain in a storm. Many of the tall oaks would be laid prostrate over the ground, and many were converted standing, or sitting on their seats." Shouting, weeping, collapsing and long periods of silence would grip entire congregations, often resulting in hundreds of conversions. Dozens of journalists would attend a single meeting, and people would flock from miles when Etter came to town. Etter must have been a loud and fiery lady. She spoke to crowds of up to 25,000 before public audio systems were available. After Etter would preach in a town, police said they had no work left to do. Crime stopped. Newspapers reported that saloons lost business.

She was arrested on several occasions, and doctors tried to have her deemed insane and institutionalized in St. Louis. She was arrested for practicing medicine without a license and for "hypnotizing" people with trances. Newspapers gave her hell. She was also criticized for predicting an earthquake in San Francisco, until an enormous shaker hit the area a couple years later and caused tremendous devastation.

Etter impacted the ministries of John G. Lake and F.F. Bosworth, among others. She preached into her 80s, and by the end of her life, she was still being carried to the platform on a wooden chair because of her age. In her final weeks, Etter even preached sermons from her bed.

Understand that at this time, miraculous gifts of healing were being restored to the church in Book of Acts proportions.

John G. Lake (1870-1935) began the healing rooms ministry in Spokane, Washington, in the early 1900s, which would document more than 100,000 healings and miracles in its first five years and result in a federal declaration that Spokane was the healthiest city in America.

Lake's healing impartation came under the ministry of John Dowie, whom he first approached in Chicago seeking healing from rheumatism. It had caused his legs to become misshapen and his body distorted. In fact, Lake came from a tragic background in many regards, which propelled him to desire divine healing.

John G. Lake

Born in Ontario, Canada as one of 16 children, Lake was sickly as a child and eight members of his family had died from a digestive illness. His wife, Jennie, was diagnosed with tuberculosis and heart disease and had become an invalid; his brother was an invalid of 22 years; his sister had severe bleeding; and another sister was dying of breast cancer. When Lake received prayer in Chicago, his own body was healed and his legs were miraculously straightened. He began bringing other family members to Dowie's healing homes in

Chicago. He brought his bedridden brother first, who rose from his bed and walked away instantly healed. His sister with breast cancer was healed next.

But by the time Lake reached his other sister, she had just died. He telegrammed Dowie in Chicago, asking for prayer.

"Hold on to God. I am praying. She will live," responded Dowie. In an hour, she was raised from the dead, completely healed. All that was left at that point was the healing of his wife, but she too was in serious condition. Friends had already begun to console him over her impending death. But Lake suddenly came to a realization that *all* sickness—not just some—was from the enemy. He then telegraphed a number of friends, telling them that his wife would be healed at 9:30 a.m. the next morning. That morning, he laid hands on her himself and she instantly recovered.

Lake had pastored a Methodist church in Wisconsin for some time, prior to these healings, but chose to enter business, founding two newspapers, making money in real estate and managing a large insurance company. Lake had become a very wealthy man, making a lucrative salary. But when the power of God swept through his family, Lake left it all for the ministry. Lake sold all that he had and moved to South Africa, where he ministered for five years. Having sold all, he arrived in port with his wife and seven children with only $1.50. But to enter the port, the family needed at least $125. While he was waiting in the immigration line, someone pulled him aside and gave him $200.

Lake's work in South Africa grew to 700,000 members and 625 church plants. In Africa, he prayed for all manner of healings and demonic deliverance. His life was also marked by charity, often giving away his own groceries to the poor. He prayed for the sick night and day, with crowds of people literally camping out on his lawn, constantly walking through his house in a single file line for prayer at the door of his study.

Lake carried such a powerful anointing, that when a plague swept the nation, killing a quarter of the population, he volunteered to help carry and bury the dead while few other medical personnel dared such a task. Lake knew that he was immune to disease through the shed blood of Christ. He literally had doctors place plague germs in his hand then study the effect under a microscope. Upon contact with Lake's skin, the living plague germs would instantly die.

Lake would eventually raise up more than 1,200 ministers and win countless souls in Africa. But this came with a price. Lake's own family suffered. His wife essentially died of starvation, as Lake would often neglect his own family for the sake of feeding others. He remarried and had more children, slowing his schedule to cater more to their needs. His children from the first marriage, however, would later resent Lake's initial neglect of the family and they grew bitter. However, later in life, Lake seemed to find a balance between the supernatural work of ministry and the natural needs of his own family. He also remarked that the extraordinary healings he saw in those early years of ministry were not worth the cost of his family.

When Lake returned to America, he opened the Divine Healing Institute in an old office building in Spokane. The testimonies of healing were phenomenal and far too many to list in a single volume. These "healing rooms" made such a splash, even in the press, that the Better Business Bureau conducted an investigation into their validity and gave the ministry flying colors. Lake was commended by the mayor, and the queen of Holland even requested prayer. She underwent six miscarriages and wanted a child. Lake prophesied that she would have one, and within a year, this came to pass.

Just to list a few of the more dramatic healings in Lake's ministry in Spokane:

A woman named Ms. Teske with a visible, 30-pound fibroid tumor running down the side of her body, described as "a twisted mass of muscle and sinew, arteries and veins, teeth and hair. The most disorganized twisted and jumbled mass that is possible," began to crunch and twist during prayer until the thing disappeared in the space of three minutes.[2]

Body parts grew into place. A missing earlobe regrew. A woman who lacked reproductive organs conceived and carried a child. Bones were reshaped after being distorted by rheumatoid arthritis. A paralyzed boy with a small, misshapen skull had his head regrown in the same instance that the paralysis left. He also gained the ability to speak. Cancers left. Broken bones were healed.

In addition to divine healings, Lake also experienced angelic visitation, as well as spirit transport to another country, where he was led to exorcise a demon. The presence of God rested so strongly on Lake that people would often fall if he shook hands with them. Sometimes, they would fall when he was six feet away. He began to simply raise his hand from two feet away from people when praying, to confirm that he was not pushing them over. And his anointing did not come easy. Lake prayed diligently for nine long months for the baptism of the Holy Spirit. When Lake finally received the baptism, he said:

> I found that my life began to manifest in the varied range of the gifts of the Spirit. I spoke in tongues by the power of God, and God flowed through me with a new force. Healings were of a more powerful order. Oh, God lived in me; God manifested in me; God spoke through me. My spirit was energized. I had a new comprehension of God's will, a new discernment of spirit, and a new revelation of God in me.

> Then a new wonder manifested. My nature became so sensitized, that I could lay hands on any man, or woman, and tell what organ was diseased, and to what extent, and all about it. I tested it. I went into hospitals where physicians could not diagnose a case, touched a patient, and instantly I knew the organ that was diseased, its extent, condition and location. And one day it passed away. A child plays with a toy, and his joy is so wonderful, he sometimes forgets to eat.[3]

Lake's testimony should be incentive for those who have longed to experience the Holy Spirit's baptism, but never seem to break through to receive it. Do not become disenchanted with the process of pressing in for God's fullness just because He doesn't seem to answer your prayers immediately. The best things are worth waiting for. Lake had to press in for nine months before it happened, but look at the intensity with which it came! Often, those who have to press in the longest and hardest for a thing are the ones God intends to fill with the most power. Also understand that Spirit baptism is not always an immediate, one-time encounter, but for some it is a gradual thing. There are usually several encounters along the way, in which God is revealed to us more fully, and we are constantly learning to become possessed more and more by God's presence anyway.

Lake always pastored a local church, although he did hold several itinerant evangelism campaigns in the 1920s and 1930s. His crusades in Africa were so successful that dump trucks were needed to carry away all the wheel chairs, crutches and other medical equipment left behind each day.

Lake's staff also suffered from severe lack in Africa, selling their possessions and even a home to fund the ministry. At a time when they were most desperately broke and hungry, Lake gave them the option of leaving the mission field. They responded by saying, "We are going back to our fields. We are going back if we have to walk back. We are going back if we have to starve. We are going back if our wives die. We are going back if our children die. We are going back if we die ourselves. We have but one request. If we die, we want you to come and bury us." The following year, Lake buried 12 men, 16 wives and children, all of whom could have lived with proper nutrition.[4] While it is easy, in retrospect, to criticize such efforts as neglecting the family, we must also remember that the Kingdom of God is paved on extreme sacrifice. We should not espouse neglect of the home for the sake of ministry, but nor should we belittle the price paid by such martyrs.

Overall, Lake planted about 40 churches in the United States and Canada, in addition to the hundreds in Africa. At age 61, after years of exhausting work, Lake was beginning to go blind. He pulled aside to speak with the Lord about it one day, telling God how it would bring shame for him to go blind after such a powerful healing ministry. After this prayer, Lake's sight was restored.

Evan Roberts

Evan Roberts (1878-1951) was setting Wales ablaze during the time of America's early healing revivalists. The Welsh Revival broke loose in 1904, and for two years, it seemed the Holy Spirit had completely consumed the nation. Churches were open 24 hours a day with constant intercession. Bars and dance halls were deserted and shut down as entire communities were converted en masse. Crime came to a halt and sports events were cancelled. Theatres and political meetings lost attendance for lack of interest.

Coal miners would go to worship services until the wee hours of the morning, then rise early to pray together before the next day's work. Then they would pray between shifts. Their cart horses had to be retrained, because the miners no longer instructed them with foul language.

And in the middle of it all was 26-year-old Evan Roberts. By the age of 20, Roberts was known as a "mystical lunatic," always with his head in the clouds. He would regularly wake to pray from 1 to 5 a.m. each night, and again in the morning from 9 a.m. until noon. In a society where religion was an emotionless, dreary thing, Roberts would walk up and down the aisles, laughing and dancing and stopping to talk to people in the pews. His face beamed with joy, and he was genuinely happy.

He also desperately grieved over sin. He was ever encouraging congregations to openly confess sin, and many would fall to the ground in repentance during his meetings. Sometimes, Evan would just begin weeping and falling over in the pulpit, pleading with God. He was also very extreme and unpredictable. He would not hesitate to jump up in the middle of a service and tell the congregation they were not being sincere.

The Welsh revival would enflame the world. People traveled from America, Africa, even the far reaches of East Asia to catch an impartation of what God was doing. Very often, they would bring revival back to their own nations.

For months at a time, during the height of the revival, Evan was sleeping only a couple of hours each night, although he said he was not tired and felt "full of electricity." Suddenly, he began exhibiting supernatural gifts of the Spirit. He would suddenly know facts about people in the congregation by divine intuition. But there was little context in his day for prophetic gifts or words of knowledge. He became very confused and the intensity of it all made him very tired. Eventually, the schedule and the spiritual warfare simply burned him out. He started having trouble discerning the voice of God, and this led to more and more sporadic outbursts. He would be very gentle one minute, then sharply turn and be condemning to the congregation. Sometimes he would storm out of a service, because he felt people were not being sincere. The newspapers began to criticize him for being unstable.

Evan Roberts

It was then that Evan fell under the influence of a woman named Jessie Penn-Lewis, who warned Evan that he and the revival were headed toward excess. She told Evan that too much focus was on him. In Evan's state of confusion, he fell under her manipulation and control. Lewis isolated Evan in her home for eight years, for him to "recover," meanwhile using her connections with him for her own personal gain. She convinced him to leave the pulpit in the height of his ministry—at the height of national revival—and curbed his opinions to reject the supernatural elements of his ministry. He would later reject the Pentecostal revival in America as well, even though it was sparked by the very Welsh revival that he ignited. Evan simply vanished from the scene. He retired to a life of seclusion and prayer, which he now felt was his primary calling. In a few decades, there was practically nothing left of the national revival he had started.

Later in life, Evan had a short "comeback tour," with a brief surge of healings and conversions, but the glory days were gone.[5]

Evan's life is a classic example of a prophetic destiny being cut short by a Jezebel spirit. The Jezebel spirit will heap fear and discouragement on the prophets, pushing them into hiding like Elijah. She seduces her way into authority. This same spirit surfaced in John the Baptist's day through Herodias. It will be important for the coming generation to learn how to defeat this foe. She is the killer of God's prophets and the supporter of satan's.

"Let it be known that, if Elijah is coming before Jesus returns, so also is Jezebel," writes Francis Frangipane in *The Three Battlegrounds*. "There is a war, a very ancient war, between the spirit of Elijah and the spirit of Jezebel. In this age-old battle, Elijah represents the interests of Heaven: the call to repentance and the return to God. Jezebel, on the other hand, represents that unique principality whose purpose is to hinder and defeat the work of repentance."[6]

Frangipane rightly points out that, to the victor of this battle goes the soul of a nation. Evan Roberts, like Elijah, had an anointing to turn an entire nation back to God. One thing we must never do with the spirit of Jezebel is to make peace with her. There is no peace or hope of reform for this enemy from hell. In Scripture, it was Jehu who eventually ordered Jezebel's death. When the kings of Israel and Judah came out to meet Jehu, they asked, "Have you come in peace, Jehu?" To which he replied, "How can there be peace as long as all the idolatry and witchcraft of...Jezebel abound?" (2 Kings 9:21-26) Jehu had the *eunuchs*—those who could not be tempted—throw Jezebel down from the tower. Then he trampled her with his horses. There can be no compromise with this spirit. Jesus Himself said to the church of Thyatira, "I have this against you: You tolerate that woman Jezebel, who calls herself a prophetess. By her teaching she misleads My servants into sexual immorality and the eating of food sacrificed to idols" (Rev. 2:20). Toleration is not an option.

We can learn a great deal by witnessing how mighty men of God have fallen. These men paved the way for us to go higher. And if we now see higher and farther, it is only because we stand on the shoulders of giants.

Stephen Jeffreys (1876-1943) was skyrocketed from the Welsh revival into one of the most extreme miracle ministries in the 1920s. While Evan Roberts was the Welsh revival's leading personality, Jeffreys exhibited far more signs and wonders. After his first campaign, it was said that "in a week or two, possibly, Stephen Jeffreys will be considered another Evan Roberts."[7]

Stephen Jeffreys

Converted at the height of the revival, Jeffreys, a 28-year-old coal miner, began preaching openly in the streets for hours at a time. He would keep going as long as the people stayed to listen. In 1907, Stephen and his younger brother George received the baptism of the Holy Spirit, which Stephen says aided his evangelism tremendously. George would also go on to minister to thousands, but not with the same power demonstrated in his brother's work.

Incredible miracles of healing followed Stephen's ministry. On numerous occasions, children with no eyes in their sockets received new eyeballs. People blind from birth received sight. Such miracles were documented regularly by newspapers, and the Vicar of Wall, Rev. J. W. Adams, M.A., came to confirm a number of these happenings, documenting his own eye-witness accounts and testimonies of healings in a book titled *Miracles of Today*. Adams watched firsthand as cancer, tuberculosis, and eyeless sockets were healed in front of him. Goiters disappeared. Many came to the meetings having been discharged from hospitals and certified as incurable, only to go home cured.

Writing of a single campaign, Adams said, "At these healing services I was privileged to witness a hundred miracles in that one week. It is the Lord's doing, and like living in the Acts of the Apostles."[8]

In 1914, a vision of Christ was seen corporately in a church planted by Stephen, and hundreds came to see it. It was visible for six hours. He was so overwhelmed that he lay before the Lord for three days, receiving a tremendous impartation for healing. Everywhere he went, the buildings would overflow with people waiting for days to enter a service. Many walked for miles over hill country to hear his preaching. Stephen's messages emphasized the second coming of Christ, as well as impending judgment, which brought many conversions. He also possessed deep humor and joy.

The opening of deaf ears and blind eyes were common. In one instance, a person's leg grew out 18 inches. Many lame and crippled people confined to spinal carriages and wheelchairs started walking. Limbs crippled from polio since birth were healed. A 36-year-old man with twisted, diminutive legs, having never before walked, was carried onstage. Stephen prayed for him, and he began to scramble on all fours. Then, the man rose and awkwardly began to walk. His healing continued over the course of several days. In Plymouth, England, an entire row of people sprang up from their wheelchairs in a service. While in New Zealand, Stephen prayed for a Maori chief who was near death and bedridden from cancer. He was instantly healed and walked away, leading to numerous conversions.

Like many healing ministers, Stephen had a "signature" healing, for which he always seemed to have the faith to effect. Stephen's signature healing was rheumatoid arthritis.

"In the middle of a service, Stephen would jump off the platform, run to the back, curse rheumatoid arthritis, for example, and scream, 'Come out of him.' People said you could hear bones pop for approximately thirty feet around as the person's bones began to relocate," writes Lester Sumrall.[9] People's crunched, contorted bodies would simply unfold and snap back into place.

Many church leaders of the day considered Stephen's to be the greatest healing ministry in existence. But sadly, like many great revivalists, Stephen's work ended on a somber note. According to some accounts, he eventually succumbed to pride in his ministry, which was flush with adoring followers. Sumrall says he once told a crowd of thousands in Africa that "the world is at my feet to worship me."

It is unclear how severe the problem became, but Stephen clearly emphasized in his earlier meetings that he personally possessed no healing power, and that the sick must expect a touch from Jesus Himself. Nevertheless, Stephen eventually became crippled with rheumatoid arthritis—the very illness over which he had once been so victorious.

"I'm so sorry to have let this number one thing that I delivered people from come upon me," he told Sumrall, after the disease had twisted his body.[10] Also, like many revivalists, Stephen maintained a punishing schedule that offered only two to three hours of sleep many nights. This could only have added to the problem, as doctors repeatedly cautioned him to slow the pace of his schedule.

Interestingly, Stephen Jeffreys' last sermon was on the "Glory of the Son," which opened with the statement "On great occasions kings put on their finest apparel, but God wrapped Himself in dust when He entered the world." This journey from glory to humility clearly marked the final days of this great man of God.

We will see throughout the lives of the revivalists that many fell to one or more of the "Three Gs." The gold, the girls, or the glory. For Jeffreys, it was clearly the glory. Nothing can bring you down faster than pride. The loss of humility signals the loss of vision. If we do not learn to humble ourselves, as God has commanded, then He will have to do it for us.

SHABA SHUNDAI

As we see, the Pentecostal Revival of the early 1900s had already been preceded by a number of mighty men of faith, who demonstrated the Spirit's power. The focus on healing miracles would remain, but the Pentecostal Revival would add the gift of tongues to modern mainstream Christianity, among other things. By relating the following accounts, I do not want to focus too heavily on the gift of tongues, but charismatics often overlook how supernaturally dynamic it is; we become so comfortable with it, we seem to consider it a "lesser" gift of the Spirit. We forget how non-Christians are utterly puzzled by this phenomenon, and even those who speak in tongues seem to underestimate its latent power for cultivating the manifest presence of God.

I cannot count how many times I have heard stories of this gift being used outside the prayer closet to actually communicate the gospel in foreign languages as did the early apostles. Carrie Judd Montgomery, a well known missionary at the turn of the 20th century, spoke in several dialects of intelligible Chinese after she received the gift of tongues. This was confirmed by several missionaries who had learned the language through study. Sometimes she could interpret Chinese into English. It is worth noting that Montgomery also was an invalid from tuberculosis, but she was supernaturally healed and later wrote about this miracle. This gained her quite a bit of notoriety, and she would go on to minister alongside a number of great faith healers in the late 1800s.

Charles Fox Parham (1873-1929) is considered, along with William Seymour, to be a founder of the Pentecostal revival. Parham effected thousands of conversions and very many miraculous healings. He was the first guy who said that speaking in tongues was someone's proof of being filled with the Holy Spirit.

The Lord was restoring the gift of tongues back to the church, so it should only be expected that some doctrines would go overboard. Tongues can clearly be a proof, but not the *only* proof of the infilling. For instance, the Lord used me to heal people and I was taken into trances before I ever spoke in tongues—but that's beside the point. Let's just say that "the Fox" was a pretty controversial guy.

It is important that we depart from some of the standard accounts that paint Parham as the virtual inventor of the gift of tongues. We should not gloss over the glossolalia king, even though he clearly popularized tongue talking more than anyone up to that point. We need to understand that he was simply riding a wave of something the Lord was already doing. We want to give credit where credit is due. For that matter, most would acknowledge that William Seymour was the real spiritual giant of early Pentecostalism.

Charles Fox Parham

We'll get to these fellows later, but if we're going to talk tongues, let's back up to a fellow by the name of Edward Irving.

Edward Irving (1792-1834) was a well-known Scottish Presbyterian minister who emphasized the supernatural in his meetings long before even Alexander Dowie. Irving encouraged parishioners to seek the Holy Spirit. He said God's Spirit would become manifest in them, and that signs and miraculous gifts, such as tongues and prophecy, would be restored to the church through them. As far back as 1830, a woman named Mary Campbell reportedly was speaking in tongues in his meetings, and Irving chose to allow such manifestations to occur in his services.

Irving put a lot of focus on the endtimes and on spiritual warfare, which is where the modern Pentecostal movement likely picked up its emphasis on these two elements. He did have some tweaked doctrines about Christ's human nature, which eventually got him booted from his denomination—although it was probably just an excuse to oust him. A lot of other preachers in his day believed the same things. The real issue was his focus on the supernatural.

Irving was one of the first men to really hammer the idea that Jesus is coming back soon. This was a truth the Lord was restoring to the church, but with every restored truth, there always seems to be extremes. Irving thought the return of Jesus was so imminent that he rejected medical help and would not let doctors treat anyone in his family. Both himself and one of his children could have been spared from death, had they turned to the medical treatments available in his day. You may remember that Dowie—who was supposedly influenced by Irving—also refused Vaseline to his own daughter, who was dying of burns.

However, women began speaking in tongues in his services. The gift of tongues would also pop up throughout the various holiness revival streams in the mid to late 1800s. It was during the days of Irving's ministry that some believe an English fellow named James MacDonald was the first modern guy to ever speak in tongues on April 20, 1830. His twin brother, George, interpreted it as, "Behold he cometh—Jesus cometh—a weeping Jesus." This also sparked a large end-time focus that was becoming popular in that day.

Now add this to the equation: A Margaret MacDonald from Scotland, in 1830, supposedly had visions and revelations that gave us the popular "pre-tribulation" rapture theory. This pre-trib theory became popular with Edward Irving and others, but it never did pass the litmus test with some of the biggest preachers of the following decades, like Charles Spurgeon, George Mueller, Charles Finney, and others. Rick Joyner points out that the sermons of Martin Luther, John Wycliffe, William Tyndale, John Calvin, John Knox, Jonathan Edwards, John Wesley, George Whitfield, and several other major theological reformers all preached doctrines opposed to a pre-

Edward Irving

trib rapture. In fact, the word "rapture" is never mentioned in the Bible, and prior to this woman's prophecy, no one had ever split up the second coming of Christ into separate parts.

"This is not the time to run—it is time for the church to draw her spiritual sword and attack the strategies and strongholds of the enemy. The doctrine of the pre-tribulation rapture has been effective in developing a retreat mentality in the church, but it will not ultimately succeed," writes Joyner.[11]

Of course, we do not want to further divide ourselves over these kinds of doctrines, and that is not my point in bringing it up. But we surely do not want to have a retreat mentality that abandons the world. We do want to be prepared for the darkness that is ahead, foremost by fixing our eyes on the light. Joyner notes that the Lord has always brought His people through trial and tribulation—through the plagues of Egypt, through the Red Sea, through the wilderness—but never did He snatch them out. We are not destined for God's wrath in the last days, but we will surely demonstrate His brilliance in the midst of a dark world.

Through many tribulations we must enter the Kingdom of God (Acts 14:22).

The supernatural generation that is coming should not adopt a retreat mentality. Nor should we be swept in the fervor of an end-times mind-set so much that we neglect sound doctrine. As we see here in the 1830s, this was a season of heightened spiritual activity, with people expecting to get beamed up any minute. But in the meantime, a doctrinal stance was unintentionally being set for years to come. Problems always arise when new doctrines are formed on the basis of "revelation." Revelation brings direction, correction, and countless means of interaction with Heaven. But we are clearly given the Scriptures as our source for doctrinal clarity. The Lord was obviously restoring the gifts and reminding the church of lost truths during this period, but it was not a theological reformation.

Now back to Charles Parham…

Now we have a bit of context to see that Parham was not the first to experience tongues in modern times; he only popularized it. Parham rightly believed the power of the apostles and early church would be restored prior to the Lord's return, and tongues were a first fruit.

Holding his first evangelistic crusades at age 18, Parham was unique in that he did not write down his sermons, but relied on God's inspiration in the pulpit. He eventually moved in healing, and after some success, opened a Bible school. It was there, in Topeka, Kansas, that his students began to experience an outpouring on January 1, 1901. They began speaking in tongues, even before Parham did. The first was a student named Agnes Ozman, who supposedly began to speak in Mandarin Chinese.

Suddenly, he began preaching on this gift and traveling the nation, seeing hundreds receive it. However, despite all this, Parham was unable to embrace the Azusa Street revival led by William Seymour, his former student, which he considered a little too radical. He had a bit of a power struggle with Seymour, which we'll discuss later.

It is important to realize that the Pentecostal denominations were birthed amid division and power plays. On one hand, Parham spoke out against denominationalism, yet he was trying to start his own separate movement. This is very common with any new move of God. Belaboring the need to deconstruct the old wineskin can often be a passive attempt at building our own kingdoms. Selfish Ambition 101.

Whenever the church gives birth to an infant move of the Lord, the enemy tries to come in like a flood and stop it. Early Pentecostalism experienced bitter divisions over minor doctrinal issues. There eventually emerged the stiffest division between the Assemblies of God and "Oneness" Pentecostals, or *Jesus Only* Pentecostals, who held aberrant views on the Trinity. But overall, there could be counted as many as 200 varieties of Pentecostals— nearly six times as many flavors as Baskin Robbins ice cream—at the height of division. Most of the reasons for splintering were absolutely ridiculous. In the 1930s, the Pentecostal Fire-Baptized Holiness church split from the Pentecostal Holiness church on the basis of wearing neck ties. Voice of Healing evangelist David Nunn later remarked that by the 1930s, "Soon they began to split their splits. Nearly every church was a split or a splinter!"[12] We'll see that much was done in the Latter Rain Revival of the 1940s to heal this. But with new moves, it is sometimes easy to blur the lines between holy non-conformity to the religious order and outright rebellion.

Charles Parham, perhaps innocently enough, had a lot to do with opening this door of division in Pentecostalism. At first, as a Methodist, he encouraged new converts to join any church they wanted. By 1906, Parham was highly popular, having established the Apostolic Faith Movement in several states; he had a following between 8,000-10,000 believers. He next sought to congeal these churches into one missionary denomination. At that time, he set his sights on Dowie's Zion City. This seemed, of course, to be the divine healing and spiritual gift capital of the world in those days.

Remember, by this time, Dowie had already pronounced himself to be Elijah, and subsequently died. His huge, citywide following there, needless to say, was still spiritually shell-shocked and disappointed. Probably a bit confused.

Parham made a splash in Zion, and his arrival was front page news. Wilbur Voliva was the man who had just taken over John Dowie's post as virtual chieftain of the town, and he also ran the local newspaper. Meanwhile, Parham began holding meetings, and before long had amassed 1,000 people in his services. He was quickly becoming a powerful influence in Zion. There began to be power struggles within the city. Parham left for a period of time, when suddenly he was arrested on sodomy charges in Texas. This would be the greatest scandal of his ministry.

The charges appeared in newspapers, but no record was ever found in the local courthouses of any indictment. Understand that Parham was severely hated by many, and his whole ministry team nearly died when someone poisoned their water, not long before this. These were also the days of small town cops, Jim Crow laws, and the like. In those days, Pentecostals were utterly despised in general in many circles—both Christian and secular. It would not be a stretch to think the charges could have been fabricated. Parham said the sodomy charges were a set up by William Voliva. Voliva was surely blasting Parham in his newspapers, and constantly added more rumor and gossip to the initial sodomy claims in his magazines. We may never know exactly what happened, but church politics surely had a lot to play in the whole situation.

Even though the accusations were crippling, Parham carried on. Though controversial in many ways, he was truly a forerunner and more hungry for the Kingdom than most men. By the time of his death, some estimate he had led two million people to the Lord.

William Seymour (1870-1922) was a student of Charles Parham's Bible school. He was a black man and segregation laws kept him from coming indoors. But Seymour was so hungry for the things of the Lord that he would sit outside the door and listen in as Parham preached about the Holy Spirit.

William Seymour

Seymour received visions from early on in his Christian walk. He was eventually invited to Los Angeles, an area that was already ripe for revival. Several of the city's leaders had traveled to Wales and picked up a vision for what God was doing in that country. Seymour was actually in a home group meeting when the Holy Spirit began to fall in LA, as people were radically filled and walked out into the streets speaking in tongues. Crowds began to grow at these home meetings, where Seymour was living with a host family. Before long, they were preaching from the front porch as people filled the streets to listen. Eventually, they moved into an old horse stable at 312 Azusa Street. It was in this stable in 1906 that the Pentecostal movement was officially born.

People would fall over and weep. They would speak in tongues. They would laugh, jerk, dance, and shout. They would wait on the Lord for hours, sometimes saying nothing. Seymour would often preach from his knees.

William Seymour

"No one could possibly record all the miracles that occurred there," writes charismatic historian Roberts Liardon.[13] John G. Lake said of William Seymour that, "He had more of God in his life than any man I had ever met up to that time."

Prayer lasted all day and all night. Firemen were even dispatched to Azusa Street, because people saw a "fire," which was actually just the visible glory of God resting on the exterior of the building. Similar occurrences have happened in a number of revivals, like the Indonesian revival, as recorded by Mel Tari in the 1970s, where firemen were also dispatched to a "glory fire" that was visible to everyone around.

Missionaries began coming to Azusa Street from around the world to catch the fire. People would fall over, get saved, and begin speaking in tongues blocks away from the building, even though no one prayed for them, and they had no idea what was going on in the Azusa mission. Parishioners would also hit the streets, knocking on doors with little bottles of oil and asking to pray for the sick.

Seymour sought first and foremost to cultivate the presence of God in his meetings. If someone felt led, they would stand up and begin to pray or preach. If the anointing did not seem to be on a particular speaker, that person would sometimes get a gentle tap on the shoulder to hush up. Truly, the Spirit of God was the leader of those meetings.

Of course, there was no precedent for this type of *participatory* ministry among laymen, either. Not only did God seem to be participating, but so were the people in the pews. It was not just a spectator sport. Of course, this freedom of expression did have its excesses. Fearful of "fleshly" manifestations, Seymour contacted Charles Parham, his former teacher, and asked him to come and help out. He would soon regret doing this. Parham was shocked at what was happening. It was definitely beyond the "shaba shundai" tongue talking he was used to. Parham began preaching against a lot of things that were happening at Azusa, and eventually Seymour had to lock him out of the mission.

I find it a bit ironic that Parham kept Seymour outside the door of his school, and Parham would eventually have to be kept outside the doors of the Spirit's move. Surely Parham was fuming. It is necessary to mention that Parham's racism seemed to manifest more in his later years. He criticized Azusa Street, which welcomed all races, because he did not like the idea of white women and black men being together. He said that it reminded him of "southern darkey camp meetings." Parham would even go on to become a supporter of the Klu Klux Klan. Most Pentecostals would reject the evils of the Klan, and Pentecostals were even subject to KKK persecution in the South, as were blacks. Much of the hatred toward Pentecostalism stemmed directly from racism, not theological concerns.

There are truly various degrees of depravity to the stronghold of racism. The depth to which Parham was affected by this demonic influence is unclear. I believe racism is inherently connected to divisiveness, which may explain why Parham's ministry was severely marked by conflict. On this note, I was encouraged to discover that John Dowie always integrated his church services and made sure to keep an African-American on his leadership board. "The time has come for this horrible so called 'race prejudice' to be wiped out," said Dowie. "There is only one race—the children of Adam and Eve."

Despite the criticism of Azusa that was leveled by Parham, Seymour always refused to speak out against his old teacher. He would lock him out of the building, but he wouldn't speak against him. The reasons he kept quiet were not very theologically sound. Seymour thought you could lose your salvation. And so, he thought that by judging Parham and causing division, he was in danger of losing his own salvation!

"If you get angry, or speak evil, or backbite, I care not how many tongues you may have, you have not the baptism with the Holy Spirit. You have lost your salvation," said Seymour.[14] Of course, this was absurd. But we must remember the electric atmosphere of spiritual gifts and manifestations which Seymour was pastoring. He was probably just trying to maintain healthy focus on Christian character, while the gifts were flooding back into the church. Nevertheless, "lose your salvation" theology may work to keep some holiness in the camp for a little while, but it always leads to more harm than good. Eventually, Seymour's flock began pointing fingers at one another and backbiting, questioning one another's salvation.

Again, we should remember that Azusa and the birth of Pentecostalism was never a theological reformation. It was a restoration of the spiritual gifts back into the church. Of course, a byproduct of this is that the gifts have to make their way back into the

Azusa Street Building

Smith Wigglesworth

theology of those who have written them off. Usually, theological arguments are counterproductive in convincing people of the power and gifts of God. They must be displayed, wherein they speak for themselves. This is why testimonies of great Christian miracle workers are important. Let us look at a few more:

Smith Wigglesworth (1859-1947) is such a well-known figure, one could write many volumes about him. His contributions to the faith were phenomenal during this period. Wigglesworth raised the dead. And his boldness was legendary. Sometimes he would punch sick people with his fist, and they would be instantly healed. He once threw a baby across the stage, and it was healed on the spot.

A British evangelist, Wigglesworth was a simple plumber who claimed to have never read anything but the Bible. He was working a job by the time he was 6 years old, and by the time he was 7, he worked 12 hours a day in a mill. Later in life, his wife was the spiritual leader of the home, an evangelist who preached in mission outreaches, while he earned the bread and butter. Then in the late 1800s, Wigglesworth was miraculously healed of a ruptured appendix. This set him on a course of ministry that would take him around the world, though he was already a middle-aged man. In 1907, he received the gift of tongues and a baptism of the Holy Spirit.

Earlier you read how the Spirit of the fear of the Lord rested on Smith. He once walked into a grocery store, and without saying a word, three people fell to the floor and began repenting. He sometimes would be led to go to a specific place, without knowing why, and an unbeliever would show up and give his life to the Lord there. Smith would sometimes simply ask "Are you saved?" to a complete stranger and they would begin weeping. But other times, he would pray and an entire congregation would roll on the floor in holy laughter.

When his wife, Polly, died of a heart attack, Smith rushed home and raised her from the dead. Frustrated with him, Polly told Smith that it was her time to go, and he unselfishly released her to go back with the Lord. His faith was phenomenal. He felt that faith mixed with compassion was the key to effective prayer and healing. He pulled numerous people off their death beds, healed tuberculosis and had people running out of their wheelchairs. Many were delivered and set free from demons. He sometimes would speak to crowds of up to 20,000, and a corporate healing anointing would fall. He would have each person lay hands on the afflicted part of their body, and when he prayed, scores were healed. As he traveled to Third World nations, it was reported that the anointing rested on him so strongly that people were healed when his very shadow passed by, as crowds thronged him for prayer.

Wigglesworth was an old school, no-medicine type of faith healer. He suffered with severe, painful kidney stones for six years, refusing surgery. At this time, he was often preaching several times a day, praying for hundreds of people. That alone is a lot of work, but Wigglesworth would often have to pull away from the pulpit, go to the restroom and pass a kidney stone, then return to finish his ministry. I don't think "tough" is an adequate word to describe this man.

Interestingly, Lester Sumrall, who spent a significant amount of time with Wigglesworth, recalls him prophesying a last-day healing revival. He said that multitudes beyond number would be saved and that no disease would be able to stand before God's people.

"I see the greatest revival in the history of mankind coming to planet earth, maybe as never before. And I see the dead raised. I see every form of disease healed. I see whole hospitals emptied with no one there. Even the doctors are running down the streets shouting," he told Sumrall.[15]

James Salter (1890-1972), Wigglesworth's son-in-law, was representative of a major overseas missionary thrust that swept the world

James Salter buries a missionary companion in Africa.

during the first few decades following Azusa Street.

Salter was a missionary to Congo, venturing to unreached people groups in central Africa where all but two of his missionary team died. He also experienced dramatic miraculous activity. Besides catching malaria, evading cannibals, and dodging bullets and arrows at times, Salter was miraculously cured of blackwater fever on several occasions, though it was an incurable disease. In addition, he reported seeing the dead raised, lepers cleansed and many other infirmities healed.

Aimee Semple McPherson (1890-1944) was a dynamic personality in early Pentecostalism who brought the tenets of divine healing into public awareness. She drew the religious ire of many church leaders in her day. She was followed by controversy, but she was also a pioneer at operating in the spiritual gifts while being open and relevant to the culture of her day. Even Hollywood was drawn to Aimee, and the public loved her.

Aimee initially incorporated healing into her services, not because she considered herself gifted for the miraculous, but she simply thought it was a requirement for any ministry to operate that way. She held revivals in major cities around the nation, opening blind eyes, healing broken bones and pulling people out of wheelchairs. The *Los Angeles Times* and the *New York Times* both covered Aimee's healing ministry, making her a household name. Thousands flocked to her revivals. She moved from tents to coliseums, and in a four-year period had traveled across country nine times. At one point she was speaking to 16,000 people two times a day, with thousands more turned away because of lack of space.

During one early meeting, a lamp exploded in Aimee's face, and she had to douse her head in a bucket of water to quench the flames. It blistered her neck and face, and she left the revival tent in agony. A heckler then jumped onto the platform and jeered "The lady who preaches divine healing has been hurt. She burned her face, so there will be no meeting tonight."

When Aimee heard this, she stubbornly rushed back to the stage and took the platform, still in pain, and began worshiping the Lord on the piano. The entire crowd watched in amazement as her face began to change color and the red blisters disappeared before their eyes.

Born in Ontario, Canada, to parents with Salvation Army and Methodist backgrounds, Aimee was frustrated with the common Christian mind-set of the times. She gradually

Aimee Semple McPherson

drifted from the church, digging into Darwinian evolution and the secular culture of her day. It was then when she became familiar with pop music, literature, and drama. But she was drawn back to the Lord after attending a tent revival with Scottish Pentecostal evangelist Robert Semple, who she would soon marry at age 17. The two traveled the world on an evangelistic tour. But Robert died shortly afterward of malaria in Hong Kong in 1910, just before the birth of their first child. Aimee returned to America, continuing evangelistic efforts on her own for some time, until she met Harold McPherson, an accountant, whom she married in 1912.

While social pressures pulled her toward domestic life as a wife and mother, Aimee for years felt a need to return to her call as an evangelist. After recovering from a near-death illness, Aimee finally answered the call. At first, she was joined by Harold, and the two traveled with Aimee often speaking eight to 10 times a day. But Harold wanted to settle down, and eventually stayed with the children to work permanently at home—reportedly he often sent her telegrams to "come home and wash the dishes."[16] Aimee's independence kept her on the field, but unfortunately it also cost her the marriage as well.

Aimee boldly challenged gender limitations, which was also a major social theme in that time period. While her call to ministry was obviously valid, it is difficult to assume whether she took appropriate actions on the home front. Nevertheless, the call needed to be answered, and she responded. Aimee did not consent to divorce until the couple had been separated for two years.

In 1923, Aimee opened the 5,300-seat Angelus Temple in Los Angeles. For an entire decade, Aimee was on the front page of Los Angeles newspapers an average of three times a week.[17] It was here that Aimee truly pioneered the use of modern arts and culture in a redemptive manner to express the gospel. While Aimee's meetings were distinctly Pentecostal in some aspects, they catered to a much broader spectrum of people. She would incorporate entertainment and drama with elaborate costumed productions and musicals in the pre-television era of Hollywood cinema. Brass bands, large choirs, and stage plays were common. Aimee felt the gospel must be illustrated through the arts, not just spoken. Her services were loaded with full-throttle theatrics. It would not be strange to see her ride down the center aisle on a motorcycle. But there would also be special healing services set aside, with acres of stretchers and wheelchairs lined up for her to pass by. Aimee started a Bible college and the first Christian radio station. In fact, Aimee paved the way for women in radio, as well as the pulpit. She eventually founded the International Church of the Foursquare Gospel. When Aimee began the Foursquare denomination, there were 1,000 pastors who signed up on the first day of membership.

Aimee sought to strike a balance between the operation of spiritual gifts and maintaining cultural relevance. She clearly saw the need and value of both. Aimee sought to keep what she considered "fanaticism" at bay, concerning the manifestations of the Spirit in her ministry, without utterly rejecting them. She set aside the 500 Room, an area apart from her main auditorium to serve as a "tarrying place," for the miraculous gifts, speaking in tongues, and divine healing. The 500 Room was known throughout the nation as a "modern pool of Bethesda."

By 1926, Aimee had attracted a great following. It was then that the infamous kidnapping incident occurred. Aimee's sudden disappearance from Venice Beach was front page news across the country. Authorities believed Aimee to have drowned at the beach, and a funeral was even held for her. Surprisingly, she reappeared a month later in Arizona, dehydrated and claiming that she had been kidnapped. Rumors began to surface that Aimee was actually having a romantic affair during this time, with witnesses claiming they had sighted her during the ordeal. She was charged with obstruction of justice and stood trial both in the courts and in the press. The charges were finally dropped for lack of evidence.

To this day, the details of the kidnapping incident remain a mystery. Whatever the facts of the case may have been, the event cast a shadow on Aimee's ministry. She bounced back with a "vindication tour," but soon had a nervous breakdown. In 1931, Aimee married again to singer David Hutton.

"Hutton, a vaudeville and cabaret performer, was known for being a womanizer and for drinking alcohol, all of which caused him to be considered inappropriate 'husband material' for a pious religious leader," writes researcher Barbara Campbell.[18] The Hutton marriage also ended in disaster within three years. The remaining decade of Aimee's life was quieter, dominated by lawsuits, church politics, and the regular ups and downs of big ministry. She died in 1944 at age 53 from an accidental overdose of sleeping pills.

Aimee defied boundaries and challenged the way church was done. Perhaps Liardon describes her best in saying, "If publicity seemed bad, she hyped it further, smiling all the way. If everyone warned her against doing something, she was apt to do the opposite, refusing to bow to fear. …Whatever it took to get the people turned to Jesus Christ, Aimee did it. She sat with the 'publicans and prostitutes,' showing up in places where the average Christian was afraid to go. The poor, the common, and the rich all loved her for it, and they showed up at her meetings by the thousands."

Aimee's life was not perfect. She was not successful in balancing family and ministry. She made great strides in balancing cultural relevance and supernatural power as tools for advancing the gospel. I believe in our day, God is now calling us to a much higher level of organically weaving the supernatural into our church communities. Not just shoving spiritual gifts into the back room. Not that I am criticizing Aimee's approach. She was still pushing the envelope for her day, and should be admired for it. The fact is, there are no easy formulas, and Aimee was a pioneer. On top of it all, she proves a good lesson—God prefers green, ambitious and slightly immature over religious, stale, and falsely mature.

Dr. Charles Price (1887-1947) was another great healer and a forerunner to the Latter Rain Revival, highlighted in the next chapter. Price was a major revivalist in the 1920s, though he died just prior to the Latter Rain outbreak in 1947. Both Price and Smith Wigglesworth died within days of one another the same year the Voice of Healing Revival began, passing the torch and the mantle to the next generation of wonder workers.

Dr. Charles Price

Born in England, Price studied law at Oxford, later moved to Canada and then came to the United States. He was a successful minister, pastoring a very modern church in California which even sported its own bowling alley, though Price would later describe himself as being "spiritually blind, leading his people into a ditch."

Prior to any supernatural experience of his own, a member of Price's congregation received the baptism of the Holy Spirit. This perked Price's interest, and he decided to investigate the Pentecostal claims, if only to debunk them. It so happened that Aimee Semple McPherson was holding a tent meeting at that time in his area. Price attended the meeting, but only as a critic, in order to take notes of what she said so he could warn his church about her claims. He went to her meetings as a hardened skeptic, vowing to discredit her. Instead, Price found himself on his knees in repentance speaking in other tongues during the service. He even responded to an altar call for the unsaved.

Price's message and ministry took a dramatic shift at that point. He began preaching an uncompromised message of the cross and the power available to the church today. He then left the pastorate for evangelistic work, where thousands would be converted and healed. Crowds swelled. It is reported that Price preached to 250,000 in a three-week crusade in Vancouver. Those were phenomenal numbers for a crowd in that era.

Price's meetings were regimented. People were required to hear three of his sermons and list them on a prayer card, before he would pray for them. This was to build their faith for healing. And his sermons were two hours in length. He would then call out certain prayer card numbers to come forward. Sometimes he would call only 50 out of a crowd of 10,000. But Price did not simply lay hands on those who came forward. He labored and persevered over each one until they were actually healed on the spot, even if it took an hour.[19] It was said plainly that "Dr. Price prayed for healing and people were healed." He also had sworn affidavits obtained from those who were healed, as well as doctor confirmation of their initial diagnoses. Many were healed during his sermons, without hands-on prayer from Price. It was not unusual for Price to pray for 1,000 people in one night, or to have a prayer line of 500 people. It is said that 95 percent of those receiving prayer would be slain in the Spirit.

Price's "full gospel" message was influential to Demos Shakarian, founder of Full Gospel Business Men's Fellowship. Shakarian tells of first meeting Price at a tent service, where cars were parked half a mile away and people were spread out on the grass, every seat having been taken in the tent. Hundreds of people wanted prayer, and

Price prayed for hours. There was a line waiting still late into the night, but the ushers were finally closing down the meeting, turning them away because of the time. Shakarian knew he would never reach Price that night.

Desperate, Shakarian dodged the ushers and called out to Price, who was already gathering up his Bible and anointing oil bottle to leave.

"Dr. Price, my name is Demos Shakarian, and my sister's been in an automobile accident, and the doctors in Downey Hospital say she can't live, and we wondered if you'd come," he said desperately. Shakarian's account is as follows:

Dr. Price closed his eyes and I saw the weariness in his face. He remained standing there a moment. Then abruptly he opened his eyes. "I will come," he said.

I hurried ahead of him through the slowly dispersing crowd, fretting each time someone stopped him. Dr. Price noticed my impatience. "Don't be anxious, son," he said. "Your sister will be healed tonight."

I stared at the man. How could he make such a blandly certain statement? But of course, I reminded myself, he hadn't seen the X rays; he couldn't have any idea how serious the situation was.[20]

On the way to the hospital, Price told a story of driving in Canada years earlier, when once he felt a strange urge to turn right. He did this, and later felt the same urge to turn left. He traveled this way, until he was guided to a Methodist Church, knowing he was to stop there. He rang the pastor's doorbell, and suddenly found that he was inviting himself to preach. The pastor agreed. When the meetings were held there, Price was drawn to a young crippled woman who was being carried in each night and placed on the front bench. Her legs were twisted and shriveled, and she had been bedridden for 10 years, having exhausted all manner of treatments from 20 different doctors. Every time Price looked at her, he felt the warmth of the presence of God.

He told the congregation that they were about to witness a very special miracle. He stepped down from the platform, laid his hands on the woman's head, and began to pray. Before the entire congregation, the woman's back drew erect, the twisted legs straightened and grew visibly longer, and although she had not taken a step for over ten years, Eva Wilson Johnston got to her feet and walked—almost danced—the entire length of the aisle. Dr. Price was still in touch with the Johnstons; the healing had been permanent.[21]

Price told Shakarian that he was about to see a similar miracle, because he felt God's presence in the same way as soon as Shakarian approached him. They reached the small hospital where Shakarian's sister, Florence, was staying. They were fitted in gowns and masks and permitted to enter, where she was lathered in salve and fitted with tubes and pulley wires. Price began to pray, and the room became thick with the presence of God. Florence began to roll back and forth, swinging the traction weights wildly around the room, although she had been ordered to stay immobile by the doctors. The next morning, Shakarian received a call from the doctor to come to the hospital.

The X-ray room was jammed when I arrived, doctors, nurses, lab technicians all crowding to see. Pinned against a lighted screen were eight X-ray plates. The first seven showed a crushed and dislocated left hip and pelvis. The bone was almost pulverized in places, the bone chips more widely dispersed in each succeeding photograph. The eighth slide, taken that morning, showed a pelvis that was normal in every respect. The two sides of the picture were identical: the left hip bone as well formed as the right. Only some hair-fine lines indicated that once—surely many years ago—this solid bone had ever been injured.[22]

This was only one of numerous creative miracles in Price's ministry. But like F.F. Bosworth, Raymond Richey, and Aimee Semple McPherson, Price had to discontinue his large campaigns in the 1930s, because of the financial hardship of the depression. The splintering of the Pentecostal denominations also played a part in squelching the campaigns. Nevertheless, at the time of his death, Price predicted the post-war revival, anticipating that the church was just on the brink of another great move of God.

There were a number of miracle-working evangelists whose ministry in the 1920s carried over into the Latter Rain Revival of the '40s and '50s. Many were influenced by the same teachers. For instance, E.W. Kenyon made a profound impact on many of the faith healers of the 20th century. Kenyon served as an evangelist, pastor, and president of a Bible school, but it was his writing that impacted a generation. While Kenyon was primarily a teacher, healing miracles were common in his ministry, and his books on the subject are still in relatively high demand. Kenyon's teachings have either directly or indirectly impacted almost every faith healing ministry today. F.F. Bosworth and John G. Lake relied heavily on Kenyon's work, and these men, in turn, impacted a subsequent generation of revivalists. T.L. Osborn, in his book *Healing the Sick*, credits Kenyon as one of the greatest teachers on divine healing.

Another major teaching influence was Franklin Hall, whose book *Atomic Power With God Through Fasting and Prayer* sparked a major wave of extended fasting and prayer from 1946 to 1947. Many undertook 40-day fasts, praying for a move of God. Then, in 1947, the Voice of Healing Revival erupted. Most of those major revivalists credited Hall's fasting methods as a key to the power they walked in.

There were many contributing factors leading up to the great revival that began in 1947. But each of the fiery saints we have discussed were forerunners to the flame that was about to ignite the world.

ENDNOTES

1. Maria Woodworth-Etter, A Diary of Signs and Wonders (Tulsa: Harrison House, 1980 ed.).

2. Liz Godschalk, "John G. Lake." (Brisbane: Anointed for Revival, 1995). Site accessed <http://www.pastornet.net.au/renewal>.

3. "John G. Lake 'A Man of Healing.'" (Healing Rooms Ministries of Spokane, Wash.) Accessed 31 Oct. 2004 <http://www.healingrooms.com/history.htm>. Article source: Gordon Lindsay, "John G. Lake–Apostle to Africa." (1981).

4. Andrew Strom and Robert Holmes, "The Life and Times of John G. Lake." Accessed 31 Oct. 2004 <http://home.swipnet.se/~w-93281/enlace.htm>.

5. For more information on Evan Roberts and the Welsh Revival, a number of resource links are available at www.welshrevival.com.

6. Francis Frangipane, The Three Battlegrounds (Cedar Rapids: Arrow Publications, 1996 ed.), 123, 119.

7. "Stephen Jeffreys." Arise Magazine (2003). Accessed 30 Oct. 2004 <http://users.110.net/~pq1550/s-jeffreys.html>.

8. Ibid.

9. Lester Sumrall, Pioneers of Faith (Ben Publishing, 1995), 92.

10. Ibid., 93.

11. Rick Joyner, The Harvest (Charlotte: Morningstar Publications, 1993), 201.

12. David Edwin Harrell, Jr., All Things are Possible: The Healing and Charismatic Revivals in Modern America (Bloomington: Indiana University Press, 1978 ed.), 18.

13. Roberts Liardon, God's Generals (Whitaker House, 1996), 154.

14. Ibid., 159.

15. Pioneers of Faith, 168.

16. Barbara A. Campbell, "A Brief History of Aimee Semple McPherson." (1997). Posted by Aimee Semple McPherson Resource Center. Accessed 4 Sept. 2004 <http://members.aol.com/xbcampbell/asm/history.ht>.

17. All Things are Possible, 16.

18. Campbell, "A Brief History of Aimee Semple McPherson."

19. Demos Shakarian with John Sherrill and Elizabeth Sherrill, The Happiest People on Earth: The Long-Awaited Personal Story of Demos Shakarian (Hodder Christian Paperbacks, 1977).

20. Ibid.

21. Ibid.

22. Ibid.

CHAPTER 12

Voice of Healing

T HE great healing revival of the 1940s and '50s brought the most extensive public display of miraculous power in modern history. Though we read little of it today, it shook North America from coast to coast. Birthed from humble beginnings, the revival started with a handful of dirt poor men coming out of the Great Depression, many of whom were from alcoholic homes, had been abandoned, or were even raised as orphans. Yet God had transformed their lives. They each operated as independent ministries, but in the heyday of the revival, they worked under the loose affiliation of The Voice of Healing magazine, and demonstrated unprecedented unity amid the fractured denominationalism of that era.

"Most were dedicated to back-breaking work and spent long grueling hours in the centers of the platforms of the big tents praying, clapping, shouting, pleading with the crippled to walk, commanding the blind to see. ...It was an exhausting, grinding, draining way of life. William Branham was a broken man after little more than a year; Jack Coe was physically exhausted at the time of his death; A.A. Allen, an incredibly tough campaigner, tottered constantly on the brink of psychological collapse; the resilience of Oral Roberts became a legend among his peers," writes historian David Harrell, Jr.[1]

Known simply as the healing revival, Voice of Healing Revival, or Latter Rain Revival, this move of God sparked perhaps the greatest evangelistic efforts the world has ever seen that carried over into the 1960s, '70s, and '80s. Its offspring either directly or indirectly included the charismatic movement, the Word of Faith movement, the counterculture Jesus People of the '60s and '70s, and later the Toronto renewal of the '90s, all of which owe their spiritual lineage to the healing revivalists. This move of God officially restored the office of the evangelist back into the church, even as the prophetic office is being reintroduced today.

No one really expected this revival before it broke, though some earlier revivalists saw it coming in shadow. Once it was unleashed, every community in the nation wanted a miracle healing service. The colossal leaders of the revival were William Branham and Oral Roberts. Yet every revivalist brought a different approach and a unique anointing to the table. Any one of these men's lives could fill volumes of books full of supernatural testimonies and unexplained phenomena. They were once household names, filling city auditoriums and massive revival tents by the thousands. Yet we have forgotten their works in a single generation. Branham was the true mystic of the movement. Gordon Lindsay was the publicist and the de facto organizer of the revival. Oral Roberts surpassed the rest in organizational skill and eventually popularity, though rough and tumble Jack Coe challenged him as the people's favorite. T.L. Osborn kept his eyes on the nations, and A.A. Allen was by far the most flamboyant. We will look extensively at this single decade of history—primarily 1947 to 1958—because theirs was a major birth pang in the body of Christ, signaling a miraculous deposit of the Kingdom which has yet to be fully delivered.

The prophetic renewal of recent years has not had a heavy evangelism focus. But as the Lord begins releasing *apostolic* ministry in our midst, we will see the prophetic merge with evangelism like never before. It's already beginning to happen. Prophetic gifts are a major evangelistic tool, as was demonstrated in the life of William Branham. Like a seed that died, the glories of his generation are already sprouting again to bring forth a harvest many times larger. The power displayed in that generation will be multiplied exponentially. Let us be prepared for what is to come.

William Branham

William Branham (1909-1965) clearly emerged as the leader of the Voice of Healing Revival beginning in 1947, moving in an unprecedented power mantle that few have ever displayed. Marked by deep humility, Branham was a meek and soft-spoken, middle-aged man. With barely any education and very little eloquence in his early ministry, Branham possessed a deadly accurate prophetic gifting and a tremendous divine healing anointing.

Born in a dirt-floor log cabin in deep poverty, Branham grew up with an alcoholic father in the backwoods of Kentucky. His family reported that a supernatural light descended and shone around him at his birth. He also remembered God speaking to him at the early ages of 3 and 7. Branham came from such an abjectly poor background, that he would piece together an old coat with safety pins, because he did not have a shirt to wear underneath as a child.[2] And while other healing evangelists were building small fortunes in his wake, Branham continued to wear cheap frumpy suits and refused a large income even when he rose to national prominence. No one could doubt his sincerity or accuse him of showmanship.

Branham's childhood home was a dirt-floor log cabin.

Branham was a true mystic. He constantly held audiences in awe with tales of conversations with God and angels. And every night, before spellbound crowds of thousands, he would supernaturally discern diseases of complete strangers and pronounce people instantly healed on the spot. Without fail, they were healed.

Branham was ordained as a Baptist minister, and briefly did tent evangelism in 1933 with marked success. He was baptizing 130 converts at that time in the Ohio River when another supernatural light came down and

Branham photographed with a halo.

hovered around him. Some fled in fear, while others fell on their faces in worship. But after that brief revival during the Depression, he returned to pastor a poor congregation. Money was tight and he preached for free, as most everyone was in severe poverty. It was during these lean years that a far worse tragedy came into his life. He lost his wife and a child in 1937 when the Ohio River flooded, causing them to contract tuberculosis. Branham watched his young daughter die in his own arms, as her eyes crossed with the severe pain she was feeling.

"Branham said that when he looked into the face of a child with crossed eyes, he saw his little girl, and it gave him compassion to believe in that child's healing," noted evangelist Don Stewart. "At the time, more than 400 children with crossed eyes had been healed in his meetings."[3]

Branham always blamed himself for the death of his wife and children.

On May 7, 1946, Branham received an angelic visitation that officially launched him to the forefront of the healing revival, and, in fact, launched the entire revival itself. The angel told Branham, among other things that, "If you will be sincere, and can get the people to believe you, nothing shall stand before your prayer, not even cancer."[4]

The angel also told Branham that he would be able to discern diseases by a vibration in his left hand. He began preaching and praying for the sick in small churches. His reputation spread like wildfire, and within a month, crowds had reportedly swelled to 25,000 in the small town of Jonesboro, Arkansas, flocking in from 28 states and across the border from Mexico. Branham first raised the dead there—a woman who was brought to the meeting in the back of an ambulance. The crowd was so thick that Branham could not open the door to get back out of the ambulance. In another meeting, a woman was struck dead outside the tent after rejecting the presence of God, which apparently rested as strongly on the meeting as in the Acts 5 account of Ananias and Sapphira. Branham prayed for her and she recovered.

Time magazine even published an article on Branham. He was once photographed with a supernatural "halo" above his head. Visitors reported seeing the tangible glory of God appear in the form of a pillar of light alongside him in some meetings. From the onset, the deaf, lame, and blind were healed. His associate Ern Baxter estimated 35,000 healings in his first year of ministry alone. Branham—not a self-promoting man—brought evangelist Gordon Lindsay alongside him, who began to publicize the revival, starting *The Voice of Healing* magazine. Very soon, the world took notice.

Branham became ever more dependent on a healing angel that would come alongside him to minister to the sick. Often, if the anointing was not present, Branham would simply cut his meetings short and walk out, leaving thousands frustrated. Branham sometimes did this if he felt the congregation was looking too exclusively at him to effect the healings. Sometimes, Branham would cancel large revivals at the last minute after feeling a leading from the Lord to do so. This frustrated many organizers who had planned extensively for the meetings. But Branham was not disinterested. He would literally spend hours praying for the sick until his associates sometimes had to drag him from the platform. There were no cases that were too hard for Branham. He raised another dead person in Finland—a young boy hit by a car on his bicycle, whom Branham had seen earlier in a vision before he left America.

In 1951, Branham was used to heal a former congressman, William D. Upshaw, who was able to walk normally after spending 59 years of his life on crutches and seven years bedridden. The king of England also requested prayer from Branham. In another dramatic case, an Indiana Bible college that was opposed to divine healing prohibited its students from attending a nearby Branham revival, with the exception of one blind student who was accompanied by a teacher. During the service, Branham spontaneously called out the girl, whom he had never met, supernaturally discerning that she was a student, that she was blind and that she was with her teacher. She was immediately healed, and the college officials were overwhelmed. They closed the school for the remainder of his meetings and mandated that all students attend the revival.

F.F. Bosworth, a widely respected and aged evangelist from the 1920s revival, fully endorsed Branham and often traveled with him. "When the gift is operating," wrote Bosworth, "Brother Branham is the most sensitive person to the presence and working of the Holy Spirit and to spiritual realities of any person I have ever known."[5] Bosworth said that in his own campaigns, it took weeks to reach the same level of faith for miracles that Branham reached in only one night.

As he would pray for deliverance from afflicting spirits, Branham's hand would begin to tremble and would sometimes become red and swollen, with a feeling of intense electricity. The power would often stop his wristwatch. But as soon as the demon departed from a person, and they were healed, his hand would quickly return to normal. Branham acknowledged that this was no special power of his own, only a gift from the Lord.

Audiences were most mesmerized, however, by Branham's uncanny gift of the word of knowledge. Countless observers noted that Branham had 100 percent accuracy. He would point people out of the crowd and call them up by name—even in foreign countries where dialects were obscure—and would tell them their disease. Branham would know the exact city they were from, exactly what they were praying about and what they were thinking, then would suddenly proclaim that they were healed without even laying hands on them. He did this extensively every night. There were no prayer cards or phony means of extracting this information beforehand. Yet, even with such a powerful gifting, Branham was often too timid to preach. He would have his associate, Baxter, preach in the early days; then Branham would come forward just to pray for people. Branham never raised his voice when he was speaking, nor did he use any showy tactics. He relied fully on the Lord and his gifting. His speaking was so unimpressive that people sometimes fell asleep during his rambling messages. But when the Spirit suddenly began to move on Branham, God showed up in a dynamic way.

No other evangelist had such prophetic authority or the ability to consistently heal the sick with a spoken word, as did Branham. His was truly a forerunner ministry that has yet to be fully emulated to this day.

Branham would often push the microphone away to discretely discuss a personal sin with someone, and they would instantly be healed before he even prayed for them. Conviction would suddenly grip his audiences as people began to repent and weep, feeling that their sins would be exposed. Branham was almost consistently compared to Old Testament seers. His gifts brought deep respect from other evangelists, who all looked up to him—including Oral Roberts—and they all admired his genuine humility. Journalists from around the globe flocked to his meetings. He would fill auditoriums hours before a service, with many camping out all night for a seat.

As the revival spread, many evangelists used hard-sell tactics to get funds, but Branham just casually passed the plate, often hesitant about taking an offering for himself. Branham literally paid no attention to the money, and while some saw this as a strength, others saw it as a flaw. Oral Roberts on the other hand was building a massive radio and television ministry, as well as a full-fledged accredited university—an expert organizer and businessman.

Branham was clearly on another wavelength. He never sold anything or promoted himself. In fact, he shunned the expensive lifestyle lived by many of the later evangelists.

Somewhat careless and clearly naïve about money matters, Branham was halted by financial problems in 1955. He suddenly faced large deficits. The Internal Revenue Service filed a suit against Branham in 1956 for tax evasion. We are used to seeing this type of thing turn into a big expose of greed on the part of the minister. But the opposite was true for Branham. Investigation showed that Branham's manager had brought in $80,000 that year, while Branham only claimed an income of $7,000. He had paid little or no attention to the massive funds funneling through his own ministry, and others had clearly been taking advantage of him. Branham had been living on a shoestring this whole time. He never fully recovered from this episode.[6]

Branham's reasoning was simple, and his lack of strong Bible knowledge eventually led him into poor doctrine. Following the financial problems—and with the revival being flooded with new evangelists by the late 1950s—he became increasingly isolated and uncharacteristically competitive. Ministry tapered off and settled down. Branham seemed almost innocently swayed by a fervent, cult-like following in his later years. While Branham was insistent about avoiding needless controversy and maintaining unity in the early years of the revival, his teachings grew increasingly divisive toward the end. He also became quick to attach "Thus saith the Lord" to minor points of doctrine—and abstract ones at that—abusing his gift.

Branham's doctrine quickly became wild and wacky. He began to believe denominationalism was the mark of the beast, and by the 1960s, openly taught the Oneness, anti-Trinitarian position of the "Jesus Only" Pentecostals.[7] He taught that hell was not eternal, that divorce was always permissible if it's the man's choice, and that Eve had a sexual relationship with satan in the Garden of Eden. The most self-absorbed of his beliefs was that one day he would have the power to speak and change physical bodies into glorified ones for the rapture. Branham felt that his own mouth had been created in a unique way to accurately pronounce the name of God, "JHVH," to enable this all to happen.

Perhaps the greatest tragedy was the unhealthy adoration Branham was beginning to receive from his followers. According to several insiders, Branham hated this and was wise enough to preach openly against it, but few seemed to listen. Followers began to call Branham "Elijah" or "the last days prophet." Still others thought he was Jesus Christ. Some even baptized converts in the name of William Branham and said he was born of a virgin. Branham despised this. Keep this in mind—as wacky as his doctrine had become, Branham never sought to become the idol of sycophants. All he had worked for in ministry was being ruined because of such activity, he said. He told followers that all of the people's blood who would otherwise have been healed or saved through his ministry would be on their own heads if they continued such nonsense and ruined his ministry. Branham confided in Paul Cain, then just a young associate, that the Lord was about to take him away because of this activity. That was the last Paul Cain saw of Branham. On Dec. 18, 1965, Branham was killed in a head-on collision with a drunken driver.

Branham's followers thought he would be raised from the dead, and they stored his body in the attic of a local funeral home from December 1965 to the following Easter Sunday 1966, fully expecting him to resurrect. Finally, they buried him. There were reportedly 300 churches at the time of his death that believed Branham to be the end-time prophet of Malachi 4. There are still cultish Branhamite churches in existence today, who hang the "halo photo" in their buildings and listen to his old sermons on cassette. All of his sermons have been meticulously transcribed by them and are used during their services. They place his words on par with Scripture.

Harrell relates that Branham became "susceptible to those who wanted to use his reputation for their own financial or doctrinal benefit. Perhaps his death saved him from obscurity or further scandal."[8]

Despite the cultish following and poor doctrine of his latter years, one cannot deny the phenomenal, genuine anointing on Branham's life that sparked the entire healing revival. It is important not to judge the man or his ministry by the small sliver of his later life that was marked by confusion. Thousands received salvation through his ministry. And he indirectly lit a fire that enflamed the world with evangelism—its effects still being seen today through the offspring of that revival. Thousands sometimes received miraculous healing in a *single* night in Branham's services. Thousands. Branham was ahead of his time with his gifts—several steps ahead of his contemporaries who moved almost solely in healing but without the powerful words of knowledge he displayed.

Even in Branham's death, we see that his supernatural gifts were irrevocable. His doctrines may have gotten bizarre, but he still carried an anointing. At the time of his automobile wreck, Branham was driving with his wife, following his son who was in another car. After the vehicle hit him, Branham lay dying, his bones broken. His son turned the other car around and came back to the scene. Branham asked if his wife was OK, but she had just died.

"Just lay my hand on her," Branham told his son. He picked up his father's hand and placed it on his mother's body. Immediately her pulse returned and she later recovered.[9]

I find it interesting that the Lord is already laying a corporate foundation of prophetic teaching in the body today that will thrust the next healing revival to new proportions. Sound teaching must accompany the prophetic. The church was not prepared for Branham's anointing, and so that level of power had to be reserved for another generation. Often when spiritual blessings are corporately withdrawn because of sin, there is literally a 50-year jubilee cycle before debts are cancelled and they are released into the earth again. That time is now for the power mantles of the Latter Rain evangelists.

Some have attributed Branham's sad ending to his gradual disassociation from Gordon Lindsay—a gifted teacher who could have balanced Branham, had he remained in closer contact with him. Branham lacked grounding in Scripture.

As for Branham's demise, prophetic teacher Paul Keith Davis relates a vision in which he was actually taken back in time to a William Branham meeting.[10] In the vision, Davis was helping to escort the crowd up to Branham for prayer, and was watching Branham's movements as he prayed for the sick. Davis then saw two serpents coming after Branham. One of them represented the *hatred of man*. Nearly every ministry that moves in great power will face intense persecution and hatred. People will utterly reject and despise you; it simply comes with the territory. Consider the death threats and murder attempts on John Alexander Dowie; the persecution of countless saints, martyrs, and prophets; and the skeptical press attacks and lawsuits against almost every miracle ministry. If we choose to pursue our supernatural Kingdom birthright, these are giants we will have to face. To pursue the miraculous takes a radical commitment to risk everything—reputation and even the respect of family and friends—for the sake of the gospel.

In Davis' vision, Branham overcame that first serpent. Persecution did not hinder him. But it was the next serpent which got him. The second serpent was the *adoration of man*. That was also the one which took out Dowie in the end, as well as Stephen Jeffreys and others. That serpent was perhaps the chief adversary of the entire healing revival. If the enemy cannot stop you with outright resistance and persecution, he will thrust you onto a pedestal. We cannot take the glory for ourselves; we cannot draw attention away from the Lord.

"When you make an idol out of man, you destroy his ministry," says prophetic minister Bob Jones. "Long ago, I was told that my ministry is a failure unless you go past me. ...When you start worshiping an idol, you'll never attain to his level. But when you listen to those the Lord is using, His main purpose is to get you on that level...so you can go on up."[11] Rather than idolizing our leaders, we must recognize that their level of ministry is just the starting point from which we can build higher! These men are the floor, not the ceiling. The nature of apostolic reproduction is that we go past them. I believe the Lord is still hesitant to release the true apostolic anointing in this hour, because we will quickly want to idolize it, instead of imitating it. Davis says we must learn from forerunners such as Branham—their successes and their failures—in order to take our birthright, which is the Kingdom dimension in which they walked.

Gordon Lindsay (1906-1973) was the publisher of *The Voice of Healing* maga-zine, which would launch most of the revival's ministries into promi-nence. Lindsay brought cohesion and unity to this movement of healing revivalists. They crossed denomina-tional lines as a loose affiliation of mostly independent ministers. Few, if any, ecumenical efforts of this kind had survived up to that point, especial-

Young Brown, Jack Moore, William Branham and Oral Roberts with Gordon Lindsay, left to right.

ly in the splintered Pentecostal churches. The unity these men expe-rienced was short lived but very fruitful—and most of this harmony is to the credit of Lindsay.

Lindsay was a healing evangelist himself, with roots in Alexander Dowie's Zion City as a child. His parents sat directly under Dowie's anointing. Lindsay himself studied under John G. Lake and was even converted by Charles Parham, giving him an impressive spiritual heritage. Lindsay held a number of evangelistic crusades prior to World War II, but then settled into a pastorate. After the war, he met the gifted William Branham in 1947. After seeing Branham's phe-nomenal gifts at work, Lindsay agreed to become his manager, and soon started the magazine to promote the revivals. The magazine began featuring other evangelists as well, and grew to be the mouth-piece for movement, quickly achieving national circulation.

The Voice of Healing featured a number of prominent ministers, many of whom history has since quickly forgotten, yet they were incredible miracle workers in their day: Jack Coe, T.L. Osborn, A.A.

Allen, and old-timers like F.F. Bosworth and Raymond T. Richey were the biggest guns of revival. But even the smaller name evangelists were drawing crowds of thousands and seeing tremendous healings: Velmer Gardner, O.L. Jaggers, Gayle Jackson, Clifton Erickson, Jack Moore, William Freeman, David Nunn, R.W. Culpepper, Richard Vinyard, Tommy Hicks, and others. These were men of intense supernatural experience. Before long, evangelists were popping up out of the woodwork, and unfortunately, competition crept into the ranks as they struggled to survive. Lindsay held a convention of healing revivalists in Dallas in 1949 with some of the bigger names. The next year, at a similar convention in Kansas City, 1,000 healing evangelists attended. There was suddenly a healing evangelist on every corner.

Lindsay's magazine gave the budding evangelists a start. Lindsay tried desperately to ease tensions between the evangelists and the established churches. This became increasingly difficult toward the end of the revival. While Lindsay was gifted in healing evangelism himself, he took a backseat to run the magazine and help guide these independent and often extreme leaders. More than any other man inside the movement, Lindsay sought to curb the revival's excesses and division. More than anyone else, he voiced caution against personal ambition and rampant monetary gain.

Lindsay shifted gears after the peak of the revival, to focus on mission work, sponsoring crusades in foreign countries and conducting radio ministry. He eventually founded Christ for the Nations in 1968, which includes a Bible training school in Dallas still in operation today. The school still produces miracle workers. He also moved from being the revival's publicist to its historian and theologian.

Lindsay brought an oil of unity and cohesion that enabled a mighty move of God to be birthed. Much fruit came simply from his own willingness to lay aside his own call as a healing evangelist, and thus take up an even higher call. Lindsay's vision was truly apostolic, in that he essentially "fathered" and released dozens of other new ministries, without focusing strictly on himself. In the coming move of God, it is essential that we take hold of this concept. Competition births striving, toil and division that more resembles the fruit of the kingdom of darkness than the Kingdom of light.

Oral Roberts (1918-present), a young man from Tulsa, Oklahoma, quickly emerged as the people's favorite among the healing evangelism movement. Many are familiar with his television and radio ministry today, as well as Oral Roberts University. However, the Oral Roberts of the late 1940s and 1950s was a much different man.

"You have to completely wipe out any impressions of Oral Roberts as you know him today. It was a different time in his life, a different ministry.

Oral Roberts praying for a child during the healing revival.

…There was much more mystique about Oral Roberts then. Today, he is overexposed," writes revivalist Don Stewart, adding that the crusade atmosphere of revival was much different than television, with people waiting for hours just to catch a glimpse of Roberts.[12]

Roberts effected thousands of miraculous healings. The continued demand for his ministry in later years always rested on the early days of supernatural works. His teaching was much more heavily oriented toward the miraculous in the late '40s. Polio, terminal cancer and countless other ailments vanished under Roberts' hands. As time and success brought greater influence, Roberts' emphasis on the miraculous waned somewhat, but never disappeared entirely.

It was Roberts' confidence that also brought him allegiance in the '40s, and his managerial skills ensured continued success. He tended to contrast the meek, mystical, and somewhat unorganized Branham. During a brief "retirement" season in Branham's crusades in 1947 (Branham's immediate success brought with it a nearly immediate season of burnout), Roberts stepped in to fill the gap. Branham had stirred a hunger in the people for the supernatural, and Roberts was right behind him, quickly adding a healing element to his own evangelism crusades. Roberts was never a Voice of Healing evangelist listed in Lindsay's magazine. He preferred to run alone. Roberts' administrative skills eventually grew a multi-million dollar ministry that expanded into an accredited college.

In the early days, Roberts was a respectable face for Pentecostals, who were a bit used to being kicked around and ridiculed by mainstream denominations. Roberts also took steps to keep accountability with funds, more so than many other evangelists, which may have helped his ministry's success. He caught flak from some later in life, when he joined a Methodist church and tried to appeal to a more moderate contingent of Christians. Roberts also garnered criticism during a fundraising drive, when he said the Lord was going to take his life if he didn't raise a certain amount of money. Regardless, one must recognize that Roberts' work has accounted for literally millions of salvations since 1947 and in subsequent decades. It also helped to bring divine healing to a more respectable forefront in the church.

Jack Coe

Jack Coe (1918-1957) was a wildcard—perhaps the boldest, most impulsive of all the Voice of Healing revivalists. He was second only to Oral Roberts as the people's favorite personality. Coe was a big man with a raw, often volatile stage presence. You wouldn't want to miss this guy.

Abandoned by his parents and raised in an orphanage, Coe learned that "it was root hog or die. For that reason he tangled," said Gordon Lindsay.[13] While Coe was warm and lovable, he could also be extremely blunt and abrasive. He was a nightmare for his denomination, and they locked horns extensively. He was also the first to bring African-Americans into his campaign, battling prejudice well before the civil rights movement. As for his miracles, the reports were often extreme.

"Jack Coe was the boldest of us all...his faith was reckless," said Oral Roberts.[14] And Coe was not above wrangling with Roberts. He reportedly went to one of Roberts' revivals, measured Roberts' tent and had one made just slightly larger. Coe would often boast about having the "world's largest gospel tent," acting as if he were being persecuted when this petty fact was called into question, and calling others "pup tents." Coe was boisterous and shocking, but he had also overcome a lot.

Coe's father was an alcoholic who gambled away not only the family furniture, but the family home. Coe eventually landed in an orphanage, telling of how he wept the day his mother left him there and walked away down the sidewalk. Later in life, Coe would become a heavy drinker and gambler. But he was eventually saved and supernaturally healed of an alcohol-induced sickness. Then, all Heaven broke loose.

When Coe was baptized in the Spirit, he had a vision of Jesus and spoke in tongues for three days straight, unable to speak English except to write it on paper. He joined the army, but was locked up in several army psych wards for being a "religious fanatic." He would walk miles every day, and hitchhike even more, to reach a church from his remote army post. He once picked a church to

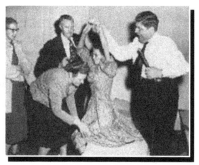

Jack Coe lifts an infirm woman off her bed, effecting an instant, miraculous healing.

attend at random by plopping his finger down in the telephone book. Another time, he approached a pastor he had never met before and told him that he had a call to preach. The pastor did not accept Coe's self invitation into the pulpit, but instead offered to let Coe first help with the altar ministry. Coe was offended and left. Later, he felt convicted and returned to the church to accept the task. But this time, the pastor only offered to let Coe serve as a janitor. Coe left again, angry, but was again unable to sleep. He returned the next day to accept the task. Starting as a janitor, he was slowly promoted to teach Sunday school. Coe was excited at this promotion, until he realized the pastor was sending him in to teach the toddlers. But Coe's humility paid off, and he ascended the ranks to song leader, youth minister and later, associate pastor.

Coe was a fighter, determined to stay on the edge. But he was also an extreme healer. At his very first healing meeting, a blind lady received her sight. News began to spread, and the deaf and lame also began to be healed at his packed-full meetings.

"Jack Coe had the strongest healing anointing of anyone in my lifetime," said Kenneth Hagin.[15] Coe was explosive. He would hit people, jerk them around, and slap them. But he was effective.

In Alabama, Coe reportedly lined up 103 people in wheelchairs and crutches and just walked down the line, snatching the people out of them. If they fell, he said they didn't have enough faith. Out of the 103, there were 63 that walked away healed that day.

Coe went for the hard cases. He was vehemently opposed to doctors. In a meeting with 350 ambulatory patients lined up, Coe prayed for them, and only 46 were not immediately healed and able to walk away. He healed all manner of "incurable" diseases. In one instance, Coe reportedly emptied 126 wheelchairs in a single meeting. Many thousands received salvation. By 1952, his ministry began to regularly experience creative miracles—the instant regrowth of missing body parts, for instance.

Coe liked to make bold statements, but he spoke the people's language. He was finally ousted from the Assemblies of God when he chose to build an independent congregation in Dallas. They had a bitter, public spat. When Assembly officials accused Coe of living extravagantly, he printed photographs of his own home compared to photos of the more luxurious houses of his denominational leaders. That was just the way Coe was. Loud, raw, and never a pushover.

Jack Coe

Coe was arrested for disturbing the peace with his campaign in Fresno, California. But in 1956, all eyes were on Coe when he was arrested in Miami for practicing medicine without a license. The entire healing movement hinged largely on that court ruling. The case was dismissed, but Coe loved the adversity. He invited healing evangelists to Miami from around the country for the proceedings, and healings began to manifest right in the courtroom while they were taking the stand! Coe also launched a short-lived television program, closely rivaling that of Oral Roberts. But Coe was suddenly struck ill with what was apparently polio or exhaustion, dying an untimely death in 1957. The public was shocked at the death of a healing minister in the midst of his prime. And to top it off, Coe checked immediately into the hospital when he became sick, although he had always preached voraciously against doctors.

One may laugh at Coe's sometimes childish antics, or cringe at his abrasive tactics. But his fruit is undeniable. Where there is no ox, the stall is clean. But from the strength of the ox comes abundant harvest (Prov. 14:4). To have the strength of an ox like Coe is worth cleaning up a few messes. Besides the radical miracles, Coe also led thousands to the Lord. In a single month in 1954, in America, 30,000 were saved in just one of his campaigns. Coe established a Bible school, an orphanage, and a faith home where the sick could receive healing through prayer.

Coe probably died because he did not take good care of himself. The work of the healing revivalist was backbreaking. Long hours of prayer lines, travel, and the breakdown and setup of the huge tents was exhausting work. Often, these men had only an hour or two of sleep each night. It was not uncommon for them to preach several times a day. In his early days, Coe stayed in private homes instead of hotels, where people would line up outside his bedroom door waiting for prayer. Coe was also overweight, which did not help his body. But it is most obvious, in Coe's hunger for a good fight, that he was motivated by insecurities, which led to strife and an inordinate amount of human effort in his ministry.

We must be a people who rest in the presence of God. It is truly the anointing of the Lord that performs ministry through us. Nevertheless, Coe's fighting spirit is admirable. His determination helped him to overcome insurmountable odds, and like Jacob, he was a wrestler who fought for all God had for him. Sometimes our "rest" in the Lord turns into complacency, but this was never the case for Coe.

In the coming wave of revival, all of the miracle working will not hinge on a single man, although leaders will still spearhead large ministries. The "nameless, faceless" generation of Joel's Army will all perform great feats, and the Lord is preparing a type of ministry that will not elevate individuals and subsequently burn them out. God alone will be elevated. As corporate anointings increase, there will be less pressure on leadership to perform, and healing, signs, and wonders will truly become a body ministry, rather than a pulpit rarity. In this way, we will not only avoid man worship, we will also learn to avoid the spiritual competition common to many of the evangelists of Coe's era. Nevertheless, when revival comes, we will *all* be busy, and it is crucial that we learn to pace ourselves in the presence of God.

One of the corporate blueprints we see foreshadowed in Coe's life, which will come upon the church, will be his sense of reckless boldness. Often, we mistake boldness for pride. But like Joshua, the Lord is calling His people to rise up, be courageous and strong, and take our inheritance. There is also a beauty to Coe's impulsiveness— a simple, childlike naivety that is devoid of any man pleasing. God honors this kind of spontaneous faith. Coe, I believe, walked in a mantle much like Peter's. He did not always analyze and think out everything he did and said. But he had a fire and a drive that got results.

Coe is one of those who received promises from the Lord, but the enemy cut short his destiny. Healing evangelist Todd Bentley feels that much of the anointing in his own ministry today is specifically related to the destiny that was intended for Coe. He clearly matches Coe in drive and zeal, and the fruit of Todd's ministry has skyrocketed to the same proportions. For instance, in a week-long crusade in India, Todd recently saw more than 300,000 commitments to Christ. And Todd is still in the prime years of his ministry.

God is no respecter of persons, and these mantles are ours for the taking.

The Voice of Healing revivalist who was focused most on foreign missions was T.L. Osborn.

T.L. Osborn (1923-present) has perhaps preached the gospel to more people face to face than any other man in history. At the time of this writing, this 82-year-old father of the faith is still holding massive healing crusades throughout the world.

T.L. Osborn speaking at a foreign crusade after decades of ministry.

Young Osborn quickly turned the spotlight of his ministry overseas during the Voice of Healing Revival. In doing so, he kept the nations in focus for the rest of the evangelists with his incredible reports from the road. He pioneered foreign evangelism crusades, and in the first five years of his ministry, he had already spoken to millions. An early service in Chile brought crowds of 100,000. In Cuba he preached to 50,000. These kind of numbers became more and more common, ranging from 20,000 to 300,000. By focusing overseas, Osborn avoided a lot of the competition that would begin to plague the revival in America by the late '50s.

"In many ways, Osborn was less controversial and more respected by other evangelists than any other man," writes Professor Harrell.[16]

Tommy Lee Osborn was born to a family of 13, and entered the ministry at a young age. He converted at 12 and felt a call to preach at 14. By age 15, Osborn was preaching, fasting, and soon working with other revivalists. He married at 18 and spent a discouraging year of ministry in India with his young wife and child at age 20. He had a vision of the Lord in 1947, and soon afterward was captivated by watching William Branham deliver a deaf-mute girl in a revival meeting. Soon afterward, Osborn was launched into a healing evangelism ministry with the help of Gordon Lindsay.

T.L. Osborn (right) with William Branham during the healing revival.

Osborn drew large crowds overseas, but he was also pioneering indigenous evangelism in the '50s, where native ministers were equipped to reach their own culture. His ministry has sponsored more than 30,000 native ministers while planting up to 400 new churches a year. Miraculous healings have always been common. For instance, in a single crusade in Jamaica, 125 deaf-mutes and 90 blind people were healed, along with thousands of conversions. There have always been other types of miracles associated with his ministry. In a crusade in Java, for instance, people saw visions of Jesus in every night's service.

Osborn has preached in more than 80 nations. His writings have been published in more than 130 languages and dialects.

These kinds of numbers can become dizzying. And, of course, a large percentage of decisions for Christ at crusades can be emotional, false conversions. Nevertheless, the scale at which the gospel began to spread, thanks to the supernatural displays of power and encounters with the divine cannot be weighed or compared to any other evangelistic methodology.

REVIVAL FIRES

We could never cover every revivalist from the Voice of Healing movement in a single volume. Revivalists you have never heard of today were bringing in thousands of souls and preaching to tens of thousands around the world. Even the "second string players" of this revival were doing spectacular things. I will list just a few more of the bigger guns, to give you a glimpse of how vast the revival spread.

F.F. Bosworth (1877-1958) was a strong influence on the healing revivalists. He was seen as a veteran elder, having been a major revivalist in the 1920s. His ministry spanned two great moves of God, and he also worked with Alexander Dowie in Zion as a young man.

Bosworth grew up in Zion and knew Dowie personally before launching out into his own ministry. He was also influenced by Charles Parham in 1906. Bosworth traveled to Azusa Street to meet William Seymour, and he even ministered alongside Maria Woodworth-Etter.

Bosworth's own meetings were full of miracles. Even without laying hands on people, many would be healed in their seats as he preached. Bosworth became very close with

F.F. Bosworth

E.W. Kenyon, and the two shared tremendous understanding of the Scriptures on the subject of healing. Bosworth's book, *Christ the Healer*, became a classic work on the principles of divine healing, selling more than 150,000 copies. Bosworth had a lot of depth that went beyond the pop theology of early Pentecostalism. For instance, he never embraced the idea that tongues were the proof of Holy Spirit baptism, although he received the gift himself. He knew that tongues, like healing, prophecy, discernment, and other gifts, was only one of many outworkings of the same Spirit. Like John G. Lake and Smith Wigglesworth, Bosworth also tried to stay away from controversial denominational battles.

Bosworth's campaigns were very successful. In 1924, for instance, 12,000 were saved in a single meeting. He also was a pioneer of radio evangelism, where he saw tremendous success. His campaigns swept the United States and Canada.

During the Depression, Bosworth retired. But when he met William Branham in 1948, revival brought him back to the forefront of ministry. For the rest of his life, Bosworth would be a major supporter of Branham.

Raymond T. Richey (1893-1968) also led a life that spanned two great revivals. He pioneered a number of ministry techniques in the early Pentecostal revival of the 1920s, and sat under John

Raymond T. Richey

Dowie as a young man in Zion City. He slowed down during the Depression, before jumping back in as a full-time Voice of Healing revivalist in 1951.

Raymond's family had moved to Zion in Dowie's day; his mother was healed of tuberculosis and his father was healed of cancer. At 18, Richey's own eyes were healed from an injury, and he gave his life to Christ. Later in life, he was also healed of tuberculosis after encountering a revelation of the Lord of Psalm 103:3: *Who forgives all your sins and heals all your diseases.*

Richey has been credited for igniting the national revival that still burns in South Korea today.[17] Lester Sumrall describes him as being a small man, without a commanding voice. But people would run down the aisles during his altar calls. People would spontaneously throw their money on the platform in sacrificial giving as he spoke. When Sumrall attended one of Richey's meetings, "We had never seen people healed in such numbers in one service." After some revivals, there were large truckloads of wheelchairs, canes, crutches and leftover medical equipment being hauled away.

William Freeman became a well-known evangelist in the revival, though he had little success in his previous years of ministry. His life was marked by visitations from God as a child, and he was miraculously healed of cancer prior to the revival. Miracles, signs, and wonders followed his ministry, and as many as 62,500 people came to the Lord in his campaigns in St. Louis and Chicago alone.[18]

A heap of crutches and braces discarded at Richey's first Tulsa revival.

Remember, we are not talking about foreign soil—these are campaigns in America.

Tommy Hicks was a popular Voice of Healing revivalist. He is best known for his work in Argentina, lighting sparks that would be flamed by spiritual leaders like Carlos Annacondia and Ed Silvoso many years later, setting the nation ablaze with revival.

Tommy Hicks

In 1954, Hicks was virtually unknown. But when he went to Argentina that year, he packed stadiums with 200,000 coming to the crusade nightly by the last week of the campaign. At one point, crowds swelled to 400,000—something that had perhaps never been done before by an evangelist.

As Hicks was first flying into Buenos Aires, the name "Peron" was coming to his mind. It was not until later that he learned that Juan Domingo Peron was the president of Argentina. Hicks felt that the Lord wanted him to speak with Peron. He learned that Peron had been afflicted with a disfiguring skin disease that was so noticeable, he would not allow photographers to take pictures of him. After hearing about Hicks' upcoming crusade, Peron asked the evangelist if he could pray for him. When he did, Peron's skin instantly cleared up in front of everyone who stood around. The eczema simply vanished. Hicks also prayed for the president's security guard, who was instantly healed as well.

The crusade brought countless thousands from miles around—from Brazil, Bolivia and Chile. The stadium quickly filled, and many would sleep there overnight so as not to lose their seat. Deaf, blind, crippled, and ambulatory patients were healed. Untold thousands were saved.

Consequently, I will mention that by the early 1970s, President Peron had become affiliated with occult practitioner Jose Lopez Rega, known popularly as "el brujo" or *the warlock*. Rega became more influential after Peron's death, and even built a public monument to witchcraft. Spiritism and occultic practices again began to flourish in Argentina until Carlos Annacondia held his first major crusade in 1982 with 40,000 saved. Tapping into those spiritual seeds planted by Hicks, national revival began to flow again. Pastor John Arnott was also strongly influenced by the Argentine revival, which contributed to the renewal that hit Toronto Airport Church in the early 1990s.[19]

David Nunn (1921-2003) entered the ministry in 1948, and began seeking God for miracles. Very soon, he began seeing miracles of healing, the first of which was a young girl healed of paralysis. Nunn hit the road and soon joined up with the Voice of Healing. Throughout the course of his ministry, some estimate that more than a million people have answered altar calls for salvation. People were healed of tuberculosis, breast cancer, and multiple sclerosis, and tumors would often disappear after prayer. Every crusade resulted in numerous blind eyes and deaf ears being opened. A single Mexico City crusade resulted in 67 deaf people hearing, 12 cripples walking away, and several blind eyes being opened.

A.A. Allen

I have not even mentioned the likes of Clifton Erickson, Velmer Gardner, A.C. Valdez, W.V. Grant and other major revivalists of this decade. As was said about the life of Jesus, there were many more extraordinary things happening than could ever be recorded. But before we move on, we should still look at one of the most important evangelists of this decade, A.A. Allen.

A.A. Allen (1911-1970) was by far the most flamboyant of the major

Voice of Healing revivalists. He did not jump into the spotlight until the 1950s, after the revival had been underway for some time, but his ministry thrived when other evangelists were going broke. The "Triple A" brought to the table some of the most bizarre miracle claims of any of the evangelists. He no doubt stirred the most controversy, and he was thoroughly blasted for his personal habits. Allen is probably one of my favorite personas of the era, just because of his idiosyncrasies. He also had a way of turning opposition to his advantage. And he was the antithesis of our modern-day stereotype of a "faith healer."

Here are a few examples of the kind of miracles recorded in his ministry:

—A 43-year-old hermaphrodite testified that he was healed, after being laid out in the presence of God during an Allen meeting. He was completely changed to a male, his large breasts went away, and suddenly he was needing to shave every day, instead of once every three days.

—A woman lost 200 pounds instantaneously as people watched it happen during a service (Similarly, this is becoming a more frequent miracle today with ministers like David Herzog and others).

—A lady who swallowed a safety pin a week before felt it come back up in her mouth during Allen's sermon.

—A man lost six cancers after a meeting, which he put in a jar and brought back to the next night's service.

—In a series of meetings in 1966, two women received their dead raised to life. During the '60s, Allen held a few programs aimed at raising the dead. Many people refused to bury their loved ones during this period and were trying to send them to Allen's home base in Arizona. After a while, Allen encouraged them to follow the law and bury their dead after waiting a reasonable amount of time.

—"Miracle oil" began to flow from the hands and heads of some who attended his services, and in some cases, the mark of a cross would appear on Allen's forehead and others in his ministry.

The Assemblies of God accused Allen of exaggerating his healing and miracle claims, and Lindsay was always pushing for verification and signed testimonies to maintain legitimacy. The press ate Allen alive. All of this would often push him to defensiveness, and he would edge further into dramatics in order to prove himself. Allen's showmanship was definitely sensational. He popularized deliverance like no one before him. For instance, he would record demonized people speaking on records—one record was titled *"I am lucifer"*—wherein Allen would carry on conversations with the demons as he was casting them out. He would ask why they wouldn't leave the person's body, etc. He also published pictures of demons, drawn by the people who were possessed. He even carried around jars of things people had coughed up during deliverance sessions, which his critics say looked like frogs. All of this was absurd, but it was typical Allen. Of course, there was not a lot of sound teaching on deliverance back then, even though a lot of revivalists were getting into it. It was understandable how it became such a spectacle.

"*Miracle* became the key word in the Allen revivals; no one outstripped his supernatural claims. When Allen's troubles with the Assemblies of God officials became heated in the mid-1950s, his miraculous claims became increasingly sensational. His detractors accused him of creating a carnival atmosphere in his meetings; he generally countered such criticisms with dramatic announcements of new miracles," writes Harrell.[20]

Despite the hype, I fully believe that Allen walked in some of the most legitimate—and some of the most bizarre—miracles of any of the evangelists. He was really a pioneer. With Allen, we have another good case of someone opening a wide door of blessing and a door of error at the same time. A lot of our modern stereotype of the white-suited, huckster faith healer comes from Allen's ministry and others like him. But it helps to understand the man, to see where he was really coming from.

An A.A. Allen campaign flyer, showing the inside and outside of his tent.

Asa Alonzo Allen had a rags-to-riches story, which appealed to his audiences. More than anyone else, he related to the poor and underprivileged. Allen was raised by alcoholics in the midst of severe poverty. His mother would put him to sleep with liquor in his bottle as a baby to keep him from crying, and she lived with several different men while he was growing up. As a child, they would often get him drunk just to laugh at him as he stumbled around. By the time he was 21, Allen was an alcoholic. He worked digging ditches, hopped trains, and drifted until he landed in jail for stealing corn.

In the 1930s, Allen was saved, and he became a licensed minister two years later. Allen chopped wood to pay for his first revival. In his first offering, he brought in 35 cents, along with an opossum for his Thanksgiving dinner. Allen was the poor man's prophet. He integrated blacks and whites in his meetings at a time when this could get him kicked out of many cities. He was even speaking out against segregation before the civil rights movement. Allen also added gospel rock music to his large tent meetings. While others were abandoning tent revivalism, Allen was purchasing Jack Coe's old tent—still the largest in the world—and Allen's boisterous claims seemed to fill the gap left behind after Coe's death. But not all was hype. There were some downright extraordinary occurrences.

Allen's associate Don Stewart later recalled watching a young boy's polio-withered leg become completely normal, among the many other miracles he saw. And he said that millions were probably saved in Allen campaigns.

"Almost every night in every city, the hospitals would bring out dying patients in ambulances. They would drive right up to the tent and wheel people out on stretchers with attendants nearby," writes Stewart.[21] "With my own eyes, I saw God instantly give a woman new skin. ...They brought a woman in on a stretcher; she was dying of cancer. When Allen pulled the sheet off of her, there was an audible gasp from the ministers on stage. The odor was unbelievable. She was all covered with this ugly thing. Her whole front was a mass of blood, puss, and cancer. The open wound extended from her chest down to her intestines."

Stewart says that, as Allen began to pray, the wound began to close and the woman's skin began to turn back to normal. "One of our ministers almost fainted. We had all seen healings every night for years, but we had never seen anything like this," he wrote. Allen always went after the really hard diseases in his healing campaigns. He would often head straight for the wheelchairs, just so that a dramatic, visible miracle would inspire the crowds and raise the corporate faith level.

The charismatic movement was beginning to sweep the mainline denominations, but Allen sought to preserve old school revivalism. Allen was committed to old-time faith healing. And his meetings were full of demonstrations of wild and exuberant worship associated with early Pentecostalism. The music was lively, and people would dance and even do cartwheels during his services. People would sometimes jump up and begin foaming at the mouth with demons, and Allen would begin shouting at them. This was starkly different to the earlier, more authoritative approach of William Branham, who would quietly give a command and the person would fall over, fully delivered. Allen did, however, understand the principle of demonic transference during his deliverance sessions. "He would warn the people that when he cast the demon out of the individual that it would seek someone else to go into and that they had better take the time right then to get their life straight with God," writes Stewart.[22] "Boy, you never saw people pray like they would at those times."

Claims that Allen was a heavy drinker seemed to always overshadow his ministry. During a revival in Tennessee in 1955, Allen was arrested for drunk driving. He always maintained that it was a set up. He told some associates that he had been kidnapped and knocked unconscious, later to wake up in a smoke-filled room with someone pouring liquor down his throat.[23] Other pastors said that Allen initially confessed his guilt to them. He denied this, saying they were trying to bring him down. Publicly, Allen always maintained that the devil was out to stop his ministry, persecuting him because of the miracles. One of his associates, R. W. Shambach, who would go on to popularity as a televangelist in later years, spoke about the incident after his death, claiming he was in the car with Allen during the arrest. Shambach said that someone may have spiked his milk at a restaurant earlier that day!

We will never know exactly what happened. Don Stewart, probably gives us the most balanced perspective of Allen behind the scenes. He says that Allen did have occasional relapses from his early struggles with alcohol. There were a few times when he found Allen drunk between meetings. He says that Allen did want help with the problem, but the competitive nature of ministry in those days and the relentless attacks from the media caused him to isolate and get defensive. Allen stepped down from the Voice of Healing group after the drunk driving incident. Evangelists were already starting to receive bad publicity at that point, and Allen chose to step down to avoid being forced from the association. Allen became a lone ranger.

Insisting on his innocence, Allen remained in ministry. To step down, he said, would appear to be an admission of guilt. But he also had to surrender his Assembly of God credentials. After this, Allen attacked denominationalism, urging other Pentecostal ministers to go independent. Then immediately, in 1956, he started the Miracle Revival Fellowship, an organization of "independent local, sovereign, indigenous, autonomous churches," which he adamantly insisted was not intended to be another denomination. He started with more than 500 affiliate ministers.

In 1958, someone donated 1,250 acres of land to Allen in Arizona, which would become Miracle Valley. Here, he established a ministry training center called the International Miracle Revival Training Camp. People were trained to perform miracles, cast out demons, and walk in the supernatural. Nine thousand ordinations were issued from Miracle Valley. Allen published *Miracle Magazine*, with a huge paid subscription list of 200,000; a daily radio broadcast on 186 stations; a foreign mission program, and his still popular tent campaigns.

We must understand that Allen was undertaking these huge efforts just as the healing revival was essentially coming to an end in 1958. Other ministers could not keep up the pace or fund big campaigns anymore, but Allen thrived. Allen always had a way of turning adversity to his advantage. In this, he excelled. Any negative press or criticism that came his way only seemed to push him further along.

Allen is also called the father of the "prosperity gospel." He was the first guy to really teach about the principles of financial blessing attached to giving. As we've seen time and again, whenever a truth is restored to the body, it always comes in extremes. The theme of financial blessing became a major focus of the whole revival by the late '50s, and was one of its major downfalls. Financial prosperity started to outweigh healing as the chief miracle people sought after. By the 1960s, overboard "prosperity teaching" was everywhere. Allen was known for making statements like this: "I believe I can command God to perform a miracle for you financially. When you do, God can turn dollar bills into twenties."[24]

Of course, 50 years and several fallen televangelists later, we see how extremely tweaked this kind of teaching can get. But we have to realize that this was just the kind of guy Allen was: He was extreme. A lot of Allen's principles would blossom into the Word of Faith movement. While everyone may not agree with everything taught in this stream—and some may have felt burned by it—teachings on faith and giving really were needed and critical for the body. That movement was necessary for reintroducing many important principles.

By 1967, Allen was being sued for $300,000 in back taxes—a lawsuit which he won. Also around that time, he divorced his wife of 30-some years. In 1970, Allen was found dead in a San Francisco hotel room—the coroner said it was from acute alcohol poisoning.

Allen had a tremendous gifting. But he obviously had character flaws as well. Gifting and character are connected, but they still develop separately. They are like the two tracks of a railroad train that are both needed for a ministry to function. We see, as the healing revival progressed, that many men possessed a powerful anointing but no depth of character. As for Allen, he overcame tremendous obstacles to make a great impact on the Kingdom. Whether he could have displayed more sincerity and done a better job is purely speculation.

FIZZLING OUT

The Lord wants the coming generation to take a long, hard look at the healing revivalists—not just their successes, but their flaws. If we cannot look honestly and objectively at their shortcomings, then their successes—as great as they were—will be our ceiling. Today, we are not seeing the same level of fruit in our ministries—except in a few pockets—because the Lord had to lift that great healing/miracle mantle which was given to the corporate church during that season. It became clear the Lord was more concerned with hearts being healed than physical bodies being healed. The Lord wants purity of heart long before He wants lightning bolts. As revivalism died out, the Lord birthed the charismatic renewal in the '70s as mainline denominations began to catch the winds of the Holy Spirit. More focus was placed on character and discipleship issues. These were needed—not because the evangelists were *failing*, but because they were called to save souls, not teach and raise them.

Whereas the healing revival restored the office of the *evangelist* to the church, the subsequent charismatic movement brought the restoration of the *teacher* back to the church. The Lord is now working on prophets and apostles, but we have only tasted a smidgen of what those offices will look like when they are functioning in their prime. There will obviously be speed bumps along the way.

In the late '50s, ministries grew to depend so exclusively on the charisma of the evangelist that most of their organizations died out with them. And as competition entered the ranks—with an evangelist popping up a tent on every street corner—there was more and more pressure to hype up revival reports at the cost of personal integrity. "Ministry" became about numbers and glitz. The church became so distraught with this, that it eventually went the opposite extreme, and threw out the importance of numbers altogether. I have attempted to highlight the vast numbers of people saved and healed through these ministries only to show how extensive the revival reached. Obviously, we cannot calculate the worth of just one soul saved, and we do not want to be desensitized by big numbers. But we should recognize how this exemplified the greatest harvest of souls in modern history, up to that point. The Lord does want the multitudes saved, but He does not want us tallying up points, as if the credit was our own. The glory must go to the Lord, not just in word but in true humility. In this respect, the early ministry of William Branham was the prototype, as he never sought personal gain, but the revivalists wandered from it. I point this out, because power is coming back to the church. The Lord is going to give us another shot, and see if we can handle it again corporately. We need to see where the revival fires were quenched, where they fizzled out. Again, the major downfall of the evangelists was the *Three Gs*—the girls, the gold, and the glory.

O.L. Jaggers was perhaps the most extreme example of problems in the revival. Jaggers emerged as one of the main Voice of Healing evangelists and was clearly one of the most gifted orators. Jaggers was the polished, handsome son of a prominent Assembly of God minister, who quickly made a name for himself in the revival. He was selling out auditoriums, and preaching to crowds of 10,000 at his height. In 1952, he established the World Church in Los Angeles.

O.L. Jaggers, once a major revivalist, has now embraced a "less than orthodox" belief system.

But Jaggers was the most erratic of the revivalists. His pride and wild imagination led him completely off the deep end. He most illustrated the lust for personal glory and lack of sound teaching that eventually crept into the ranks. For instance, Jaggers once made a claim that he had supernaturally appeared on television all over the country, which was just one of the things that caused Gordon Lindsay to start doubting his revival reports. Jaggers claimed that his 3,000-seat church had 10,000 members, and that God was going to give him 100,000 members. Jaggers eventually abandoned the healing revival. In the mid-'50s, everyone was shocked when he released a book entitled *UFOs and the Creatures That Fly Them*. Jaggers had gotten more and more unorthodox in his beliefs. Ironically, it was William Branham, not himself known for superb doctrine, who actually tried to get Jaggers to "Come back and stay with the Gospel."[25] Jaggers only went further into delusion. He invented some kind of three-fold way to be born again. Up to the present day, Jaggers has believed his World Church is building the golden altar of the Book of Revelation. Those who have seen it, say it looks like "spray painted macaroni, the color of fresh Velveeta." His wife, Velma, supposedly has a secret anointing oil that brings perpetual youth. She has used this "fountain of youth" on the aging congregation since the '50s, but it hasn't seemed to stop them from dying over the years.

I don't want to belabor the point that Jaggers is confused. But it is absolutely essential that we understand that even the most gifted, promising leaders among us can become utterly deluded. The healing revival is a great case study of what we will be dealing with in the next move of God, so we have to learn from their mistakes. There is no degree of confusion that is off limits, especially when power and influence are involved.

Jaggers would later describe himself as a "doctor of divinity; doctor of science; Litt.D; LL D.; Ph.D. in human genetics; professor of human genetics in the University of the Universal World Church; teacher of the human genetic sciences; human cellular biology; genetic ingredients of DNA, RNA, the neuclear-histones; the chromosomal elements; biophysics; nuclear biology and biochemistry; research fellow of Biblical and historical manuscripts and their languages, Hebrew, Chaldee, Greek, Latin and Aramaic; scholar, scientist, university professor; pastor, revivalist and author of some 300 books and hundreds of scientific papers distributed throughout the world, including the landmark treatise, **UFOs and the Creatures That Fly Them**." He also thinks he is the "builder of the holy of holies and the temple of God on earth, the greatest endeavor ever attempted by modern man," which is, by the way, a $100 million project. His church is full of elaborate Christmas lights, shiny tinseled decorations and golden spray-painted altar gizmos. He appointed 24 elders who wear robes and golden crowns—they are "the governing body on earth." Jaggers also thinks he is "endowed with all the supernatural gifts of the seven-fold Holy Spirit," as well as "The most knowledgeable and superlative preacher on the American platform today." I am not making this up.

We must understand that Jaggers was a nationally renowned leader of revival in his heyday. Most of the revivalists simply left him alone after he lost his sense of reality. As for all of this fantastic stuff he claims about himself, A.A. Allen once explained to his associates that, "The problem is boys, he really believes it."[26]

Jaggers is obviously an anomaly. By no means was your average revivalist running off to start a UFO cult, or anything close to it for that matter. He is a very extreme example of how small embellishments began to stretch into outright lies when an evangelist brought too much attention to himself. Most revivalists who fell into this trap exhibited far more subtle problems, never intending to go there in the first place. The beauty of Gordon Lindsay's *The Voice of Healing* was the detail he gave to verifying the miracles and avoiding excess. He also tried to hold together the splintering movements, but by the end of the '50s, division had again reared its ugly head. So many revivalists were going independent, that accountability was lost and healthy relationships suffered.

By 1958, the revival was only a shadow of its former glory. People were hearing a lot of big claims and a lot of pleas for money. Ministers depended on their own skills to bring people to their services. They even depended on their own skills to change people's lives. Revival became formulized, with high-powered motivational speaking techniques. Valid miracles were overshadowed by gimmicks. The corporate faith and awe that marked the mystical ministry of Branham and the early revivalists was shattered. It only took a few spiritual abuses to turn the public to extreme cynicism. There was a lot of packaging, but not a lot of substance.

"Miracles became too commonplace, claims too unbelievable, prophets too available. Honest participants in the revival were disturbed by the popularity of frauds and extremists," writes Professor Harrell.[27]

During this period, however, the charismatic revival began to blossom. With good teaching, the church began to realize that the Holy Spirit was available to everybody, not just the man in the pulpit. Tent campaigns were replaced by charismatic conferences. This was also the age of the televangelist. There was clearly a strong anointing on TV ministry for several decades. We are quick to criticize the glitzy showmanship of televangelism today. But often we fail to recognize that there really was a glory that the former generation was tapping into. We usually just see the old package, the old style, that once surrounded that glory. But in its heyday, there was a tremendous supernatural dynamic that captured the world's attention on the tube.

Kathryn Kuhlman was not the least of these who carried ministry to the airwaves. Kuhlman began broadcasting television programs in 1965 on CBS. She would pray for people on air and they would fall over on camera. This phenomenon was utterly unique for many who had never seen the power of God move in such a way. The nation watched miracles on a major television network. Many people were healed, but she was always quick to point out that Jesus, not Kathryn Kuhlman, was doing the healing. Kuhlman became a very popular figure. She was written up in *Time* and *People* magazines. She was interviewed by Johnny Carson, Merv Griffin, and others. She was controversial, of course, because she operated in a supernatural ministry. But Kuhlman ushered in a very important element. Healing was not really the focus of her meetings. She used her gifting only to turn the focus of the people back to the presence of God. Kuhlman sought to provide an atmosphere where the Holy Spirit was present and up front.

One of the reasons television ministry has not progressed to its full potential is because the Body of Christ has criticized it, rather than interceded for it over the past two decades. As a child in the early '80s, I remember even my non-Christian relatives watching television ministry. The church, when operating in power, offers the best show in town. But right now, there is obviously much that must be restored.

There is going to be a fresh wind of God's Spirit blowing on television ministry, as prophetic power encounters are filmed on the street with ordinary people. "Reality television" will go to whole new levels as Christians are recorded live, preaching everywhere from bars to foreign villages—all sorts of strange places. Sometimes they will be physically assaulted on camera. Sometimes they will perform miracles. I mean bizarre, undeniable creative miracles. Things so extreme that critics will have to write it off as CGI animation. It is going to be so raw and cutting edge—almost completely opposite of our concept of Christian television today—that viewers will be dumbfounded and drawn to the screen. But it will go far beyond the filming of preaching—especially just the preaching of church services in Christian lingo. The church has not even begun to explore the medium of film. I have noticed in recent years that many secular movies have been much more anointed than many church services. Whether script writers have recognized it or not, many movies have held deep prophetic symbolism recently, and this has been the Lord's doing.

Televangelism was indirectly birthed out of the healing revival. Some would say that bad press contributed to the healing revival's downfall, but journalists only fed the public with what they already wanted. Society was tired of seeing a guru behind the pulpit. They were tired of demigods. They wanted to see the real humanity of these miracle-workers. Religious fronts had always veiled the minister's human struggles from the public, and this is why scandal tasted so sweet by the time of the televangelist debacles of the '80s. For once, the ethereal clergy was brought down to the level of the common man. I don't think the church wanted to see its leaders deposed. But I do think they wanted a supernatural experience that was available to the ordinary man.

Marjoe Gortner (1944-present) resounded the death knell to old-time revivalism in 1972, when he released the expose movie *Marjoe*. Marjoe was groomed by his parents as a sort of revival oddity, who began preaching at age 4 as the youngest-ever ordained minister. He was touted as a miracle child, named for Mary and Joseph, after being nearly strangled by his own umbilical cord. By age 8, he had performed a wedding ceremony, and he held evangelistic crusades across country through his teens.

Marjoe Gortner, groomed as a revival oddity by his parents, would later film an expose on the movement.

Marjoe got out of revivalism for a while, dipping into the counterculture movement and playing in a rock band, once he was old enough to make up his own mind. Then, he decided to go undercover as a revivalist again, to document the corruption, greed, and exploitation that had become rampant under the big tents. Marjoe preached the gospel with flair. He showed how easily he worked the crowds, zooming in on their emotional responses—the singing, laughing, crying, and swooning. He talked about the money, sex, and even drugs that corrupted a number of the revivalists. But the Christian experience had never become a personal reality for Marjoe. He instructed his film crews how to act religious and pretend they were saved while they were filming inside the meetings. Although he had led thousands to the Lord, you could never quite tell if Marjoe ever believed for himself.

The film was a sort of confessional to the showmanship and fraud he had always been a part of. It also cast a stigma over those ministries which were legitimate, and painted all healing ministers as charlatans in the public eye like never before. The movie won a major award, and at the end, it leaves Marjoe the lost, confused byproduct of greed and religion. He turned completely to secular entertainment after that, making a number of B movies before he was forgotten.

Obviously, Marjoe aired a lot of dirty laundry. Marjoe's story shows how a complete unbeliever can step into a ministry role, say the right words, perform the right way, and get positive—even supernatural results. Marjoe clearly had a gifting, and the Lord used him even though he was lost. Let us remember that God used Balaam's ass as well—ministry is not about the minister. For many, this was a new revelation. Some were so used to glorifying the "holy man," that they were left completely disillusioned.

Marjoe openly attacked ministry (which needed a good kick in the tail at that point), but he never could deny that miracles were really taking place! This is the irony that really confused him.

"I don't have any power," said Marjoe. "And neither do any of these other guys. Hundreds of people were healed at my crusades, but I know damn well it was nothing I was doing."[28]

Marjoe saw the miracles happening, but even he didn't understand it was really about God—not himself. As a youngster, Marjoe was so confused, he thought he was performing the miracles *himself*. When he figured out he had nothing to do with it, he became disillusioned. Called the whole thing a scam. But that never explained how the miracles were happening! In his confusion, Marjoe finally just wrote the miracles off to psychosomatics, or the big, vast unknown. The film caused many to reject healing ministries altogether. But it was an expose on greed and crowd control—it was never an indictment against *miracles*. Journalism has never been able to explain doctor-verified, documented miracles. This is why Jesus said, *"Believe Me when I say that I am in the Father and the Father is in Me; or at least believe on the evidence of the miracles themselves"* (John 14:11). There will always be criticism and spiritual warfare around miracles, because they are the clearest outward validation of the truth of the gospel—that Jesus is God; He is one with the Father.

Psychosomatics became a popular term—many claimed that healings were rooted in *positive thinking*. Some evangelists became so afraid of this pseudo-scientific criticism, that their own healing messages turned into little more than a positive affirmation trip. "Miracle" became a fluffy, sentimental word associated with the "power of positive thinking." But to believe in psychosomatics is the most idiotic stance one could take to "scientifically" explain a miracle. There is no scientific explanation for how someone can be "psychosomatically" healed. To think the human brain can heal broken bones and tumors, dissolve metal plates, or grow out a shortened limb is far more ridiculous than believing God did it. The spontaneous creation of a new limb, for instance, actually suspends the physical law that matter can neither be created nor destroyed. Much less can it explain the spontaneous appearance of feathers, gold dust, gems, and diamonds, clouds of smoke and even literal, edible manna—all of which are beginning to spontaneously appear at a number of revival meetings and conferences today.

Call psychosomatics an alternative "religious" explanation for those who cannot face the reality of a living God, but please do not call it science. The problem is many people will jump to any conclusion that leaves God out of the equation. To invalidate God is to extract any personal responsibility to Him.

To say a person was spontaneously healed (or raised from the dead!) by the power of suggestion is just as non-scientific as saying God did it. That is just simply not science. Nevertheless, that is how the American Medical Association wrote off miraculous cures. As society became disenchanted by the faith healers, there was a huge gap left behind that science could never fill. It was perhaps the excess of the later revivalists that helped turn Western society toward a general disbelief of the miraculous in general. Society's appetite for true spirituality was turned askew, and all manner of metaphysics, astrology, and pseudo-spiritual practices were quickly ushered in, gaining popularity in the 1960s. With today's generation now beginning to ask "Where is the God of Elijah?" it is important to put the '60s into perspective a bit. That is where American society really started to abandon Him. On one hand, the West began to embrace the spirituality of Eastern religions, ushered in by the counterculture, while on the other hand, public institutions began to rabidly embrace evolutionary science and secularism. Today, science is the largest government-funded religion in North America. I am not speaking about true science, but about the Darwinian pseudo-science that has corrupted nearly every major branch of scientific learning.

American society moved more heavily toward moral ambiguity and popular atheism in the mid-1960s—as witnessed by the removal of prayer from public classrooms and the eventual legalization of abortion a decade later. The sexual revolution and an explosion of drug culture, crime rates, divorce rates, and teenage pregnancy followed. You cannot boil all these societal problems down into one, single root cause. But if you wanted to take a stab at the main problem, it is this: The American church grew apathetic. As goes the church, so goes the society. Judgment begins with the house of God, but so does blessing begin with the house of God. If we catch a burning passion for the Lord, it will rub off on the world. We need fire. The sleeping church needs to awaken with a hunger for God like the world has never seen, and society will follow in our wake. America is not too far gone for revival fires to be kindled again.

How can we best prepare for the coming revival? The number one way is to prepare our hearts with oil and have His holy flame stirred up in our inner man on an individual level. We must cultivate lifestyles of abiding in the secret place, until our hearts and lives are fully captured—fully possessed—by the Lover of our souls.

ENDNOTES

1. David Edwin Harrell, Jr., *All Things are Possible: The Healing and Charismatic Revivals in Modern America* (Bloomington: Indiana University Press, 1978 ed.), 6.

2. Don Stewart, *Only Believe: An Eyewitness Account of the Great Healing Revivals of the 20th Century* (Shippensburg: Revival Press, 1999), 36.

3. Ibid., 40.

4. *All Things are Possible*, 28.

5. Ibid., 37.

6. *All Things are Possible*, 39-40.

7. Ibid., 163.

8. Ibid., 165.

9. Roberts Liardon, *God's Generals* (Whitaker House, 1996), 342.

10. Paul Keith Davis, "From Preparation to Demonstration," conference audio recording.

11. Ibid.

12. *Only Believe*, 57.

13. *All Things are Possible*, 59.

14. Accessed 16 Oct. 2004 <http://www.jackcoe.org>.

15. Ibid.

16. *All Things are Possible*, 64.

17. Lester Sumrall, *Pioneers of Faith* (Ben Publishing, 1995), 131-138.

18. *All Things are Possible*, 76.

19. "Miracles Bring Pentecost." (Jesus Army/Jesus Fellowship Church). Article source: Edward R. Miller, Cry for me Argentina (Sharon Publications, 1988) and Peter Wagner with Chris Simpson and David Little, "The Awesome Argentina Revival–Lessons in Evangelism and Spiritual Warfare from Argentina" (International Revival Network, 2002).

20. *All Things are Possible*, 69.

21. *Only Believe*, 74-75.

22. Ibid., 80.

23. *All Things are Possible*, 70.

24. Ibid., 75.

25. Ibid., 79.

26. *Only Believe*, 120.

27. *All Things are Possible*, 7.

28. Flo Conway and Jim Siegelman, *Snapping: America's Epidemic of Sudden Personality Change* (1978).

CHAPTER 13

Mystery

T HE unparalleled lives of miracle workers and supernatural God lovers are a testimony of Jesus. He is saying to us that these things are available to us today—from bizarre miracles like levitation, to the simplicity of hearing His voice for ourselves. Furthermore, the testimony of Jesus is the *spirit of prophecy* (Rev. 19:10). His followers' lives are prophetic signposts, and this is why we are drawn to a hunger for the supernatural when we read of them. It is quite normal for us to desire extreme supernatural encounters. We were made for interaction with the divine. Joel's Army will be a prophetic generation, the recipients of Jesus Christ as He is poured out on all flesh. This will not be a church of *spectators*, but a people whose lives demonstrate and manifest the mysteries of Heaven.

There is a mystical dimension of our faith that has been largely lost in evangelical fundamentalism. Not that we reject fundamentals, but we worship a living God, not a set of doctrines. The modernist theologian seeks to provide an answer for everything, line upon line, precept upon precept. Simple, rote explanations for divine, eternal realities. But there is little spiritual depth or experiential substance to much of it. Today's postmodern generation is calling out for intimacy, reality, and relevance. They are not seeking a religion of distant theological theory. They want hands-on interaction with a tangible, emotive God. In place of supernatural experience, the church has been given formulas and pat answers. But the age of pat answers is over. The age of divine dialogue has begun.

The mysteries of Heaven are the subject of divine discontent and paradox. While God longs to reveal hidden secrets to His friends, it seems that with every answer comes a multitude of new questions. Understanding Heavenly mysteries requires much more than knowledge. *"Knowledge puffs up, but love builds up"* (1 Cor. 8:1). Only the Holy Spirit can reveal the secrets of Heaven. And so, by pressing into His presence and friendship, we are able to receive new levels of comprehension of Scriptures and God Himself that supercede the ability of the natural mind. To many, the radical supernatural encounters you have read about here seem foreign to their Christian experience. Many dismiss those things which are not readily explained or easily understood.

"When I came to you, brothers, I did not come with eloquence or superior wisdom as I proclaimed to you God's mystery," states the apostle Paul (1 Cor. 2:1). Paul moved in a demonstration of supernatural miracles, not just a message of talk. He was very clear that the gospel consists of more than just words, but power. Furthermore, his words themselves had power, because they were revelatory. And while Paul provided a whole host of answers to Heavenly mysteries, he also opened the door to a swarm of new questions. The Christian walk is not just a matter of reiteration of old principles. It is a walk of exploration and new discoveries.

We must understand that even the greatest mysteries can be unveiled to the simplest believer. Furthermore, God *wants* to unveil them, and then show us new ones. Paul says the grace was given to him *"to preach to the Gentiles the unsearchable riches of Christ, and to make plain to everyone the administration of this mystery, which for ages past was kept hidden in God, who created all things. His intent was that now, through the church, the manifold wisdom of God should be made known..."* (Eph. 3:8-10).

> *As it is written: "No eye has seen, no ear has heard, no mind has conceived what God has prepared for those who*

love Him"—but God has revealed it to us by His Spirit. The Spirit searches all things, even the deep things of God (1 Corinthians 2:9-10).

God does not present us with any mystery that cannot, in some measure, be revealed. This is not to say God will reveal His mysteries in the precise context in which we are asking. Sometimes we are not getting an answer from God because we are asking the wrong questions. C.S. Lewis once remarked, "Can a mortal ask questions which God finds unanswerable? Quite easily, I should think. All nonsense questions are unanswerable."

As we exercise and mature our spirit man, we can move on to the meatier things of Heaven. Spiritual matters can only be discerned spiritually—not logically. *Revelation* is the unfolding of Heavenly mysteries—it is a "revealing" of things that were hidden. The God-given solution to the puzzle. The *mystery* is the shrouded, unsolved puzzle itself that becomes revealed. The puzzles of Heaven usually have many layers of meaning, and so we never want to presume easy answers to spiritual unknowns. However, we must never think God is so cloaked and aloof that He cannot be touched. That He no longer talks. That He especially won't talk to me. God is completely mysterious, yet through the cross, His love and wisdom has been completely revealed.

Following the healing revival and the subsequent charismatic movement of the 1970s and '80s, the prophetic movement was birthed. The Kansas City prophets came onto the scene, with renowned men of revelation like Bob Jones and Paul Cain. Men who have prophesied earthquakes and floods with precision. Men who are called by senators and congressmen for direction from Heaven. Men who have received the president's personal telephone number by revelation, and have the ear of the White House. Men who keep company with angels.

The Toronto Blessing further accelerated the spread of prophetic equipping in the 1990s, and today, the church is blessed by many powerful, upstanding prophets like Rick Joyner, Bobby Conner, John

Paul Jackson, and others who are on the vanguard of preparing the Bride to hear the voice of the Bridegroom. There are so many prophetic voices in the church today that we are rightly beginning to understand that hearing from the Lord is not a *novelty*. It should be a regular expectancy. It is normal Christianity.

The prophetic movement that is currently sweeping the church is not really a *movement*. This is about habitation with the Lord. Not just about a few prophets being raised up, but about the Lord establishing for Himself a prophetic people. The mystical dimensions of our faith are being reawakened. A revival of contemplative, soaking prayer has been key in this hour, because the Lord is first of all returning us to the place of His presence. The place of intimate abiding, out of which all revelation flows.

THE RED PEN: MYSTERY VS. REVELATION

We live in exciting times, because the church is finally shaking off its disdain for new revelation. God is longing to reveal to you things that have been locked up for the ages. This does not mean there is "new truth," for there is really nothing new under the sun. The new word is the old word lived out in the context of today. Revelation He has held in reserve for this hour is being realized. Truths that have been misunderstood, misinterpreted, or sealed up for centuries are becoming clear in the present day.

It is strange, however, how we so *devalue* the present, as if God can work in the past and the future, but not today. In fact, it may even be your calling not just to get a "word" from God, but to unlock some aspect of His very *nature* that has never before been discovered. This is your hour. The life you have lived has been lived by no other, and the experiences you have encountered have likely come your way to shape you into a living example of who He is. The lives of the saints each give us glimpses into different angles of the same God. God is so multi-dimensional, that even all of us cannot reflect His full image, yet each individual somehow reflects Him distinctly.

The Lord is calling each one in this hour to discover his or her own call and to step into their destiny.

As simple as this may sound, if God is going to do anything, He is going to do it *right now*. God is a *living* God. He is present tense. Interactive. He is a God of today, and today is really the only time we can truly experience Him. There is no period of time, whether today or 2,000 years ago, in which He is not present. He's a pretty phenomenal Lord to have as a buddy. He is both utterly nebulous, yet completely tangible.

The mysteries of God hold an intrinsic beauty, which is intended to draw us in. Signs and wonders are meant to make us *wonder*. And it's all for the purpose of engaging us. When we cease to ponder a thing and think we've figured it all out, we miss the mark. I think that one of the dangers of the prophetic movement today, is to settle for easy answers and cheap solutions to deep theological questions, and tag, "Thus saith the Lord" on it. Why? Because as revelatory people, we have come to believe that we know God inside and out. As Bobby Conner says, "We are way too familiar with a God we barely know."

We need to recapture our awe over this God of ours. God doesn't always expect us to know a thing. Often, He wants us to ponder over a thing for a given time. On the other hand, He doesn't want to leave us in the dark, either. As confused as I get, the Lord never leaves me in that state of confusion forever, as long as my heart is to know Him. One touch from Him and the whole universe seems to make sense, although I could never explain it! The things He reveals to us through the eyes of our spirit often seem impossible to describe to the natural ear. But in this hour, the Lord is giving language to those mysteries like never before since the earth's foundation. It is all possible because of the work of the cross, where Heaven was sheared open.

Skeptics often fail to ponder the mysteries of Heaven because they think it's pointless—that God will never answer their questions. Others become so engaged by the beauty of mysteries, that they reject revelation when it comes. The Pharisees had tremendous insight into the word of God, but they missed Jesus when He came. The key is to be quick to listen and slow to speak. Press into the presence. Know the heart of God and the voice of God and follow the way of love. Love and humility open vast doors in the seer realm. Revelation is not our goal—it is Jesus, the *Spirit* of prophecy, who we truly seek.

Yes, we *can* hear from Heaven about any given thing. The mysteries of Heaven have all been revealed to us at the cross, if we want communion with *The Mystery*. Apart from the work of Jesus, all of Heaven's secrets are beyond us, but in Him, we have been given access to all.

To say God is mysterious is not to say He is distanced or confusing. Ever-present Emmanuel is constantly interacting with us today. We must acknowledge that it is OK to embrace unknowns until we hear from Heaven, rather than shuffling about trying to figure out everything in our own understanding. On this point, the postmodern mind can agree. We need to have the eyes of our heart enlightened by the Holy Spirit. It is better to still have questions than to have wrong answers. How many demonic doctrines have crept into the church because of theologians who interpreted the Bible out of human wisdom, with a predetermined theological agenda? True mysticism is not an enemy to theological answers, neither is it afraid of paradox and theological problems. In fact, the ironies work powerfully to push us to hear from God. All mystery then should be conceived as the infinite stuff of exploration—opportunity for spiritual pioneering—a last frontier of sorts. Questions only intimidate the one who does not believe God answers them. But mysteries are revealed through the heart, not the mind.

This is a generation that is braced for discontinuity. A generation that will not be intimidated by the enemy's veil of confusion. I always get excited when I encounter some vast unknown in the Spirit, because I know there are new depths of the Kingdom to discover. And when we inquire of God about a thing, we can believe in faith that He will answer, because He is a rewarder of those who diligently seek Him. To fix our eyes on our meager limitations is just as blinding as presuming we know it all. We must look at Jesus, then all things become possible.

With humility, we recognize that all our understanding falls short, so we don't get ruffled when things do not make sense. We can embrace mysteries, without embracing confusion. And just because a question is beyond us, our faith is not in peril and we do not feel abandoned by God. Our eyes only see adventure.

> *For now we see through a glass, darkly; but then face to face: now I know in part; but then shall I know even as also I am known* (1 Corinthians 13:12).

The apostle Paul spoke continually about the *mystery of Christ*. Paul showed that this mystery was already revealed through the prophets before him, was presently being revealed in Paul's day, and would continue to be revealed in the future. We serve a past, present, and future God who abounds in hidden treasure. Paul tells the Ephesians that these riches are unsearchable and that they surpass knowledge, even as he invites them into the *fellowship of the mystery* (Eph. 3:9). It is clear that Christ Himself is the ultimate Mystery, and while He surpasses our ability to grasp Him, we can still have relationship with Him. He is ever the more revealed on the Emmaus walk of life's sojourn.

> *Ask and it will be given to you; seek, and you will find; knock and the door will be opened to you. For everyone who asks receives; he who seeks finds; and to him who knocks, the door will be opened* (Matthew 7:7-8).

Searching out the frontiers of Heaven is as simple as asking God for insight. There are paths to which you are called to explore that have never been bushwhacked by anyone else. Never let the abundance of theology, the reams of books already written, or the 2,000 years of existing Christian thought intimidate you. Not all of God's mysteries have been revealed. He is still breaking open new revelation today.

Consider the verse: *I will open My mouth in parables, I will utter things hidden since the creation of the world* (Matt. 13:35). We see that there are things hidden from the earth's foundations. Many of these are still waiting to be revealed in our day. There are many insights in the prophetic books that are still shrouded, that you and I are called to understand. And you do not need a seminary degree to hear from Heaven. In fact, God can supernaturally download information into your head in a single encounter! He did that with Roland Buck and others.

Roland Buck (1918-1979) was born in Everett, Washington, and pastored several churches before settling in an Assembly of God church in Boise, Idaho. One day in the late '70s, as Buck was sitting at his desk at work, he put his head down to pray and was suddenly sucked up to the throne room of Heaven. Buck was shown the file rooms of Heaven, where he was allowed to look at his own file, as well as those of Paul, Abraham, and others.

Roland Buck and his dog, Queenie.

"God truly gave me a glorious glimpse of the hidden secrets of the universe of matter, energy, nature and space, all bearing the same beautiful trademark. As He gave me this dazzling over layer of truth, He added a new beauty and unity to the entire Bible, which I previously did not have. Certain biblical truths, which I have seen darkly were now perfectly clear," said Buck.[1] To confirm his visit, Buck was given a scroll with 120 prophetic events that were about to take place in his own life and the lives of others in his church and elsewhere. Buck was able to supernaturally remember every one of them, backward and forward.

"He wrote down 120 events which he said would happen in my life in the future. It wasn't like you and I write; the information just suddenly appeared! I did not even need to read it, but right now, I can tell you everything that was on that paper, because it was instantly impressed on my mind like a printing press prints on paper," wrote Buck.[2]

When Buck returned to his desk, there was the scroll, still physically in his hand! He just laid it down, overwhelmed, and walked home. When he returned the next morning, the scroll was still there on his desk. Others in his ministry also saw the scroll, confirming it was real, and over a matter of days, it slowly disappeared, dissolving in thin air like ash. All of the prophetic events were fulfilled before his death in 1979.

What was even more incredible, was that the Lord had supernaturally burned 2,000 Scriptures into Buck's mind. He could quote them from memory without opening a Bible. He did not have an exceptional memory prior to this experience, but he could recount any of these verses at will. After that day, it is said that to have a conversation with him was like speaking with a living concordance. While I would love this gift more than just about any other, this barely scratches the surface of what Roland Buck experienced. I still recommend studying the Scriptures in the meantime, and not waiting for a lightning bolt experience like his! But it is the *fruit* of study and discipline which we pursue. We do not pursue study for its own sake, or else it is an idol.

Over the course of 18 months, Buck had 27 separate visitations with angels, including many with Gabriel and Michael. Much of what he experienced was recorded in a book, *Angels on Assignment*. We must realize that a visit from Gabriel is not a thing to be taken lightly. He is the messenger angel that announced the birth of Jesus. What was God doing with Roland Buck to merit such a thing?

Prophetic teacher Paul Keith Davis feels that God sent Gabriel, because He wanted to move corporately with this type of visitation anointing in Roland Buck's day, but since the church could not receive him, it had to be postponed for a later date. Davis says that the experiences of Roland Buck are now being offered as a signpost of what our generation can walk in.

One thing is for certain—if Almighty God is willing to live within us and even die for us, how much more willing is He to send an angel to visit us.

"Possibly the questions asked most often are, 'How did it happen that God chose you?' 'Was it through deep hunger on your part?' 'Was it through prayer and fasting?' I would honestly have to say, 'I don't know!' I fall short in all of these areas," wrote Buck.[3]

At first, Buck was very uneasy about sharing these visitations, because he knew the persecution that comes from talking about such things. People from around the country who did not even know him began to call him to confirm that he was to share the messages publicly. One man was not even a believer, but he had heard an audible voice while he was in bed say "Call Pastor Buck in Boise, Idaho." The man did not know who Buck was, but he called the operator and found a Pastor Buck in Boise. He called, bewildered, and Roland led the man to the Lord.

Buck knew he had to talk about the visitations. Buck was quickly ridiculed for these things. The church at large made a mockery of him. The Body of Christ was not prepared for something that was so radical and unusual for that time.

Many of Buck's visitations were in his own home. Angels would just be sitting around talking to him. They were relaxed, and conveyed to Buck that Heaven is much more carefree than our religious strife dictates. Once, Gabriel said that God had sent Buck a gift for his strength and energy. He gave Buck a small wafer, which looked like bread but tasted like honey.

"When I finished the bread, he gave me a silver-like ladle filled with what appeared to be water. I drank every drop of it, and an overwhelming desire to praise and worship God instantly came over me. Rivers of praise billowed up to God, bubbling up out of my innermost being, and for days after I drank this liquid, there was a sensation of 'fizzing' inside of my veins," said Buck.[4]

The day after he ate this food, he lost five pounds. The next day, he lost five more. This continued for four-straight days, then began to taper off to one pound a day. Eventually, Buck was no longer overweight, and his breathing stabilized, where before he had shortness of breath when he jogged.

Roland Buck is not the only man to receive a supernatural memory download from Heaven. And while there is no formula for receiving such a gift, we can all ask for this type of thing. Healing evangelist Todd Bentley was virtually given a photographic memory, although he made failing grades and was expelled from school prior to his conversion.

"I struggled with being able to apply myself and even grasp some of the simplest concepts," he said.[5] In addition, he used drugs extensively, which did not help. But after encountering the Lord through dramatic visitations and receiving a groundbreaking anointing, his memory is such that he can flip through six books in a matter of hours and retain most of what he reads.

Finis Dake

Finis Dake (1902-1987) secured the great healer John Alexander Dowie's home in Zion, Illinois, after his death, where Dake was president of Great Lakes Bible Institute. Dake would stay up for days at a time working on an annotated Bible he was writing. It took 100,000 hours to write the notes for his Bible. Obviously, Dake acquired a habit for study.

As soon as Dake was baptized in the Holy Spirit at age 17, he immediately noticed that he could quote hundreds of Scriptures by memory, though he had read very little of the Bible previously. He said that his memory was slow in other matters prior to that experience. Later in life, he was able to quote the entire New Testament, from Matthew to Revelation, verbatim without opening a Bible.[6]

Memory supercharges and supernatural information downloads are only one small taste of what we will begin receiving by divine impartation in these last days. Christians will again become the world's top innovators and inventors, and the brightest minds and leaders of every major field of arts and the humanities. There is an unprecedented download of Heaven-sent knowledge (the very Spirit of Knowledge) coming to the church, as the massive outpouring of the Holy Spirit is released to the world in these days. Did you know that every major branch of science was begun by a Christian? Although much has been corrupted in these fields through skepticism and atheistic world views, the Lord will restore them. The Lord not only wants to release new spiritual insight, but he wants to disclose new, creative discoveries for the natural world as well through His church. God has the sole market on creativity. The enemy can only copy and counterfeit.

Did you know that, in a spiritual sense, we already know *everything*? That sounds trippy, but not only do we have the *mind of Christ*, 1 John 2:20 says, "you have an anointing from the Holy One, and you know all things." Somehow, through our knowledge of Christ, we have come into a knowledge of all truth in our spirit man. This is how, at any given time, we can access Heaven and receive insight or a word of knowledge about any given situation. Here, in the information age, believers will discover a broadband Heavenly connection that will release tremendous power. It's already inside us; we just need to tap into that anointing. This passage goes on to say that the anointing *teaches* us all things. We all have the Holy Spirit of Almighty God latent within us, but there will be a body of people who begin to manifest it more regularly. Greatest of all, we all have the potential within us to know the Lord for ourselves, without the aid of any man.

> *After that time...I will put My law in their minds and write it on their hearts. I will be their God, and they will be My people. No longer will a man teach his neighbor, or a man his brother, saying, "Know the Lord," because they will all know me, from the least of them to the greatest* (Jeremiah 31:33-34).

I believe that the invisible realm was created together with the earth, because we are specifically to search it out and occupy it. In fact, most do not realize that God made the Heavens and the earth at the same time. While we look at Genesis as an account of the earth's creation, we forget that it is also an account of Heaven's creation, as well as the Heavenly hosts (Gen 1:1– 2:1). God never intended that the two should be separated by sin. We often think the Heavenly realms are off limits to the average person, but the opposite is true. The greatest mystery of all is that God bridges that separation of Heaven and earth in Christ, even *"the mystery that has been kept hidden for ages and generations, but is now disclosed to the saints. To them God has chosen to make known among the Gentiles the glorious riches of this mystery, which is **Christ in you, the hope of glory**"* (Col. 1:26-27). What could be a greater revelation than to know God Himself is living inside of me, and that I have access to every spiritual blessing in Christ (see Eph. 1:3)? Or that *"all things are possible for him that believes"* (Mark 9:23)? To fully grasp any of these single truths would revolutionize the world.

The Kingdom of Heaven is in you. Our hearts are the doorway, and we are constantly learning to overcome the battleground of the mind to enter. Accessing Heaven within is the key to receiving revelation. The difference between worldly mysticism and Christian mysticism is that one seeks to discover the inner self, while the other seeks to discover the inner Christ—the very portal of Heaven. Jesus is both the gateway and the model for accessing Heaven. Jesus was in Heaven on earth—at the same time. This is our archetype. Even now, we are seated in Heavenly places, although we walk planet earth. Now is the time to access the Mystery.

[God's mysteries are] to be put into effect when the times will have reached their fulfillment – to bring all things in Heaven and on earth together under one head, even Christ (Ephesians 1:10).

HIDDEN MANNA

The Catholic old-church tradition speaks of the mystagogical journey of life, wherein the "mystagogue" is one who interprets mysteries, and "mystagogy" is the practice of interpretation of mysteries. The Lord will be releasing a new breed of mystagogues in this day. They will understand their royal authority to reach into Heaven and taste of the Lord's hidden manna.

Who interpreted mysteries better than Daniel? He had boldness in the presence of kings because he understood the supreme authority of his God. Most of us are familiar with the passage of Scripture in which the prophet Daniel interprets King Nebuchadnezzar's dream. None of the king's astrologers, magicians, or sorcerers could interpret the dream because the king made the stakes high. He expected them to first tell him what the dream was, and then interpret it. He threatened to kill them if they could not do so. *"But if you tell me the dream and explain it, you will receive from me gifts and rewards and great honor,"* he told them (Dan. 2:6). The same principle is true today. For those who press into God for revelation, there will be blessing that follows. Revelation is essentially the same as understanding and wisdom, which we are fervently exhorted to seek. Without it, all roads lead to ignorance and death, just as was ordered for Babylon's wise men. Without vision the people perish.

"What the king asks is too difficult. No one can reveal it to the king except the gods, and they do not live among men," said the wise men (Dan. 2:11). Like Daniel, however, our God does dwell among men—Emanuel, God with us—provides an open stream of revelation for all who seek. The cross opens a door for us to hear from Heaven. Daniel was tapping into this access by faith, long before the crucifixion physically took place, because he tapped into God's fore-ordained plan from the foundation of the earth. During the night, after seeking God for help, the mystery was revealed to Daniel in a vision. He praised God, saying:

"Praise be to the name of God for ever and ever; wisdom and power are His. He changes times and seasons; He sets up kings and deposes them. He gives wisdom to the wise and knowledge to the discerning. He reveals deep and hidden things; He knows what lies in darkness, and light dwells with Him" (Dan. 2:20-22).

Daniel then testified to the king that *"No wise man, enchanter, magician, or diviner can explain to the king the mystery he has asked about, but there is a God in Heaven who reveals mysteries"* (Dan. 2:27-28). This caused Nebuchadnezzar to admit that *"Surely your God is the God of gods and the Lord of kings and a **revealer of mysteries**, for you were able to reveal this mystery"* (Dan. 2:47).

The word *revealer* here in Hebrew is "galah" or "gelah" (gel-aw) which means to denude in a disgraceful sense. It implies sending one into exile, because exiles were usually stripped of everything by the overcoming army.

God literally wants to strip away and nakedly expose every mystery of Heaven, every shroud and cloud of smoke that covers our eyes from seeing Him in all His glory. There will be a violent tearing open of secrets, and it is the Lord's heart to overcome the darkness of our understanding like a king set out to battle who strips his enemies bare. Even now, the Lord is revealing and exposing powerful truths that have laid dormant for ages, until the given time for their unveiling. It is not that God has wanted to keep things hidden from us, but it is "the glory of kings" to search out these secrets. Mysteries are not intended by God to remain hidden. Rather, He longs to aggressively tear away every roadblock that keeps us from knowing Him more intimately.

This word *gelah* also means to reveal: advertise, appear, *plainly publish, shamelessly tell, uncover.* Because of the shed blood of Jesus, we are called to boldly approach the throne, boldly rip open the mysteries of Heaven like the unwrapping of gifts, and plainly publish them for all to see. Jesus tore every veil that separates us from entering the secret place of the Most High. In doing so, He gives us inner access to the most treasured things of God. He gives us the right to rule and have dominion over Heaven and earth alongside Him. A king understands authority. He takes up the power that has been given to him; we have access to all mysteries as heirs of the throne and recipients of an eternal inheritance.

Miracle workers are about to start crawling out of the rocks. The remnant of the Lord who are hidden away in caves are about to shake off their slave/orphan mentality. They are going to begin walking the earth boldly as sons and princes. They will *boldly approach the throne of grace*.

Isn't it Jesus' heart to reveal God to us? God so exposed Himself—making Himself vulnerable—that He let us nail Him to the cross. He allowed *Himself* to be stripped down, even physically on the cross. We were like children puzzling over a butterfly stuck to a pin board. The cross was the ultimate example of God *allowing* man to put Him in a box. He entered humanity and voluntarily let us take a concrete hold on Him. God let us strip Him and even kill Him. But of course, He could not be contained there. Death lost its sting, and in the resurrection, we see Him leading us all back out of the religious/tomb/box and into a vast realm of Heavenly understanding.

There are a vast number of wonderful truths being restored to the church today, regarding the gift of prophecy and understanding Heavenly secrets. But there is simply not a formula for hearing God. God is releasing mystagogues who will know Him like never before, not because they are superbly trained, but because they burn for Him like no one has burned for Him before. Do you want to walk in revelation and the supernatural power that accompanies it? Learn to love God. If you somehow grew to love God more than anyone else in history, you would become the greatest wonderworker the earth has ever known. The love of God is our target as well as the fuel that gets us there. No matter the depth of our learning, experience, or gifting, understanding Heaven's deepest mysteries requires intimate fellowship with the Bridegroom.

We must become friends with God like Abraham, of whom the Lord said, *"Shall I hide from Abraham what I am about to do?"* (Gen. 18:17). God is always revealing His plans to someone, whether we realize it or not, because *surely the Sovereign Lord does nothing without revealing His plan to His servants the prophets* (see Amos 3:7).

Intimacy brings insight. God will show us His secrets as friends; they are not for everyone. Jesus said in Mark 4, *"The secret of the Kingdom of God has been given to you. But to those on the outside, everything is said in parables...Don't you understand this parable? How then will you understand any parable?"* All parables have the same root key to their understanding. Love unlocks every door. Desire. Without it, we remain on the outside.

Parables are used to cloak mysteries of the Kingdom, because the Lord does not throw bread to dogs. He requires faith and a hungry heart. Do you want the inside scoop on Heaven? Get close to Jesus. There is hidden manna, solid food, reserved for the mature, who by constant use and training of their senses have learned to discern good from evil (see Heb. 5:14). The Lord does not withhold Himself from some, and not others, for reasons of elitism. He loves all equally, but His *favor* spills over onto some more than others, based on their responsive desire for Him. It is a matter of responsibility because of the power at stake in what is revealed. God does not have *favorites*, but only those who choose to draw near and follow Him closely get the best goods. Jesus spoke to the multitudes. Out of all these, He only sent out 70 to minister. And still, there was an inner circle of 12 who really got the best downloads. Better yet, there were Peter, James, and John—His three closest acquaintances—who got nearest to Jesus and thus were privy to the coolest miracles and revelation of all. John, *the disciple Jesus loved,* was the Lord's best friend on earth, even laying his head on Jesus' breast. He would later go on to receive the greatest prophetic revelation ever released in the church age—the *Book of Revelation.*

Revelation and spiritual gifts are all byproducts of holy adoration. We are only permitted to seek spiritual gifts because they all part of His Kingdom, and therefore an extension of Jesus. Prophecy is only an extension of the Living Word. Healing is only an extension of the Healer. We must seek first the Kingdom of God, then all else will be added to us. But the underlying fabric is friendship—as we get close to Him, He reveals things to us. We do not go to Him strictly for revelation. We go to Him because we are His friends, His children, His Bride. Anything else is a backward approach, which can even lead to divination. One of the very reasons that instrumental worship is so conducive to releasing prophecy, is because the Lord likes our hearts to get focused and impassioned *before* He gives us a word.

Overcoming the orphan spirit is critical to receiving revelation. We all want more prophetic authority. Authority comes from kingship. And kingship is tied to sonship. An heir of the king is a king. We are sons not because of our works, but because of God's pleasure toward us.

> ***In love*** *He predestined us to be adopted as His sons through Jesus Christ, in accordance with His **pleasure and will**—to the praise of His glorious grace, which He has **freely given us** in the One He loves* (Ephesians 1:4-6).

Understanding a son's acceptance gives us the confidence to risk going higher and closer toward the Father. The passage continues:

> *In Him we have redemption through His blood, the forgiveness of sins, in accordance with the riches of God's grace that He lavished on us with all wisdom and understanding. And He **made known to us the mystery** of His will **according to His good pleasure**, which He purposed in Christ* (Ephesians 1:7-9).

How often do we face a brass Heaven, thinking we must twist God's arm for Him to speak to us? Just to hear from Him on simple matters is difficult, without first understanding our acceptance and the pleasure He takes in us. God does not want us to have a mind-set of isolation, fear and rejection, thinking that He doesn't care to speak to us. For here, we learn that it pleases the Father to make known the mystery of His will.

The spirit of Elijah is being released in our day to draw the hearts of the sons to the fathers. This sonship—the spirit of adoption—will break the orphan spirit that prevents us from approaching God as heirs to the throne and recipients of the King's counsel. Father is King. As the mysteries of the Book of Daniel are unfolded in our day, the church will be released to walk in kingship. Like Daniel, we will boldly approach the King of Kings, who is a revealer of mysteries. It is our glory to search these things out.

But God does not simply want us to have revelation and vision. He wants to activate the things He shows us. He wants us to bring the realm of vision into the realm of reality. The church is a womb to bring the invisible realm into the visible, to birth Heaven into the earth. This is the substance of apostolic reformation. Many prophetic people have vision, but it is an apostolic work to make the vision happen.

God is releasing princes who will *rule in righteousness*. That means they will not just operate to their own benefit, but they will rule on behalf of the poor and fatherless. The tangible power they will possess is beyond the realm where the prophetic movement has operated over the past decade. This regiment of people will possess such power in their spoken word, that when they speak a thing, it will happen. As they decree the righteous verdicts of Heaven, their words will have power to release Heavenly restoration into the earth. Supernatural stuff will happen, just because they speak it aloud. Where the Word of Faith movement went astray with this kind of thing toward personal gain in years past, there will be a body of people who will operate in it justly and sacrificially. This is a *kingly anointing* that is coming to bring freedom to the captives, sight the blind, blessing to the poor and widow.

IN OUR DAY

The times are now reaching fulfillment. When we compare the great historical moves of God with the present darkness around us, we often wish the Lord would bring us back to the glory days. But God is interested in doing something much better. The capacity for restoration will not be limited by the degree of darkness around us. And God will not just give back to us that which was lost. Restoration has *no* limits, because a thing that is restored is actually *better* than its original condition.

Restoration is greater than the return of something lost. It represents bringing that lost thing to a whole new level of glory and multiplication. God wants to do more than just give back what the enemy has stolen from us through sin and deception. He wants to force the thief to pay back seven times what he has taken (see Prov. 6:31). Restoration is not an even exchange. It's better than even.

If I borrow your old Subaru and wreck it, I am obliged to do more than repair it. Though it may function and look the same, it has still taken a loss in value. You probably wouldn't trust me to ever drive your car again. If I got you *another* Subaru, the exact make, model, and mileage—the same Blue Book value—that would be an even exchange. That would be good, and you would probably let me drive your car again. But God is better than good. Restoration is not just replacing your Subaru. Restoration is giving you a brand new Lexus. In that case, trust is also fully restored. You would probably even make me a separate set of keys and let me borrow your whole house and everything in it for that matter.

God is not interested in paying our accounts evenly for all we have lost to evil, both individually, and in the corporate church as a whole. He is a God of abundance and overflow. After the enemy took Job's family and possessions, his losses were restored double (Job 42:10). He is a God of unmerited favor, and so the principle of restoration is the very nature of His grace. Likewise, we do not earn it. We will not be a church that is striving to rebuild from the ground up what has been robbed from us in the area of spiritual experience, emotional trauma, health, or finances. We will simply find that, as we surrender to the Lord's presence, *He* accelerates the outflow of anointing in our lives as a byproduct of that intimacy.

Many of us who are anticipating the glory of the last day church have the wrong idea about how we are going to get there. We see the great men of God in years past, and we think that somehow we will have to run harder, die deader, and make ourselves holier if we are ever to catch up with them. But I have news for you: God is the one who is going to pull this thing off. His grace will be multiplied in these last days like never before. Many feel they must pound hell to take things back from the devil. But satan will not be restoring our fortunes; he has nothing to offer us. We want nothing his hands have tainted. God will bring restoration. And satan will be utterly powerless to restrain the abundant rains of blessing that God will release on His last day church.

LATTER RAIN

The revivalists of the 1940s and '50s were experiencing such a tremendous outpouring, they felt they were seeing the latter rains of God's Spirit being released on the face of the earth. James 5:7 tells us to "be patient therefore brothers unto the coming of the Lord. Behold the farmer waits for the precious fruit of the earth and has long patience for it, until he receives the early and latter rain. Be also patient, establish your hearts, for the coming of the Lord draws nigh." The revivalists also felt they were seeing the release of the end-time army prophesied by Joel, who mentions these latter rains. The rains are related to harvest and end-time revival.

> *Be glad then, you children of Zion, and rejoice in the Lord your God; for He has given you the former rain faithfully, and He will cause the rain to come down for you— the former rain, and the latter rain in the first month. The threshing floors shall be full of wheat, and the vats shall overflow with wine and oil* (Joel 2:23-24).

The move of their day was even called the Latter Rain Revival, but what these men saw was only a foretaste of the latter rains we are about to enter. Another major wave of healing and power evangelism is already beginning to erupt, but this time coupled with a deeper perspective on intimacy, and a corporate embrace of the spirit of prophecy. These men's stories should stir within us a hunger for what is to come. They should provoke us to faith on one hand, and on the other hand, they should instill within us a patient endurance to wait on the Lord. The things we will see would boggle even their minds. It will surely boggle ours. Faith and patience go hand in hand. But it is one thing to wait on the Lord's season for revival. It is another thing to spark a revival yourself—to be the front-runner and bring it into your community. Often we are waiting for the Lord's permission, or someone else's, before we step out in faith. But more often, it is the Lord who is waiting on us. We can set our own harvest season into motion by allowing our hearts to be purified before Him.

> *Let us now fear the Lord our God, who gives rain, both the former and the latter, in its season. He reserves for us the appointed weeks of the harvest. . . . Your iniquities have turned these things away, and your sins have withheld good things from you* (Jeremiah 5:24-25).

In fact, no one of the Voice of Healing generation—like every other, from the mystics of the Middle Ages to the missionary streams throughout the early centuries of church history—stepped into the fullness of what God had for them. Understand, they were seeing tens of thousands saved, thousands healed and the world being set aflame. But they still could have gone further. It will take purity and holiness for us to go beyond them. But not the kind of purity that comes from form and legalism. We must return to intimacy. We must return to the presence of the Lord. As great as the miracles and power encounters are—as much as we need them to effect change in the world—truly the love of God is the greatest pursuit of all. This is the mantle of the end-time church. This is the revival fire that cannot be quenched.

> *Come, and let us return unto the Lord; for He has torn,*
> *but He will heal us; He has stricken, but He will bind us*
> *up. After two days He will revive us; on the third day He*
> *will raise us up, that we may live in His sight. Let us know,*
> *let us pursue the knowledge of the Lord. His going forth is*
> *established as the morning; He will come to us like the*
> *rain, like the latter and former rain to the earth* (Hosea
> 6:1-3).

Sin and excess, warfare and apathy brought an end to every revival before us. But only for a season. Each wave of God's Spirit has been a birth pang before the coming of the Lord. A deposit of greater glory has been set aside for us to walk in. There is coming a people of repentance who will also be a people of inheritance. Turning back to the Father always brings a release of inheritance. Consider what Solomon prayed over the new temple just before it was filled with a latter glory that superceded anything before it:

> *When Your people Israel have been defeated by an*
> *enemy because they have sinned against You and when*
> *they turn back and confess Your name, praying and mak-*
> *ing supplication before You in this temple, then hear from*
> *Heaven and forgive the sin of Your people Israel and bring*
> *them back to the land You gave to them and their fathers.*
> *When the heavens are shut up and there is no rain*
> *because Your people have sinned against You, and when*
> *they pray toward this place and confess Your name and*
> *turn from their sin because You have afflicted them, then*
> *hear from Heaven and forgive the sin of Your servants,*
> *Your people Israel. Teach them the right way to live, and*
> *send rain on the land You gave Your people for an inheri-*
> *tance* (2 Chronicles 6:24-27).

And this is how the Lord answered Solomon's prayer:

I have heard your prayer and have chosen this place for Myself as a temple for sacrifices. When I shut up heavens so that there is no rain, or command locusts to devour the land or send a plague among My people, if My people, who are called by My name, will humble themselves and pray and seek My face and turn from their wicked ways, then will I hear from Heaven and will forgive their sin and will heal their land (2 Chronicles 7:12-14).

Will we see the last of the latter rains? Is our present generation just one more birth pang before the end? Like Elijah, let us pray until we see clouds on the horizon. The harvest is ripe for revival. *Ask the Lord for rain in the time of the latter rain.* Where past revival fires were quenched, the last days forerunner fire is like the fire rained down at the word of Elijah—it not only burns the wood and sacrifice, but it consumes the stone and even the water poured over it. The fire of God's love is that unquenchable fire—the fire of burning passion. His love is stronger than death.

The church will recover all that has been lost. But that which is yet coming is altogether new. We learn from the forefathers, and we seek to re-dig their old wells. But the Lord wants you to dig your own well. Your entire life is still ahead of you to pioneer great and untold feats of the Kingdom. There are pages of testimonies yet to be recorded in the annals of Heaven. We imitate men of old, yes—but this is your hour, and it is my hour. Let us press into what God has for us today. Let us become innovators. The baton is in our hands. The mystical flame of God's presence is in our court. Where will you ignite revival?

ENDNOTES

1. Charles and Francis Hunter as told by Roland Buck, Angels on Assignment (1979). Online version accessible <http://angelsonassignment.org>.
2. Ibid.

3. Ibid.

4. Ibid.

5. Todd Bentley with Jackie Macgirvin, Journey Into the Miraculous Todd Bentley: An Ordinary Man Touched by a Supernatural God (Victoria, B.C.: Fresh Fire Ministries, 2003), 30.

6. Lester Sumrall, *Pioneers of Faith* (Ben Publishing, 1995), 67-72.

About the Author

John and Lily Crowder are the founders of Sons of Thunder Publications and The New Mystics Ministries. Their passion is to minister foremost to the presence of God, to equip the church for works of service and to bring the gospel of Jesus Christ to the nations.

The two have been involved with local mission work in Alaska for several years. John speaks at churches and conferences across North America as an itinerate revivalist. Their work also branches to the nations, with a strong focus on healing and miracle evangelism.

The couple has a vision for global harvest through a demonstration of God's presence and power in the lives of believers.

John is a prophetic minister as well as a writer, having published more than 1,500 articles and the recipient of 15 Alaska Press Club awards. Lily often ministers alongside him.

For more information on the ministry, please contact us:

Call toll free: 1-877-DIE-DAILY
Email us at: info@thenewmystics.org
Visit us online at: www.thenewmystics.org

Ministry Resources
and Information

FREE WEEKLY TEACHING

Stay connected with our ministry by signing up for free, weekly online teachings from John Crowder. Simply visit our Website: **www.thenewmystics.org** and enter your Email address for our Word of the Week to be automatically sent to you. You will also receive updates on our new products and upcoming conferences.

HOW TO BOOK AN ENGAGEMENT

Would you like to request John Crowder or a Sons of Thunder team member to speak at your church or a conference in your area? Mail, phone, or Email your request with details of your engagement at the contacts listed below. John and his team will pray regarding your request, and you may expect a prompt confirmation.

HOST A CONFERENCE IN YOUR AREA

For more information on hosting John for a meeting or conference, click on the "Itinerary" link on our home page. John does not charge a fee to minister. Whenever possible, it is appreciated if a special offering could be received at the meeting. The host group is responsible for providing transportation to and from their ministry destination for John, in addition to accommodation. Hosting groups often like to charge a registration fee when booking a conference or retreat, to cover expenses.

Our team will be praying for your ministry, for the meeting itself, and for follow up as you foster the fresh impartation brought into your community. We would be appreciative if your intercessory team could also meet to pray prior to the meetings.

Audio & Video Resources

PROPHETIC SCHOOL

CD series $40 plus $4.50 S&H Six equipping teachings from John to hear the voice of God, receive the Spirit of Revelation and understand the prophetic office. Caters to all levels of prophetic development.

BIZARRE MIRACLES

CD series $15 plus $3.50 S&H A two-part teaching from John whets your appetite for supernatural Christianity with phenomenal stories of miracle working saints, seers and mystics.

Visit us online at **www.thenewmystics.org** to order

Shake the Nations With Us—
Become a New Mystics Monthly Revival Partner

Financial giving is one of the foundational ways we worship the Lord. By investing the substance of our labor into His Kingdom, we not only bless others, but also position ourselves for breakthrough both in our spiritual and natural lives.

Without the help of our partners in ministry, we could not fulfill the call and commission of the Lord to reach the nations with His saving, healing, and delivering power. The Lord regularly calls His servants to a certain dependence on the people. He did this with Elijah, with His first disciples, and with countless other holy men throughout history so that the Kingdom blessings that rested on their own ministries could be shared and transferred over onto those who supported them—to those who gave cheerfully, with expectant faith. God still bestows radical blessings on hilarious givers.

Ours is an international ministry, focused on harvest. We are also dedicated to equipping the church, and most of all ministering to the presence of the Lord Himself. We believe that by investing your financial resources with us, you are sharing in the same fruit and the same reward with which the Lord blesses us. Not only do you help us to reach souls—we believe our partners tap into the same favor and spiritual mantle the Lord has placed on our ministry through their prayers and support.

For these reasons, we extend to you an invitation to join us in the shared privilege of partnering with the gospel. We are constantly seeking to advance the Kingdom of God at home and abroad. If you like what you see in our ministry and feel that The New Mystics is good ground in which to plant your resources, consider standing with us with a monthly gift.

Partners who donate $25 or more each month also receive regular teaching CDs and discounts on our products and conferences. We thank God for you, and pray for rich blessings and multiplication in your lives for your heart of giving!

—John and Lily Crowder

Become a monthly partner with The New Mystics
by calling toll free:
1-877-DIE DAILY

Become a partner online at **www.thenewmystics.org**
and click on "**Partners**"

Additional copies of this book and other book titles from DESTINY IMAGE are available at your local bookstore.

Call toll free: 1-800-722-6774.

Send a request for a catalog to:

Destiny Image® Publishers, Inc.
P.O. Box 310
Shippensburg, PA 17257-0310

"Speaking to the Purposes of God for this Generation and for the Generations to Come."

For a complete list of our titles, visit us at www.destinyimage.com